From Magic and Myth-W...
to Care an...

From Magic and Myth-Work to Care and Repair

Essays on the Fiction of the Self and Other Devices

Simon O'Sullivan

Goldsmiths Press

Copyright © 2024 Goldsmiths Press
First published in 2024 by Goldsmiths Press
Goldsmiths, University of London, New Cross
London SE14 6NW

Printed and bound by Short Run Press Limited, UK
Distribution by the MIT Press
Cambridge, Massachusetts, USA and London, England

Text copyright © 2024 Simon O'Sullivan

The right of Simon O'Sullivan to be identified as the author of this work has been asserted by him in accordance with sections 77 and 78 in the Copyright, Designs and Patents Act 1988.

Every effort has been made to trace copyright holders and to obtain their permission for the use of copyright material. The publisher apologises for any errors or omissions and would be grateful if notified of any corrections that should be incorporated in future reprints or editions of this book.

All Rights Reserved. No part of this publication may be reproduced, distributed or transmitted in any form or by any means whatsoever without prior written permission of the publisher, except in the case of brief quotations in critical articles and review and certain non-commercial uses permitted by copyright law.

A CIP record for this book is available from the British Library

ISBN 978-1-915983-04-6 (pbk)
ISBN 978-1-915983-03-9 (ebk)

www.gold.ac.uk/goldsmiths-press

Goldsmiths
UNIVERSITY OF LONDON

For Tom

Contents

Acknowledgements — ix

Introduction — 1

Part I On Magic and Myth-Work — 5

  1 Avatars, Egregores and the Writing of the Self — 7

  2 Fiction as Desiring Work — 23

  3 On Acéphale and Having No Head — 33

  4 Time Circuits and Temporal Loops — 43

  5 Landscape, Trauma and Myth-Work — 57

  6 On Magic and Place — 69

  7 A Thousand Devices — 83

Part II On Care and Repair — 99

  8 On Teaching and Writing as Care and Repair — 101

  9 On the Non-Human — 115

  10 Archaeofictioning — 127

  11 Dreaming as Method — 139

  12 On Tabletop Role-Playing Games and Fictioning — 153

  13 Memories of a Buddhist — 165

  14 Notes on Performance Fiction — 181

Afterword — 191

  Bibliography — 195
  Index — 207

Acknowledgements

Thanks to: Tom O'Sullivan and Norman James Hogg who both read an early draft of these essays and gave valuable and insightful feedback; John Cussans, Helen Palmer, Lucy A. Sames, Kristen Kreider and Neil Chapman, each of whom reviewed a later draft and offered many important comments and suggestions; Eldritch Priest and Gary Genosko who also gave constructive feedback at an earlier stage of my project; Ola Ståhl for our many conversations around the themes of this book; David Burrows for our ongoing collaboration that has also fed into this book; Plastique Fantastique and its myth-work (and especially David, Alex Marzeta and Vanessa Page); Jon K Shaw for his ever-attentive proof reading and indexing and ongoing conversations around writing and the themes of this book; Adjoa Armah, Verity Birt, Neuschloss, Mark Leckey and Sophie Sleigh-Johnson for images of their work and permissions (and to Auto Italia, Cabinet Gallery and Arcadia Missa); Sarah Kember, Angela Thompson, Ellen Parnavelas and Susan Kelly at Goldsmiths Press who have been supportive and attentive to this book project; my colleagues in the Department of Visual Cultures at Goldsmiths who continue to be an inspiring and supportive community of teachers and researchers; and finally the BA and MA students at Goldsmiths who took my courses on 'Occulture' and 'From Art Writing to Theory-Fiction' from 2020–23 and whose conversations and contributions have also fed into this work.

More general thanks to the following for all sorts of different things (and devices) that have contributed to the writing of these essays. In no particular order: Mark Rohtmaa-Jackson; Nick Thoburn; Maggie Roberts; Lesley Guy; Adnan Madani; Bridget Crone; Samudradaka; Anna Weaver; Joe Collins; Thomas Mannion; John Cowton; Alexis McGlone; Mikey Tomkins, Robin Mackay; Mandarava and Nagasiddhi.

Finally, thanks to Hannah for all the discussions about (and practices around) care and repair (many of which have obliquely found their way into this book) and to Hannah, Luke and Kit for putting up with the absences and other stresses that writing a book (for me) invariably involves.

Parts or earlier versions of three of the essays have been previously published as: 'On Tabletop Role-Playing Games and Fictioning', *Vector*, 21 December 2022 (https://vector-bsfa.com/2022/12/21/on-tabletop-role paying-games-and-fictioning/); 'A Thousand Devices', *Michiko Itatani: Celestial Stage*, Chicago: Wrightwood 659, 2022, pp. 40-3; and 'Avatars and Egregores and the Writing of the Self', *Journal of Writing in Creative Practice*, 16:2 (2023): 229-41. Many thanks to the editors (Jo Lindsay Walton, Ashley Janke and Lucy A. Sames) for permission to re-use this material.

Introduction

Gathered together in this book are 14 short essays that I wrote either during or immediately after writing an experimental novel titled *The Ancient Device* (O'Sullivan 2024a). I use the term essay here not just in the sense of a written composition, but also in the sense of an initial or tentative attempt at something (and, as such, as a verb as well as a noun). Certainly each of the essays that follow operates as a sketch (some more than others) in relation to its thematics. The first of them—'Avatars, Egregores and the Writing of the Self'—is the most closely aligned with the content of the fiction I mention above and with the various devices that are in play in it. It was the first to be written and arose directly from reflections I had whilst writing that other work, but concerned ideas that seemed to me in need of being developed outside the genre of fiction. Many of the other essays, especially in the first half of the book, return to and expand on some of the material in that first essay and most of them are constellated around ideas of writing and magic, especially in relation to the fiction of the self or what I also call 'myth-work'. At the same time they increasingly develop the idea of the device I mention above (so there is a logic to the order of the essays in this sense). The final essay of the first part—'A Thousand Devices'—also attempts a more abstract working through of this concept of the device (drawing on the work of the previous essays) so as to further set things up (and not least my own account, in the last essay, on what David Burrows and I call 'performance fiction'). All of the essays circulate around certain key figures and fictions—ciphers in a way for my own myth-work—which means there are more than a few repetitions and refrains (albeit with different inflections), as well as various traverses across essays.

This also relates more directly to the question of method. Although theoretical—at least to a certain extent—the essays were not written as

I have written other books and articles. The method was to use a question or phrase that had foregrounded itself as important. Sometimes this became a provisional title, but in any case, it worked as a prompt to see what might follow. After writing a draft the process was then to edit and bring in as context other theoretical references and reflections, many of which appear in the endnotes. All of these references—in the endnotes and the main text—were from reading I was doing at the time, but also from the book *Fictioning* that David Burrows and I had relatively recently published (hence some of the repetitions and close resonances with that work). A second prompt was certain contemporary art practices I had encountered that it seemed to me might be gathered together under this banner of magic and myth-work. This was especially the case with more performative practices that were concerned with transformation in some senses (often through a looping or layering of references) and which also involved a kind of fictioning of their author within the practice (see especially those discussed in 'On Magic and Place').

The other key resource and important prompt for the essays was the reading and teaching I was doing in relation to a new course at Goldsmiths on 'Occulture'. In fact, looking back at the essays, it's clear that much of the eventual content—and, indeed, the overall tone—arises directly from that teaching situation and from discussions with the students who attended those seminars. I go into this in more detail in the first essay of the second part of my book—'On Teaching and Writing as Care and Repair'—so won't repeat that discussion here except to say that that essay's title (which also partly works as a title for the second part of my book) relates to those intense Covid years and, as such, this book is also the result of a collaboration with the many amazing students who attended my seminar (sometimes virtually) during those especially difficult times.

As far as the echoes of *Fictioning* go—especially in the first set of essays—what follows might also be thought of as a supplement to that longer collaborative work insofar as the essays generally involve themes I was keen to develop further or that didn't find their way into that longer book. This therefore means that much of what I say in those essays is indebted to my collaborator. David will recognise many of the themes explored in what follows, but the more personal tone and the essays that involve more personal reflections are, of course, my own. David and I are working on a second volume of *Fictioning*, tentatively titled *Fictioning Community: The Non, the Ill and the Dead in Contemporary Art and Philosophy*, in which we will shift some of the focus of our work together to questions around difference, diversity and the production of community.[1] Or, to put that in terms of what I have written here, we will move to other devices, certainly beyond the one foregrounded in this collection of essays and especially those in the second part of my book.

Indeed, the essays in this second part are generally more personal. They tackle some of the same themes, but they give more personal context or make more of an attempt to 'situate' their particular perspectives (it might be that a reader interested in this approach turns to part two of my book first to set a context for the other essays).[2] In many cases these essays move away from academia and art to other worlds and to my subjective experience within them. One way I have thought about this second set of essays especially—which relates to the genre of autotheory—is as a further working out of the device I have or the device that I am. There is certainly a sense that subjectivity in general is a kind of device—as I suggest in various essays—but, in addition, that each of us is also their own unique device. It seemed to me that in order to use this device—perhaps for other purposes?—it would first need to be more thoroughly mapped out (and then, moreover, simply seen as one).

Some of the essays in the second part of my book also involve an account of devices that have been useful or important to me, not least in terms of my own mental health (albeit sometimes obliquely).[3] So, group and myth-work or performance and collaboration for example. They attend too to ideas of care and repair more generally and in a wider context (and look at some further artistic case studies, for example in the essay on 'Archaeofictioning'). It seems to me that myth-work, whether personal or more collective, needs different devices in order to do its work.[4] The second set of essays also return to a key theme or motif that is in play in the first set of essays, that of landscape. This is understood in different ways throughout my book. In terms of actual landscape, but also as a way of thinking the fiction of the self—as itself a kind of landscape—and then again, more simply, as naming an imaginative resource.[5]

Another way of putting all this is that different genres are at work in what follows but also that this gathering together of different writings attempts to work across genres too (for example from the academic to the therapeutic). Looking back it is this, ultimately, that seems interesting and at stake in what I have written. A desire not to be captured by a particular genre, but also to understand what genre one is working in—or that already constitutes one's subjectivity—and where the edges of that might be. And then even perhaps what is beyond those edges. Are there, for example, other genres yet to be invented? In this way these essays evidence a further refrain of my work—the dictate that a magician must make their own tools (or, in my case, write them). In terms of the title of my novel that I mention above, the writings collected here are an attempt to gather components so as to construct a further device whose function is yet to be determined. Indeed, the principle in this case has been to build the device *and then* see what follows.

Notes

1 See also David Burrows' own forthcoming work on *Fictioning Devices* that explores some of this terrain in relation to cosmopolitics and cosmotechnics (Burrows 2024).
2 See Donna Haraway's essay on 'Situated Knowledges' (1988) which makes the case for acknowledging positioning and affirming partial perspectives in relation to our objects of study, but also in relation to self-knowledge ('We are not immediately present to ourselves. Self-knowledge requires a semiotic-material technology to link meanings and bodies' [Haraway 1988: 585]).
3 I want to acknowledge Tom O'Sullivan here as many of these devices were discovered or made with him—as I mention in some of the essays themselves—and certainly our ongoing conversations and sharing of interests and archives has fed into the present work (as have his own practices around art and writing).
4 This follows but also turns away from some of the material and arguments in my first book, *Art Encounters Deleuze and Guattari* (O'Sullivan 2006). At stake there were practices that operated against or beyond representation. In the essays collected here representation is instead figured as an important device that allows another kind of perspective to be taken on.
5 In terms of this idea of landscape I should mention a further collaboration with Ola Ståhl as, during the writing of the second set of essays, we were involved in a parallel project of what might be called 'eco-therapeutics'. I will briefly return to this in 'Dreaming as Method' but want to thank Ola here for the many discussions we had and, indeed, for the explorations we carried out together.

Part I
On Magic and Myth-Work

1

Avatars, Egregores and the Writing of the Self

This first essay is concerned with writing as a creative technology of the self or, more simply, as a form of self-authorship. This is a key theme in many of the essays that follow in the first part of my book. Related to this is the way writing can involve summoning other agencies that disrupt or sidestep the self (so writing as a technology of the non-self too). Before I get to this, however, my essay begins by laying out some more general terrain about the 'fiction of the self' and, even more generally, about how different fictions can and do take on a reality. It also contains some initial reflections on why this particular theme of the fiction of the self has foregrounded itself in my life (so, more generally, what my investments in this book project are).

Avatars and Egregores

The term avatar is often used within video/computer games where it names a persona or character of some kind that is taken on within the game. Generally, one selects a pre-made avatar, though increasingly one is able to design one's own (within set parameters). In contemporary art practice it's a less common term, although some practices—including the one I am involved in—use the term for the invented fictions that are taken on or 'channelled', especially in performance. The term originates within religious discourse—and specifically Hinduism—where it names the material manifestation of a deity (and, as such, 'avatar' is an example of how a religious term can become secularised as it is taken up in the West). In each of the above the general meaning seems relatively clear. An avatar is an alternative presentation of a pre-existing entity. What, however, about an avatar that has no pre-existing entity behind it? We might be reminded here of different neuroscientific takes on the 'fiction of the self', from

Thomas Metzinger's account of the 'ego tunnel' (Metzinger 2009) that, for Metzinger, we are necessarily travelling in and through, to Ray Brassier's 'nemocentric' subject/perspective (Brassier 2011)—a term he borrows from Metzinger—which explores similar territory but also names the speculative possibility of a mode of being in the world without a self. These are two philosophers—and their associated ideas—that I will be returning to more than a few times especially in the first few essays of my book. The term 'fiction of the self' implies this lack of a 'real' entity (although that is not to say that there is not *something* behind or beneath the fiction).

The term egregore also relates to a non-physical entity or 'thought-form', one that has been collectively produced or has arisen somehow through collective endeavour. The term is an occult one, often used in relation to chaos magick, although it has also recently been 'applied' to memes and to the way in which they can acquire a certain power through collective investment (specifically with 'meme magic' and the weaponisation of memes by the alt-right) (see Asprem 2018).[1] Egregore is a term even less found in contemporary art discourse—despite the recent turn to magic[2]—but it does seem an appropriate one to describe those beliefs and practices—and specifically collective fictions—that are produced by a group and/or invested in by the latter. Certainly, with the art practice I am involved in the fiction (of the group and of the avatars within the group) has taken on its own life. It's a collaboration between individuals (alongside other agents), but also something else. Something that has its own autonomous existence besides our involvement and that, as such, we then 'step' into. I will turn more explicitly to this kind of 'performance fiction' and to the group I am part of—Plastique Fantastique—in the final essay of my book.

Hyperstition and Being 'Compromised by Magic'

In relation to fictions taking on a life, two other contemporary sources seem especially relevant (at least in my own working through of these ideas). First, the philosopher Isabelle Stengers' idea of fictions having an effect within a given milieu. Stengers writes about this in her essay 'Reclaiming Animism' (Stengers 2012) which, in part, is concerned with her own attempts to be 'compromised by magic' or, put differently, how she might productively relate to and engage with magical systems of thought even though she is a modern and, as it were, a scientific subject. For Stengers this is crucial in relation to being able to explore and perhaps inhabit other modes of existence besides those that have brought about the many issues of our Anthropocene. Part of her argument in that essay is simply that what we might understand as fictions (from a certain perspective) can nevertheless be active agents. If they have real effects within a given milieu then they are, to that extent 'real'. Stengers' prompt here is thinking about the healing properties of a statue of the Virgin Mary but, more generally, also the beliefs and practices of witches. It seems clear that those fictions which are collectively invested in will have the most purchase on a given reality (or the most purchase for the largest group of people).

This extends the kinds of entities that one can have a productive relationship with beyond other persons. Or, put differently, it extends the idea of 'personhood'—as in Viveiros de Castro's writings—to include non-human beings (see for example Viveiros de Castro 2014).[3] In fact, it broadens this out even further to include other objects and then also different fictions in any given field or milieu.[4] Indeed, here the boundary between fiction and so-called reality becomes blurred. For Stengers magic is a name for this expanded field of agency/desire and for the practices that are implied by it (so, crucially, magic is not to be understood as simply a regression from science). Broadly speaking then, magical practice concerns other agencies (whatever they might be) and involves a pragmatic engagement with them. Again, I will be returning more than once in what follows to this important essay by Stengers.

The second source is the concept of 'hyperstition' from the Cybernetic culture research unit (Ccru), a para-academic group set up in the Philosophy Department at Warwick University (and then existing outside of it) in the 1990s (see Ccru n.d.).[5] Hyperstition—to give a very short and succinct definition—names fictions that make themselves real.[6] In fact, hyperstition names a strange kind of retro-causality in which the fiction works back on its conditions of emergence, bringing about its own reality.[7] A particular idea of time is in play here—a flat, cybernetic one—with hyperstition being a name for the workings of these various time circuits and temporal loops (something I look at explicitly in another essay in this first part of my book). For the Ccru the term hyperstition is also connected to the occult insofar as it involves a secret or hidden knowledge (in this case, about time)—a knowledge that comes from a perspective that is not typically available; or, at least, not to a subject as they are typically constituted in the modern West.

To a certain extent the Ccru might itself be understood as an egregore. The apocryphal quote originally ascribed to Warwick University—where the Ccru was first conjured—namely that 'Ccru does not, has not and will never exist' points to at least the semi-fictional nature of the group. Certainly, it was an entity that was collectively produced and invested in. And certainly it had an effect (and is continuing to have one), not least within some of the art and theory worlds that I am familiar with (both positively and negatively, depending on your perspective). Moreover, it was itself involved with the naming/summoning of other agencies and entities—specifically demons—something the term hyperstition also refers to.[8]

Elsewhere David Burrows and I have written about how fictions can be instantiated or materialised within art practice and especially how such embodied fictions can then have a traction in a given world (Burrows and O'Sullivan 2019). We used the term 'fictioning' to refer to this kind of work, when work names both the object/practice in question and what the latter does. We also referenced the Stengers essay mentioned above (alongside various writings by Donna Haraway) as offering a parallel concept to fictioning especially in relation to 'worlding' practices (See Burrows and O'Sullivan 2019: 264–5). Hyperstition is also a form of fictioning in this sense although the Ccru were less concerned with art practice as such and, certainly, hyperstition is of a more philosophical character. Once again, I will be returning to the Ccru in some of the essays that follow in this first part of my book.

Having briefly laid out some terrain around fictions taking on a reality, I want now to turn away from contemporary art practice myself and reflect more on the practice of producing avatars and egregores especially in relation to the fiction of the self.[9] This is a further theme of my book and follows from an interest I have had for some time in understanding this fiction and even in dislodging it in some manner. It's not entirely clear to me where this interest comes from, but certainly there is something around the possibility of transformation (that arises from seeing the self as a fiction) which has always appealed. This is partly to escape from—or at least see more clearly—what is an especially anxious set-up in my case, but it is also to foreground the possibility of producing (and performing) other fictions.

I think it is this sometimes unconscious intention that has motivated many of the seemingly disparate themes of my essays and the choices about the texts and other materials I look to (and indeed why I so often return to the same references). In terms of the two sources introduced above, attending to the fiction of the self in this way is to attend to a very particular kind of fiction and the effect it has in a given milieu and then also to how the production of a fiction can bring about a certain reality. I want to briefly consider five examples or case studies to see where this might lead and to further set up some of the themes of subsequent essays.

Neuroscience and the Fiction of the Self

It is increasingly being scientifically demonstrated that the self is a fiction and that behind this fiction there is something else entirely different going on. On one level it is simply the physical and chemical processes of the body that are 'going on', more or less irrespective of what we might think or narrate to ourselves or to others. The self, which is partly this process of continuous narration (to drastically reduce down this particular aspect of the process of self-formation) is then a fiction that is often interrupted or outflanked by these other material processes. The uncanny feeling one can have of having done something or arrived somewhere for example without consciously planning or even being completely aware would seem to anecdotally point towards this other bodily intelligence that is always already at work beneath our conscious narration.[10] Indeed, the conscious explanations—or rationalisations—tend to come after the event even if they might seem to come before.

This fiction of the self is only one aspect of what a self is of course. There are other processes that are involved in self-formation when this also includes the formation—or selection—of the world which that self moves through. Most of these are 'sub-representational', part of the material processes mentioned above. Neuroscience is increasingly able to map out this terrain or, at least, map out the neural correlates to certain subjective/emotional states. A fully scientific account of the self seems to be on the horizon in this sense. Or, put differently, a bridge is being constructed piece by piece across the gulf between the scientific and more manifest images of the self. Brassier also refers to this—following the philosopher

Wilfred Sellars—as the development of a 'stereoscopic' synthesis (Brassier 2014: 74).

Might it also be the case that there are feedback loops between these two images or worlds? Can, for example, the narrative—or the fiction—work back on these other, more material processes? It seems clear, on one level, that a given fiction can affect a given body. Witness, for example, the placebo effect in medicine. More pertinently for this essay, is there a sense in which seeing the fiction *as* a fiction (so having a kind of perspective back on the self from some other place) might allow some flexibility—or open up some space as it were—around a given fiction of the self? Or even prompt the writing of a different fiction?[11] In other essays collected here I look at this change in point of view in relation to Buddhist technologies, but it seems to me that neuroscience can also offer this kind of view back on ourselves. It offers a scientific perspective on our more typical one, but additional to this, and more interesting for myself, is the way it sometimes necessarily proceeds by the positing of various thought experiments. Metzinger (from whom the above brief neuroscientific account of the self has been taken) offers up an especially compelling example here—a thought experiment that involves the production of a fiction within a fiction—in the part of his book *The Ego Tunnel* on 'Lucid Dreaming' (Metzinger 2009: 139-48). The self-aware dream avatar is able to give us some reflective or recursive information about the fiction that we are always already within (the ego tunnel, for Metzinger, being akin, in some respects, to a dream). Following Metzinger, Brassier also suggests that the self is a nested fiction—a phenomenal self-model that is always already in a world-model produced by and for it—albeit the self necessarily cannot see this because the modelling is transparent.[12] It is in this sense that the self exists in a 'special form of darkness' (Metzinger quoted in Brassier 2014: 15). But as I gestured to above, Brassier also makes the argument that this need not necessarily be the case, that there might be other kinds of non-self-models that are possible—other kinds of agency and, with that, the possibility of experience without a self. The production of Artificial Intelligence (AI) seems to be a case in point here when this involves not only an entity with a different self-modelling (for example a modelling system whose processes are opaque rather than transparent), but also one that allows us some purchase on the fiction that we ourselves are. Like the lucid dream then, here the making of a fiction (the AI system) allows us a kind of outside perspective on that other fiction we necessarily inhabit.

Psychoanalysis and the Sinthome

In typical understandings of psychoanalysis, the fiction of the self—or, in psychoanalytic terms, the ego—'masks' desires and drives that also arise in and from the body. In Lacan's formularisation, the self can be thought of as a linguistically constructed subject, produced in and through the web of the Symbolic that is spun over the Real. This Real will often assert itself, or certainly exert pressure on the Symbolic (and thus on the conscious subject), but it is not readily accessible—or not directly 'seen'—by the subject (so the subject exists in another kind of darkness in this sense). Indeed, in Lacanian psychoanalysis, the subject is more or less defined by being cut off from the Real. This originary wound (to speak figuratively) is not something which can be healed or sutured in any straightforward sense. There is always already a gulf between the body (the Real) and the Symbolic (the fiction). It is this gulf—or cut—and how a subject deals with it that defines their particular set-up or fiction of the self.

In the later Lacan the fiction of the self becomes more complex. Here it is understood more as a knotting together of the three registers of the Real, Symbolic and Imaginary (the Imaginary involving a prior moment—before the Symbolic—of ego formation that happens, crucially, through a misidentification).[13] This knot can, however, become undone or, in some cases, was never effectively tied to begin with. Lacan defines analysis in these later seminars as a kind of 're-tying' of the knot. He calls this work of repair the sinthome (a play on the more familiar 'symptom') (2018). It involves some kind of pursuit (by the subject concerned) which can bind the three registers together. The sinthome is not the production of an avatar or egregore exactly, but it is the production and practice of a fiction (broadly understood), one which is invested in and that then has real effects (in this case offering some cohesion and consistency for a subject). Crucially it is a fiction that is self-authored and, as such, follows Lacan's dictate we find elsewhere (for example in the seminar on *The Ethics of Psychoanalysis*) that the work of analysis might also be framed as prompting the subject to 'become a cause of themselves'. This is to claim one's own causality away from external agents (so it involves another kind of retroactive feedback loop) (Lacan 1992).

Writing the Self

Lacan's 'case study' of the sinthome is the body of works which produce the author/name 'James Joyce' as a kind of repair (Lacan's claim here—to be very brief—is that Joyce faced a crisis because of an absent father and thus the lack of the 'name-of-the-father' that might have cohered his sense of self) (see Lacan 2018). In Lacan's reading of Joyce, writing—or using the register of the Symbolic in a very particular and creative manner—is a practice that is able to stitch a self together. It can give consistency to a life that otherwise threatens to come apart. Writing might be understood as a practice of repair in this respect.[14] It is especially the way in which writing can allow a claiming of that Symbolic register that has determined the subject in the first place that can give it this character.

Especially interesting here are those writing practices that are specifically concerned with the self (Lacan's point of departure is Joyce's *Portrait of the Artist as a Young Man*). This is not simply autobiography, but writings that narrate the self in some way (Joyce's book is a fictioned account of his own self-formation). It certainly seems as if writing can be a technology for producing the egregore of the self. A more contemporary example than Joyce is Kathy Acker who wrote fictions about her life, but then also narrated her life as a fiction (and so might be understood as a key forerunner of the 'genre' of autofiction). Or, put another way, Acker, the person, invents Acker the fiction (which then—we can presume—fed back on the person). Also compelling here is the way in which different registers—especially drawings and diagrams—can augment this self-narration. See, for example, Acker's magnificent dream maps in *Blood and Guts in High School* (Acker 1984). These offer a further level of 'actualisation' of the fiction (or, to return to a psychoanalytic register, they introduce the Imaginary into this self-formation). A further and related aspect here is the way in which other fictions have also been written about (the fiction of) Acker or have folded Acker's fiction into other fictions (including other fictions of other selves).[15] If Acker is an egregore, then they are one that has been—and is still being—collectively written.

Acker is another of the key figures I will be returning to in some of the following essays.

Schizoanalysis

For Gilles Deleuze and Félix Guattari fiction is also a key resource for the practice of schizoanalysis and the production of subjectivity. Here the method is less the interpretation of symptoms and the 'speaking cure' and more the following of a symptom—as if it is a bird tapping on the window[16]— and, with that, the working on more affective, even atmospheric registers. Schizoanalysis also proceeds with very much a pragmatic attitude. So, not necessarily what is true but what works.[17] We might even say that the intention is to invent fictions—again, broadly understood—that will allow a life to continue (Daniel Schreber's *Memoirs of My Nervous Illness* being a key case study for Deleuze and Guattari here) (Schreber 2000). More broadly, schizoanalysis might be understood as a kind of fictioning of the self—or of subjectivity—in this sense, when the latter is understood as a very broad term, covering the more larval selves that make up an individual and/or a group that a number of individuals might make up.

In fact, in *Anti-Oedipus* the subject is less of a focus and is understood as being secondary to a process of desire that is primary. Deleuze and Guattari write about different 'celibate machines' that express or incarnate different relations between this desiring process and a principle of non-desire (what they call, in this book, the Body without Organs). These celibate machines (which might also be understood—following Freud—to incarnate different kinds of relation between the death and life instincts) are complex diagrams or again different fictions of the self. In *A Thousand Plateaus* the pragmatic and constructive aspect of schizoanalysis is further emphasised, especially in plateaus like 'November 28, 1947: How Do You Make Yourself a Body without Organs?' (Deleuze and Guattari 1988: 149-66) where the latter—a Body without Organs—shifts its meaning and names a practice or set of practices for accessing an outside to the self and, as such, is something that a subject might themselves make (against themselves as it were). This pragmatics is also in play, for example, in the central becoming plateau where becoming itself—understood, at least partly, as a kind of magical practice (or a practice of sorcery)—is aligned with the practice of schizoanalysis.[18]

In his solo writings on the production of subjectivity Guattari writes in an even more abstract manner about certain entities—might we call them fictioning machines?—that operate at the interface between the registers of chaos and complexity or allow an emergence of the latter from the former.[19] These fictioning machines are forms of processual and proto-subjectivities. There are connections here with the more usual psychoanalytic terms—and relations between—the Real and the Symbolic although, crucially, Guattari's model follows an asignifying logic and, as such, his entities maintain a more intimate relationship with the chaos/the Real that they emerge from. Put differently, Guattari attends to how a fiction can operate to spin and cohere a subjectivity around itself. As I have put it elsewhere, fiction operates as the friction in this process (see O'Sullivan 2012: 108). Images might also work in this way, as kind of 'key-points' in the production of subjectivity. In other writings Guattari explores this in relation to the writer Jean Genet who deploys this kind of 'image function' in relation to subjectivity (Guattari 2013: 215-30).[20] Images operate here across different regimes or can have a traction beyond the regime they are written (or made) in. This idea of fictions crossing over from art to life (or from an imaginary space into a real space) is a recurring one in these essays and has been important to me in relation to my own myth-work (more of which in the second part of my book).

Magick

I have already briefly mentioned magic above in relation to Stengers but it seems to me that the more particular magick (with a 'k')—which especially follows Aleister Crowley and Austin Osman Spare's practices and definitions—has a parallel intention to analysis (both psycho and schizo).[21] In resonance with Lacan's ethics of psychoanalysis there is a similar goal to 'become a cause of oneself' (and, in this sense, the Ccru's hyperstition is also magickal insofar as it attends to this retro-causality).[22] In relation to schizoanalysis there is a similar pragmatic attitude in play as well. A desire and intention to see what works and then to claim (or 'write') one's own self.[23] There are many different kinds of practice involved in this self-determination, for example sigil magick which, to a certain extent, is also a practice concerned with the Symbolic (and even with 're-writing' parts of it). There is in addition the practice of naming and re-naming or, once again, the re-claiming of one's own determination (so, self-narration again)[24]—although, following some of my comments above, it might be more accurate to say that this claiming of identity is really a claiming of a fiction or even a series of them. Then there is the important tradition of the magician making their own tools that I mentioned in my Introduction. This seems especially pertinent in relation to the 'metamodeling' method of schizoanalysis (the way in which it looks to other models as resource) but also to any genuine practice of self-analysis.

More generally magick is a name for practices of self-transformation.[25] In this sense it is a 'technology of the self' to borrow a phrase from Michel Foucault (see Foucault 2000). But it is also a technology that treats 'reality' as something that can be manipulated or, to turn to a more contemporary magickal practitioner—the writer and experimental novelist William Burroughs—that can be cut in to. Reality here, it seems to me, is not quite the same as the Lacanian Real and is more akin to the Symbolic (although it might also be the case that this distinction is itself undone through magick). In fact, might we say that the self is a particular script that can itself be edited? Here magick dovetails with writing. Or writing— in its experimental form (as in Burrough's practice of the cut-up)—can be understood as a magickal technology.[26] Insofar as it disrupts linear temporality and cause-and-effect sequencing then it is also a cut into space and time. The cut-up might be understood as a kind of accompaniment to the production of an avatar or egregore then. If the latter is to do with the conjuring of another entity or entities, then the cut-up cuts into the existing set-up (or what Burroughs termed 'control') and, as such, provides material for this summoning (as well as opening a gap through which the entity might appear). Burroughs is another of the figures that I will be returning to in many of the following essays.

Writing 'Speaks Back'

The above practices are all concerned with seeing the self as a fiction to some extent and thus, very broadly, as something that can be rewritten. They constitute a toolbox of sorts for this kind of constructive and creative work (when this also involves different methods and devices that produce a shift in perspective). This is not to deny the specificity of the above practices, but, rather, to foreground a general pragmatics that is certainly always already in play with schizoanalysis and magick. A pragmatics that also means using different resources in ways for which they were not intended perhaps or as a method for something that is not strictly speaking part of their milieu.[27] After all, the intention here is not necessarily to get things right or to become an expert in this or that or, indeed, to produce knowledge (at least as that is usually understood). It is, rather, to produce transformation.

So much for theoretical exegesis and for a type of writing that attempts to explain and persuade (even, in its own way, to control). So much too for writing *about* these other writing practices (broadly conceived). The actual business of 'writing the self' cannot but also attempt a circumnavigation of all this. It is in this sense that this essay—and those that follow—can only be a kind of preparatory work or operate as a parallel to another kind of writing that is more performative. After all, if writing remains the writing 'of' a self that is already there then it operates only as a (reassuring) mirror of that self. Crucially, writing can also disable this kind of image and 'reality effect'. It can 'speak back' to its author as if it has arrived from somewhere else. It has very real—and often unexpected—effects in this sense. This is because writing does not belong to anyone (there is no entity behind it). It does not come from you, but, rather, you come from it. Ultimately it will always undo a sense of origin and, with that, any secure sense of self. Or, put more positively, writing can open a given self up to an outside and thus allow a different self—or different avatars and egregores—to step forth (which means it will necessarily sometimes be bloody).

Coda

I realise what I have written in this first essay does not involve the more performative writing that it calls for and, indeed, in many ways follows the style and 'voice' of the typical academic essay (and thus might be said to reinforce a particular fiction of the self). It's not easy (at least for me) to change a writing habit and style or to know how to introduce that other kind of writing into a more academic register. It's more straightforward when this other kind of writing happens elsewhere (as it does, for me, in relation to Plastique Fantastique). But on the other hand I think that any and all writing—including the academic—can have a performative function especially when it is concerned with another intention beyond meaning (for example the construction of a device). I am also aware that this essay—like some of those that follow—repeats many of the ideas and tropes of previous work I have written. I've figured this to myself as a case of opening all the cupboards to see what resources are already in there (or as a looking back to see what it is that I've been about). I think this turning around and revisiting materials and methods—and even a re-versioning of previous themes—is also partly what myth-work is about. Finally, in each of the following essays I will add a short coda like this that involves a reflection on what I have written and thus attempts too to address more of my own personal investments in the themes of this book. In the second part of my book this will also occasionally involve an attempt at a more performative style of writing or at least one that involves the presentation of images rather than concepts or explanations.

Notes

1 'Meme magic' refers to the way in which internet memes can have real-world effects, as is the case, for example, with the alt-right 're-purposing' of the Pepe the Frog meme—especially with the folding in of the cult of Kek—and the part that might have played in the election of Trump (see the discussion in Burrows and O'Sullivan 2019: 481–4).
2 See as indicative the recent anthology of writing on magic—a 'gramarye' for artists—edited by Jamie Sutcliffe which foregrounds a 'magical-critical' tradition in amongst the more superficial (and often right-wing) turns to magic (Sutcliffe 2021a). See also Sutcliffe's introductory essay which warns against a focus on 'rediscovery' and 're-enchantment', but additionally attends to the ways in which the magical-critical tradition can dovetail with identity politics and political activism (as well as art practice) (Sutcliffe 2021b).
3 In relation to Stengers' argument about other forms of agency see also Viveiros de Castro's definition—following 'Amerindian perspectival ontology'—that 'whatever is activated or "agented" by the point of view will be a subject' (Viveiros de Castro 2004: 467) and a little later in the same article: 'A good interpretation, then, would be one able to understand every event as in truth an action, an expression of intentional states or predicates of some subject' (469).
4 And as such this understanding has something in common with Bruno Latour's 'actor network theory' (See, for example, Latour 2007).
5 My encounter with the Ccru and their writings had a deep impact on my own academic trajectory (it has been pointed out to me more than once that I often return to this scene). In particular I attended the 1995 Virtual Futures conference at Warwick University (and then again in 1996). I've written more about this experience in a long review essay (see O'Sullivan 2014a), but would repeat here that it was the particular combination of Deleuzian-inflected talks and presentations, alongside more counter-cultural content (and especially dance/rave culture) that had this formative impact.

6 For a fuller discussion of hyperstition in relation to fiction (and myth) see O'Sullivan 2017a.
7 To quote the Ccru from the essay 'Lemurian Time War':

   for practitioners of hyperstition, differentiating between 'degrees of realization' is crucial. The hyperstitional process of entities 'making themselves real' is precisely a passage, a transformation, in which potentials—already active virtualities—realize themselves. Writing operates not as a passive representation but as an active agent of transformation and a gateway through which entities can emerge. '[B]y writing a universe, the writer makes such a universe possible'. (Ccru [and quoting Burroughs] 2017: 36)

8 In relation to the summoning of demons see also the 'Syzygy' collaboration between the Ccru and the collective artist 0[rphan] d[rift>]—themselves a kind of egregore—at Beaconsfield gallery, London in 1999 (see 0[rphan] d[rift>] n.d.).
9 And, as such, this essay develops some of the ideas and themes discussed in the 'Overcoming the Fiction of the Self' chapter of *Fictioning* (Burrows and O'Sullivan 2019: 49–62).
10 This is what N. Katherine Hayles calls the 'cognitive nonconscious' or simply 'unthought' (Hayles 2017). Crucially for Hayles this is not just a capacity of humans ('cognition happens outside of consciousness/unconsciousness'), but 'extends through the entire biological spectrum, including animals and plants' and, further, includes machines and our relation to them: 'technical devices cognize, and in doing so profoundly influence human complex systems; we live in an era when the planetary cognitive ecology is undergoing rapid transformation, urgently requiring us to rethink cognition and reenvision its consequences on a global scale' (Hayles 2017: 5). See also the discussion of Hayles (in relation to 'Machine Fictioning') in Burrows and O'Sullivan 2019: 435–40.
11 There is also the way in which neurological diseases and what Catherine Malabou calls the 'new wounded' show us something about how our identities are both fragile and can be 're-written', for example in those cases where a new personality emerges after disease or trauma (see Malabou 2022).
12 To quote Brassier's definition of consciousness and the self (quoting Metzinger's own definition):

   Once consciousness is minimally defined as the activation of an integrated world-model within a window of presence, then self-consciousness can be defined as the activation of a phenomenal self-model (PSM) nested within this world-model: 'A self-model is a model of the very representational system that is currently activating it within itself'. (Brassier [and quoting Metzinger] 2011: 15)

   The self is, however, a modelling that cannot see itself as such because its processes are transparent.
13 This is Lacan's famous 'mirror phase', a developmental stage a child goes through and which involves their identification with an image (for example in a mirror). This imaginary stage of the formation of the ego is thus based on a fundamental misrecognition (for example, insofar as this image is inverted).
14 For a recent lucid and rigorous discussion of repair in relation to Lacan (the sinthome), Guattari ('automodelling') and 'post-transgressive' art practice, see Theo Reeves-Evison's *Ethics of Contemporary Art: In the Shadow of Transgression* (Reeves-Evison 2020).
15 See for example Chris Kraus' *After Kathy Acker* (Kraus 2017) and Olivia Laing's *Crudo* (Laing 2018).
16 This phrase is in fact Guattari's from his solo work *Chaosmosis* (Guattari 1995a) where he is writing about what he calls 'Schizoanalytic Metamodelisation' in relation to the

production of subjectivity. Here is the full and more technical quote: 'The lapsus, for example in this perspective is not the conflictual expression of a repressed Content but the positive, indexical manifestation of a Universe trying to find itself, which comes to knock at the window like a magic bird' (68).

17 This pragmatics is especially in play in *A Thousand Plateaus* (Deleuze and Guattari 1988). As Brian Massumi says in his translator's foreword (writing about how one might approach this book): 'The question is not: is it true? But: does it work? What new thoughts does it make possible to think? What new emotion does it make possible to feel? What new sensations and perceptions does it open in the body?' (Massumi 1988: xv).

18 An indicative quote:

> x starts practicing piano again. Is it an Oedipal return to childhood? Is it a way of dying, in a kind of sonorous abolition? Is it a new borderline, an active line that will bring other becomings entirely different from becoming or rebecoming a pianist, that will induce a transformation of all of the preceding assemblages to which x was prisoner? Is it a way out? Is it a pact with the Devil? Schizoanalysis, or pragmatics, has no other meaning: Make a rhizome. But you don't know what you can make a rhizome with, you don't know which subterranean stem is effectively going to make a rhizome, or enter a becoming, people your desert. So experiment. (Deleuze and Guattari 1988: 250-1)

19 See especially Guattari's essay 'The New Aesthetic Paradigm' in *Chaosmosis* (Guattari 1995a: 98-118).

20 See the fuller discussion of this image function in Burrows and O'Sullivan 2019: 21-3.

21 What follows also relates to Chaos Magick especially as practised by groups like Thee Temple ov Psychick Youth (for more detail on the latter see Burrows and O'Sullivan 2019: 159-63).

22 Although it should be said that the Ccru were less interested in the human (and its claims to self-determination) and more in the processes of which the human is a blockage or drag. See also note 25 on the work of the Gruppo di Nun.

23 See also Gary Genosko's recent article on 'Schizoanalysis and Magic' which tracks through Guattari's own interest in magic as method (Genosko 2022). Crucial here is that magic must be subject to metamodelisation or, which amounts to the same thing, become just one further model that might be utilised by schizoanalysis. In general, Genosko shows how Guattari's interest in magic was part of his turn away from overly scientific accounts of the production of subjectivity and how this turn must also involve disrupting various dualisms and binaries (including that between science and magic).

24 For a discussion of these different practices of sigils and re-naming—especially in relation to contemporary art practice—see, respectively, Burrows and O'Sullivan 2019: 63-82 ('Mirror Work: Self-Obliteration') and 155-169 ('Scenes as Performance Fictions').

25 The writer and chaos magick practitioner Phil Hine has recently developed a more nuanced take on this, suggesting that two impulses are in play within chaos magick. A productive one (or, simply, the deployment of various techniques so as to get what one wants) and then something more akin to wonder (or an opening to the world) (Hine 2022). Hine relates the first of these to neoliberal governance. The second, for Hine, connects magick up with affect theory. In relation to psychoanalysis, we could

also say that the first of these impulses involves a willed transformation, whereas the second, like psychoanalysis itself, involves an attempt to sidestep this will so as to allow a different 'voice' to foreground itself. A further take on these two paths is the Gruppo di Nun's recent *Revolutionary Demonology* which, in Amy Ireland's understanding, develops the Ccru's interest in the dissolution of the subject, specifically in relation to entropy (Gruppo di Nun 2022 and Ireland 2022c). The Gruppo di Nun are explicitly mapping out a 'Left Hand' path for magical practice that is concerned with the insignificance of the human as opposed to the more usual 'Right Hand' path (within the Western esoteric tradition) that is more concerned with the transformation of the human into the divine (in their reading). Magical practice, for the Gruppo di Nun (and for Ireland), is then necessarily feminist and queer (insofar as it operates contra heteronormative patriarchy).

26 Once again see the Ccru's writing on Burroughs that figure him as involved in this editing of reality. An indicative quote:

In the hyperstitional model Kaye outlined, fiction is not opposed to the real. Rather, reality is understood to be composed of fictions—consistent semiotic terrains that condition perceptual, affective and behavioral responses. Kaye considered Burroughs' work to be 'exemplary of hyperstitional practice'. Burroughs construed writing—and art in general—not aesthetically, but functionally,—that is to say, magically, with magic defined as the use of signs to produce changes in reality. (Ccru 2017: 35)

27 And, as such, this pragmatic (and heretical) attitude has something in common with François Laruelle's project of Non-Philosophy (see the discussion in O'Sullivan 2017b).

2

Fiction as Desiring Work

This second essay continues with the theme of writing the self, but homes in further on the question of desire. In particular it explores the idea that fiction—especially in its mobilising of different figures—might be understood to be involved in a kind of desiring work, but that preparation for this writing (or other kinds of writing around and about fiction) can be a kind of desiring work as well (which might be the case too with these essays in the first part of my book). Towards the end I also relate this to methods like mapping that enable a perspective to be taken on the particular fiction—or even a kind of landscape—of the self. What follows was prompted by my own attempt at writing fiction (and reflections on my writing process more generally). Or to put this differently, the connection of desire to my own myth-work.

On Desire

To what extent is it important in and for a given life that our desires are fulfilled? Lacanian psychoanalysis (as well as more general folk psychology) suggests that we be wary here. That not getting what you desire might be bad, but that getting it can be worse. Why is this? Partly because what we get never really satisfies our desire even though we might have presumed it would. The thing we desire, whatever that might be, invariably disappoints. It turns to dust in the mouth as the saying goes and, as such, desire moves on to the next thing (hence consumerism). But might it also be that getting what we want is unwelcome in a further sense or can be figured in another way? Simply, that it can halt the desiring process itself, producing a kind of stasis in and for the subject.

If this is the case, then is to be in a state of desire—to be always desiring something which one does not have—itself desirable? And, perhaps more crucially, is such a state of moving towards what we desire, but not arriving at the destination, somehow sustainable? Pre-psychoanalytic ethics often foregrounds the idea that, really, it's a question of managing our desires. Marcus Aurelius, for example, suggests that we should work on desiring only what we already have. For Spinoza, desires—and more particularly affects— also need to be regulated or, at least, organised. Lacan himself traces this pre-psychoanalytical understanding of ethics even further back to Aristotle ('The cleaning up of desire, modesty, temperance, that is to say, the middle path we see articulated so remarkably in Aristotle' [Lacan 1992: 314]). Certainly desire can cause problems. But, following Lacan, is there a sense that these older theories—pre-Freud—are a kind of wishful thinking (that desire can be controlled effectively) and that the 'managing' of desire might be understood differently? Can what could be called this 'desiring work' be reconfigured in terms of the circulation of fictions? Here, the desired object (to reduce down whatever the 'thing' might be) might be figured as a fiction that pulls forth or conjures a world—the world of the desiring subject—but also as a fiction that sustains that subject *as* a desiring subject. In psychoanalytic terms such a fiction would then be 'an unconscious theme' in an individual's life. Something that 'is specifically our business' (Lacan 1992: 319). And analysis here would be about coming into some kind of relationship with this fiction—or these fictions—or even claiming them in some sense.

The Preparation of the Novel

A good example of this desiring work as sustaining fiction, especially as this relates to writing, is Roland Barthes' *The Preparation of the Novel* (2011). This book, which is composed of lecture notes for a course at the *College de France*, sets out Barthes' programme of preparation (for the writing of his novel) but also defers the actual starting of the novel. So here a fiction, at least of a kind, defers the beginning of another fiction. This is not a failure, however, but more a way of keeping desire—in this case the desire to write a novel (what we might call Barthes' more or less unconscious theme)—in circulation. Barthes refers to this preparation as the 'fantasy-of-the-novel stage' and then also 'the fantasy as an energy, a motor that gets things going' (Barthes 2011: 11). Failure, at least to some extent, would be to arrive at the point of writing, with all the inevitable disappointments and moments of stasis that this can involve. It would signal the end of a particular desiring process. Is it coincidental that the desire in this case is also to narrate a self?

There is then here a gesturing towards something to be started at a point in the future whilst at the same time a putting this off in the present. In fact, to repeat the key point here, this projecting ahead is itself a way of mobilising or animating desire. Again, for Barthes the planning is the real work—preparation as a form of desiring work—which writing the novel would signal the end of (Barthes is clear that there is a definite difference between planning the novel and writing it). Anyone familiar with starting a long writing project will, at least to some extent, be familiar with some of this. The sense of openness and everything to come that often characterises the planning and early stages before a certain kind of commitment has been made and with that a certain kind of grafting must begin. Indeed, this pre-beginning state can be very generative indeed, especially as there is nothing that has been produced that has had the chance to disappoint. I think this is also the case with other practices besides writing, not least art.

All this does need to be weighed against the satisfaction of getting things done, however (for example completing a piece of writing such as a novel). To fully meet a challenge—to come up against a limit, and to either pass that limit or, at least, understand it as a limit—are all important and meaningful things, not least insofar as they can also produce self-knowledge. As is working on a creative project more generally or simply having an ongoing relationship with the latter (which I think is itself a form of desiring work). This desiring work needs to be disentangled as well from a near enemy, procrastination, which can involve diversion and distraction as a means of avoidance (although, again, might procrastination be figured as a kind of sustaining fiction?). These caveats aside, however, there does seem to be something about intentionally circling around the thing (that is also specifically avoided) that is important. In Barthes' case circling around his own planned narrative which then—to say it again—itself becomes a further narrative. *The Preparation of the Novel* is like an autofiction in this sense but also a kind of psychoanalytic 'case study'. Or, at least, an exercise in self-analysis.[1] Ironically, it shares some characteristics of an experimental novel as well, especially in its style and form of presentation.[2]

The Ethics of Psychoanalysis

In Lacan's seminar on *The Ethics of Psychoanalysis* (1992) this desiring economy is figured as a ring—or torus—with *das ding* in the centre. This is the 'The Thing' we are attracted to and moving towards (as if we have been hooked by it) but are also *very* keen to avoid or, at least, various obstacles are put in place (by us) to prevent us getting there.[3] Indeed, it is not really a question of arriving at this destination (which would certainly mean the end of a process). Rather, it is the journey itself—the various encounters and side-tracks 'on the way'—that are important and, indeed, meaningful. Desire keeps all this moving along, as on a carousel.

Again, might these various encounters (with different figures perhaps?) and tracks (other loops and circuits?) be thought of as fictions? Certainly, they are wrapped up with our desire. In many ways they are conjured by it as signposts on the way, but also, again, as obstacles. Seeing these figures and tracks clearly—relatively speaking—seems important in understanding how desire circulates in a given life. But understanding them as fictions seems important too, not least as this suggests that substitutions might be possible, if only to get things moving at times of impasse. This is partly what Lacan meant by his term 'traversing the fantasy'.[4] The substitution of other fictions which might then have more traction on and for a life at a given moment or move things on in some manner. A kind of doubled attitude seems important here. To take the fictions as real (and thus as animating), but then to also understand them as fictions (and thus as substitutable). Is this also to take these fictions as both serious *and* comic? Certainly it is to both believe the fiction and not believe it at the same time (or, at least, to oscillate between these positions).

There is something important in play here too that relates this desiring work (as I have attempted to define it) to magic.[5] To take a fiction 'as if' it's real suggests the possibility of transformation (of a world and of a subject in that world). After all, are we not always already involved in this practice of living out various fictions? And then to treat reality as a fiction also opens up some space and, again, the possibility of transformation. This idea that reality can be transformed in some way seems to be a key principle of magical practice. Returning to the theme of the previous essay here, it also means that the writing of fictions can have what might be called an ontological weight. After all, if reality is already composed of other fictions (most of them not authored by us) then it would seem fair to assume that it can be re-fictioned, at least to some extent.

Returning to the subject and turning to another of Lacan's seminars, might we also understand these fictions as 'quilting points' that give the subject cohesion and coherence (these are the 'key-points' I mentioned in the previous essay)? For Lacan any given subject in order to be as such necessarily has a number of these quilting points, or particular set-ups of signifiers/signifieds. Indeed, for Lacan, the question is to know how many are needed to stop psychosis.[6] It is these points that maintain a consistency for the subject. It seems to me that these points can also be understood as fictions and figures in some senses (if we are allowed to broaden Lacan's own formularisation out somewhat). A project of analysis—and especially self-analysis—might then be about mapping out these points and, with that, getting some perspective on any pattern they mark out. In many ways this is also the work of writing and, indeed, preparing to write (in the sense Barthes discusses it). This identification of quilting points—or specific figures and locations on a landscape—has been a key component of my own myth-work as I suggest in some of the essays that follow.

Anti-Oedipus

Might it also be that there is no subject before or outside of these fictions and figures? Or that the subject is secondary to them? In *Anti-Oedipus* (1984) Deleuze and Guattari suggest that the subject is produced as a kind of side effect of the process of desire. For Deleuze and Guattari the subject is a 'residuum' of desiring-production that then identifies with, but also misrecognises itself in the various figures and tracks. This is the infamous retroactive identification in *Anti-Oedipus*: 'Ah, so *that's* what it was!' (Deleuze and Guattari 1984: 18). For Deleuze and Guattari, schizoanalysis becomes a method for mapping out these figures and tracks (and attending to any sequence they are part of). It is less about the interpretation of symptoms within a signifying economy—or utilising any pre-set interpretive framework—and more a pragmatic following of those symptoms to see where they might lead (the bird knocking at the window once more [see Guattari 1995a: 68]). The goal here, if that's an appropriate term, is less the production of a fully functioning ego (as in some other therapeutic techniques and technologies), but rather a kind of strange self-authorship—a claiming of these figures and other images through making a connection (and then maintaining a relation) with this desiring-production. This is also what Deleuze and Guattari call 'materialist psychiatry'. *Anti-Oedipus* is at the intersection of Marxism and a radical

Freudianism in this sense, but it can be brought into relationship with Lacan's *Ethics* too (despite what Guattari thought about Lacan's signifier enthusiasm) insofar as both works are concerned with the subject assuming their own causality.[7] Although, again, for *Anti-Oedipus* the category of subject is certainly more thoroughly interrogated and distributed.

For Deleuze and Guattari it is in fiction that we see most evidence of this self-authorship and thus can find resources for our own practices. For example, with Schreber and Beckett in *Anti-Oedipus* and Woolf and Lovecraft in *A Thousand Plateaus* (1988) (amongst many others). The two volume *Capitalism and Schizophrenia* project can be defined in one sense as the utilisation of non-philosophical materials and especially literature for philosophical (and analytic) ends.[8] As I also mentioned in the previous essay, for Lacan too literature evidences this 'self-construction' as paradigmatically the case with James Joyce and the sinthome (2018). Writing—and especially the writing of fiction—seems to always be a kind of autofiction in this sense, even, perhaps, when it appears to be about something else.

On Writing and Mapping

What then is the relationship of the writing of fiction as the writing of a life to the process of desire that throws up fictions as a way of enabling a life to carry on? Perhaps it is simply that they are the same process, albeit with writing one assumes ownership of those images and figures or, at least, sees them more clearly. And then also represents and mobilises them in some manner. Or follows them to see where they might go (so, once again, one takes them seriously even if they are comic). Put differently, one listens so as to hear what they might 'speak back' to us, their author. Indeed, it is this 'speaking back' that seems crucial insofar as some kind of knowledge or information not readily available to the more usual—or self-conscious—subject is offered up by a writing process. There is a connection here with Freud and the speaking cure, and especially with the idea of 'overhearing' ourselves speaking or 'listening in' to the unconscious. It is certainly the case that desire can be hidden or, once again, that it is not completely under our control. And as such it needs must be approached obliquely through mediators and other masks.

There is also a sense that writing this out—or mapping it in some manner—allows a different perspective on the process of desire more generally. As if one is invariably in this process, being tugged along by it, but through writing (and other forms of representation) one is also able to shift so as to have a different perspective on the circuits and loops, the various tracks, images and figures. To *see*—from above as it were—the map (or the landscape) of desire that constitutes a particular self. Or even to see the self as simply a region within that terrain. This idea of a switching or shuttling of perspective is a further theme of some of my essays. It is also this that allows a certain orientation and, following this, the identification of other areas hitherto outside a given territory (as well as the possibilities for the substitution of fictions and figures—and images—I mentioned above). It is not, however, as if this map pre-exists the enquiry exactly (or, at least, it is never complete). Rather the map is always there to be made. The unconscious, if that is 'where' desire is 'located', is always to be constructed in this sense. This is one of the key messages of Deleuze and Guattari's *Capitalism and Schizophrenia* project.

Might this also mean that other maps besides those of a given subject can be made as well? More collective maps for example? Following Guattari's solo work here, more 'micro' or molecular maps that can be drawn 'below' the register of the typical or habitual subject (see Guattari 1996b). So below a signifying consciousness and, as such, concerned with more pre-personal intensities. And then perhaps there are more 'macro' maps which can also be drawn 'above' that register. Hence the importance of groups and collectives and the work associated with them (something I will return to in later essays). The typical—or habitual—subject is just a midway point here. Or, put differently—and to return to some of my earlier comments—different kinds of map might operate on and at different registers (signifying and asignifying). Any map in this sense—or, again, any landscape to change the perspective slightly—involves a selection of images and figures. Certain details are always foregrounded that allow the production of a particular fiction of the self. Perhaps it is also the case that this selection has been made before the subject, and, in that sense, was made *for* the subject? Here part of the work is to be able to *see* this and work out what details and narratives were always already in play and whose interests they serve. And then to identify as well what material might be repurposed and made available for other more creative forms of self-narration.

This means a practice of analysis and a critique of previous narratives—and, crucially, the seeing of these narratives *as* fictions—but also one of pragmatics and creation. What other maps and landscapes can be drawn and what other figures summoned or encountered with or within the material available? And, for that matter, with whom (when this 'whom' is not only other selves, but perhaps other non-human persons or even other objects and props)? What paths and passageways lead to impasses and dead ends (the halting of the desiring process) and which of them open us up to further areas and adventures? How do we summon these different figures that are both of us and not of us at the same time? And then what relation do these have to the maps (and landscapes) of others?[9] It seems to me that strange and contradictory strategies might well be required in this kind of work that is partly about getting ourselves out of the way so that the desiring process can get on and do its work. What might be called this negotiation (and play) with fiction as mode of existence is a further definition of what I have been calling myth-work.

Coda

I mentioned the fiction I have recently written in my Introduction to this book. That writing project involved a tracking of desire with its various figures, landscapes and other images and narratives. I am not naturally a fiction writer, being more comfortable with ideas and concepts than images and narratives, but certainly the process of writing that work helped map out a particular landscape of myself, one that I am still working on (or listening back to). In fact, this second essay has partly been a retrospective attempt at figuring out further what that other writing was about (and why I had undertaken such a project). But more generally this essay—and the others in this book—involve another take on desiring work. That it can involve a kind of commentary or reflection on what it is that has been done and thus gesture forwards future possibilities. Might it also be the case that sharing this kind of work can operate as a trigger or prompt in some way for others to pursue their own myth-work? This has been one of the intentions (and hopes) behind gathering together these essays and presenting them here (both the theoretical ones and those that involve more personal reflections).

Notes

1. In relation (and contradiction) to this see also Élisabeth Roudinesco's efforts to disentangle autofiction—as overly concerned with ego and identity—from the practice of analysis (Roudinesco 2014: 42-4).
2. In relation to this see also *Roland Barthes's Party* by the Roland Barthes Reading Group (2020), which operates as a fictioned commentary on a fragment of Barthes' text, but also demonstrates the way in which a text can be folded into other texts and, indeed, can call a community forth (in this case a reading group).
3. For a more detailed engagement with this particular seminar of Lacan's (in relation/contrast to Foucault) see 'The Care of the Self versus the Ethics of Desire' in O'Sullivan 2012: 59-87. My diagrammatic understanding of Lacan's seminar on *The Ethics* is indebted to Jean Mathee.
4. It also resonates with a definition Alain Badiou gives of analysis (and the psychoanalytic cure), which is:

    supposed to unblock a situation that is initially experienced by the analysand as an impotence (I am separated from my desire, caught up in the hardness, the stagnation of existence), so that it leads to a real point where the subject, bogged down in the imaginary, can once again recover some of its power of symbolization. (Badiou in Badiou and Roudinesco 2014: 16-17)

5. For another metamodeling of transformative magic (this time voodoo) with Lacanian psychoanalysis see John Cussans' composite diagrams in his contribution to *Performance Fictions* (Cussans 2010). See also the performances—for example the work *+HRdpN+)(BAHNBAMOOIRA+* made and performed with Roberto N. Peyre as part of *There Is Not and Never Has Been Anything to Understand*, curated by David Burrows and Simon O'Sullivan, ASC Gallery, London in 2012—where Haitian veve are brought into encounter and productive relation with Northern Soul. Could Cussans' expanded ritual/art practice be described as a form of myth-work?
6. To quote Lacan:

    I don't know how many there are, but isn't it important that one should manage to determine the minimal number of fundamental points between the signifier and the signified necessary for a human being to be called normal, and which, when they are not established, or when they give way, make a psychotic. (Lacan 1983: 268-9)

7. Another way of putting this is a subject refusing the narrative of being born of parents (or of being Oedipalised) as is the case with both Artaud ('I believe in neither father/nor mother,/aint gotta/daddy-mommy' (Artaud 1995: 237) and Sun Ra ('I wasn't just born; I had been somewhere before I was born. I'm not a human. I never called anybody "mother"...I never called anybody "father". I never felt that way' (Sun Ra quoted in Szwed

2000: 6). For a further discussion of Sun Ra along these lines see 'Myth-Science: Alien Perspectives' in *Fictioning* (Burrows and O'Sullivan 2019: 199–216).

8 For a fuller discussion of this point see my essay 'Memories of a Deleuzian: To Think Is Always to Follow the Witches' Flight' (O'Sullivan 2017c).

9 Although it has not been the focus of this essay, reading other's fictions (or traversing their landscapes) also seems to allow some understanding of the fiction that we are—and thus can produce some flexibility around the latter—especially when that other fiction is both engrossing and alienating at the same time. See my essay 'Fictioning a Pilgrimage (or Fieldwork on the Fiction of the Self' (O'Sullivan 2022) that concerns just such a reading of a fiction, Russell Hoban's *Riddley Walker* (1980). In that essay I also draw out the connections between walking and writing, both of which seem to allow an understanding (and activation) of different fictions (and landscapes), especially when there is a nesting of one fiction within the other.

3

On Acéphale and Having No Head

What does it mean to lose one's head or to explore a mode of being in the world without a self? This essay begins with a brief look at Georges Bataille's Acéphale project—the group and their writings—especially in relation to ideas of self-sacrifice and 'headlessness.' It then goes on to explore this thematic in relation to other accounts of non-self, for example within Buddhism and neuroscience. I end with some very brief and speculative comments about the relationship of this material to theorisations of Blackness (a theme which will be picked up in subsequent essays). Once again a key concern here is the 'fiction of the self' and, alongside that, the idea that there might be other modes of existence—or other fictions—that we can experiment with.

Headlessness

The headless figure of Acéphale represents a mode of being in the world that is set against reason and even a more general cerebral intelligence. In its place Acéphale asserts an embodied or libidinal take on thinking and the self (if those last two terms are still appropriate). Georges Bataille's idea of 'base materialism' and of an affective 'communication' that occurs in limit experiences foregrounds this idea that there is something else going on besides what we presume is going on, at least conceptually speaking (see Bataille 1985). There is a whole 'other' bodily intelligence at work that parallels and often usurps the sovereign subject (hence Bataille's interest in Nietzsche who was also concerned with this other intelligence).[1]

For Bataille this base materialism is set against 'project' understood as that which we do in terms of utility in all its forms.[2] Indeed, it is set against the human—when this figure and fiction is the embodiment of project—and all that follows from that (the 'good life' for example). Bataille is radically anti-theological in this sense and, more particularly (and following Nietzsche once more), affirms the death of God as a liberation of the human animal. Those extreme moments when humans experience themselves—or experience something—outside of project are especially valued and Bataille's writings and life revolve around seeking them out and affirming them.[3] Indeed, might we say that Bataille's writings—the (anti-) philosophical work and the fiction—are a kind of communication to us and, as such, summon something else from within the fiction we invariably occupy? They are certainly not to be read for typical knowledge or to provide information for the self as it typically is.

Acéphale also names both the journal and the secret society set up by Bataille and others. As far as the former goes, writing is often used to call forth and then bind a group. It can be both *from* a group and *for* a group in this sense. The manifesto form is key here, but other kinds of writing that contain instructions, protocols and so forth can also perform this function (as perhaps fiction can too).[4] As far as the latter goes—the secret society—there is a connection between this headless mode of being and the collective—a headless group—that is called forth. Both subvert the control of the self-conscious sovereign subject (in fact, membership of Acéphale involved various gestures of self-sacrifice as well as talk of actual sacrifice). Or, to put this differently, both modes operate at a different register to this sovereign subject which is situated between but also to one side of the molecularity of both the body and the group.

There is as well a less esoteric and less theoretical account of a person suddenly realising that they are headless. Edison Harding's *On Having No Head* (1961) gives their account of walking in the mountains one day when it occurs to them, with crystal clarity, that they have no head. That there is, in fact, a hole where their head should be. True, they could look in a mirror, but that would be to just see a reflection (it would be a misrecognition in Lacan's terms). The truth of the matter—for this particular self out walking—is simply that there is a kind of 'non-place' from which one looks out. Or even does not look out (after all there is no head so there are no eyes). It is more, simply, that they are in the world somehow. Or that something is in the world. Some kind of point of view.

Having a 'realisation' like this has further implications. If there is no head, then is it also the case that there is no one there behind the head? No self at all? To quote from the very beginning of Harding's book: 'Reason and imagination and all mental chatter died down...I forgot my name, my humanness, my thingness, all that could be called me or mine. Past and future dropped away...Lighter than air, clearer than glass, altogether released from myself, I was nowhere around' (Edison Harding 1961: 1-2). This shift in perspective—that, again, is invariably experienced suddenly—seems to allow a kind of seeing through or *dispelling* of the fiction of the self. Or, put differently, a certain kind of framing of experience suddenly drops away and, as such, is seen (retroactively) *as* a framing.

There are other 'traditions' too that involve producing this shift in perspective so as to snap an individual out of the illusory sense of self. In Zen Buddhism for example, there are different techniques and methods for producing sudden moments of 'insight'. There are also other non-dualist Buddhist traditions that involve a rigorous discipline of rational enquiry that leads to the unseating of this fiction (questions are posed in a series, such as 'who raises this hand?', and so forth). From all accounts this can produce a moment of clarity—a 'stepping through the gate'—after which, again, the fiction of the self is seen retrospectively as a fiction (ultimately the questions asked lead towards a realisation that there is no author 'behind' the various parts—and actions—of the body). Traditionally, once seen this 'sight' cannot be unseen. Once the illusion is broken then that's that (hence the idea of stepping through the gate). Crucially, for these Buddhist traditions, holding on to a fixed sense of self is the source of our suffering in the world insofar as it is a desire for permanence in a world marked by impermanence. I will return to this in a further essay—on my own experiences with Buddhism—in the second part of my book.

This tradition and these practices are certainly different to Bataille's base materialism and to Acéphale, but like the latter they do affirm another place or a kind of experience outside of the self and from which—looking back—the self can be seen as a fiction. Indeed, the two strategies—of asceticism (Buddhism) and abandonment/excess (base materialism)—arrive at the same place. As if all that is needed is the affirmation and occupation of a mode that is either more or less than that which the human more typically occupies or experiences. Or, put differently, a mode where one is more in the world or certainly less extracted from it.[5]

Neuroscience and the Nemocentric Subject

Dispelling any illusory sense of the self is not the end of the story. After all, there is still an entity in the world that is doing something. There is still a perspective at work. Elsewhere (in relation to François Laruelle's Non-Philosophy project) I have written about the way in which this seeing of the frame I mentioned above might produce a little wiggle room around a self and even prompt the possibility of shifting to other selves (or other fictions) (see O'Sullivan 2017b). In fact, I think that it is not exactly the 'space' beyond the self that should hold our attention (in many ways there is not much to say about that), but rather how this space can allow for the possibility of other selves. It announces the possibility of what might be called a 'generic' creativity and, with that, a kind of experimental pragmatics (although we need to be wary here—following Bataille—of reintroducing project). There is also something about removing the head—and dispelling the fiction—that relates to that other neuroscientific idea of the 'nemocentric subject' (see Brassier 2011). As I briefly laid out in my first essay, the latter names a mode of being in the world without a self understood here as a particular kind of organising—and filtering—mechanism. In fact, it is to make that which is typically transparent—the fiction when it is not seen as a fiction (or, to repeat the point above, the frame when it is not seen as a frame)—to make that opaque. There is a kind of radical gestalt at play here and, with that, a foregrounding of that which was background. And once again, becoming aware of the fiction means it is retroactively seen as one.

Certainly, again from a neuroscientific perspective, there is a whole lot going on besides this filtering mechanism or 'ego tunnel' as Thomas Metzinger calls it (Metzinger 2009). Again, as I mentioned in my first essay, there is an intelligence that gets things done despite what the head intends. It is science, broadly understood, that has shown us this. The scientific image of the human as an incredibly complex bio-chemical organism sits 'beneath' the more manifest or 'folk' image we have of the self (and of our own self). The latter is then a kind of device that sits atop all this (to speak figuratively). There are different accounts of how and why this device came about—why a certain form of self-consciousness emerged—but there does seem to be strong evidence that it was in part useful in some senses, at least at some point in our species' history (which is to say, it is—of course—an evolutionary development). It certainly seems to be a cohering device. It gives consistency—and an agency of sorts—to an entity in space and, crucially, through time. It is then also a 'time-binding' device, to use a term from William Burroughs who was himself intent on dismantling or at least disabling this device (so, it might once have been useful, but for Burroughs at least, it is restrictive and limiting as well).[6]

It would seem then that our bodies—our headless bodies—do what they do and then, after that, the fiction or device performs the interpretation. There is an altogether different intention at work behind or besides what we consciously intend or think we intend. The question of free will also foregrounds itself here. If we go along with many of the scientific theories and explanations (which are based on empirical evidence) then our sense of making certain choices and of being a free agent are not exactly correct. Again, the conscious decision comes after as a rationalisation of some other prior intention. We are always following some other agenda (or 'deep assignment') in this sense.

The neuroscientist Anil Seth suggests that the brain is a 'prediction machine' in this sense, operating through inferences it draws from sense data (Seth 2020). Our perception is then less of what is actually out there and more a 'controlled hallucination' which, again, is determined by what is useful to us or ensures our survival. Seth applies this theory of perception to the self which is then seen as the regulatory system of our bio-physical existence. In fact, Seth turns to cybernetics here to frame our perception of the self as a form of feedback and control that has been shaped by evolution. Our various experiences of first-person perspective, of having a body, intention and free will are all part of this system (as is personal identity) beneath which is simply the fact of instability and change. Once again then, the self is part of a control system that allows the body to continue or subsist through time. Importantly, this scientific account of the self, Seth suggests, can open up some space so as to allow for the possibility of change. Scientific explanation can produce some distance or a different perspective on our immediate experience (in much the same way as Buddhist meditation can also produce this productive gap).

This other kind of perspective that decentres the self is present elsewhere as well. As I suggested above it relates to Buddhist thinking and practice, but from a Western perspective Freud also decentred the individual in relation to the drives (and in this analytic enquiry Freud followed the scientific method of hypotheses and empirical evidence). In his own 'beheading' Freud demonstrated that there is an unconscious that operates beneath or besides our conscious motivations and rationalisations as evidenced by the symptom which, in this context, is the headless body 'speaking' back to the head. In Lacan's reading of Freud the human is further decentred in relation to language or the Symbolic. If not exactly beheaded, the human is certainly always already alienated from themselves. And then, as I have briefly outlined above, there are Bataille's writings that perhaps most violently decapitate the human. For Bataille it is only through this sacrifice—a kind of will to our own headlessness—that something else can come to be born.

Algorithms and Other Fictions

From another kind of scientific or technological perspective there is also a sense in which the individual has been beheaded. Put bluntly, the actions of individuals—when seen together as a population—can be predicted by big data (hence the successes of the algorithmic turn). Here, once again, individual agents might feel or think they are autonomous and in control, but from a wider perspective, they are predictable, or, at least, tendencies can be identified. So, once again, we see a fiction at work here. The fiction of an autonomous subject that makes decisions. The question here is whether there is a limit to this tracking of the subject by algorithmic governance and prediction. This is not to reinstate the head, but, rather, to suggest that the particular body that is being tracked—by whatever corporate or state mechanisms—is simply a reduced version of that other bodily intelligence I mentioned above (as, for example, when algorithms reductively track 'us' as only consumers).

Medical technology and discourse can also track us as bodies with various genetic dispositions, nascent illnesses and so forth. Again, the science attempts to track—and predict—whatever it is beneath the fiction. Certainly illnesses tend to surprise us. There can also be a further reduction here, especially within medical discourse that treats the body as simply that which can be observed when it is clear that the body is far more complex than our perspective on it (as Spinoza has it, we do not yet know what a body is capable of). This is not necessarily to instate an essence to what we are (although Spinoza does use that term), but it is to state—once again—the fact of the vast complexity of the body which, it would seem safe to assume, goes beyond our current medical or scientific knowledge. We are not reducible to the fiction we have of ourselves, but neither are we reducible to the image that medicine gives us of ourselves (although this is not to say for a moment that that image does not have value, simply that it has limits).[7] Indeed, it seems clear that other accounts of the body—and of the world it moves through—will involve other medicines and cures. Other ideas of what illness—and what 'health'—actually is (and, with that, other ideas of what constitutes care). Indeed, these other accounts might also foreground other entities and agents besides the fiction of the autonomous and self-sufficient subject.[8]

The idea of a complex bodily intelligence aside (and, with that, the scientific image as well), is there a further way of mitigating against the algorithmic turn that tracks us? So, not to have our selves predicted as specifically consuming subjects or, indeed, reduced down to any one image? Here the possibility of holding the self more lightly—understanding it *as* a fiction— seems important. That said, the device of the fiction of the self is nothing if not robust. As I have mentioned in both of the previous essays, it works on all sorts of sub-representational levels that are less easy to shift (and here the question of feedback loops between these and other representational levels becomes important). Seeing the self as a fiction is then perhaps less about identifying something that needs completely dispelling (so as to get at a 'deeper' reality), but rather recognising that the device—a complex fiction that performs many important functions—is something that can be tinkered with, at least to some extent. Might this perspective and attitude in itself enable some experimentation? Might, for example, other fictions be tried on? Again, not a dispelling exactly, but a kind of proliferation of devices. Or perhaps a certain kind of dispelling—again a seeing of the frame as a frame— that allows the proliferation. Laying one's head upon the block means that other heads (or non-heads perhaps?) can be put in its place.[9]

Writing and art practice more generally seem to be pursuits where some of this experimentation can take place (at least this has been my experience). There is something important about how these creative practices can offer up a liminal space away from more typical or habitual realities (so, again, they allow a distance to be opened up between our experience and then a reflection or representation of that experience). There can too, for example, be the possibility of performing different fictions (which also gives us that reflective perspective back on our own fiction). And then there is the possibility as well of entering into more collective fictions through collaboration and other kinds of group set-ups (I go further into this idea in some of the essays in the second part of my book). What do these other kinds of fiction allow? And then also what are the limits here? For example around gendered, classed and racialised bodies? There is also the business of writing fiction more generally and how this allows the exploration of other fictions of the self or, indeed, the speculative exploration of other modes of being. Bataille's own fictions—and more generally his use of the first person in his writings (which means his own identity is in play in his texts)—would be a case in point.[10]

As well as affirming these experimental possibilities we need be wary of moving too fast when many people have no flexibility or are living out fictions overly determined for them. One thinks here of those colonial fictions in particular and their institution of their others. There is a crucial place for work that attempts to show or describe a reality that has at times been obscured behind these different fictions (as well as for more straightforward ideological critique that attends to the fictions themselves). But there is also the important business of producing 'better' fictions when better simply means those fictions—or other kinds of device—that enable a different mode of being and acting in the world (and this might also mean reclaiming and refiguring those fictions hitherto imposed from outside).

It is here that we can speculatively bring both the base materialism of Bataille and Brassier's nemocentric subject into relation with 'Black Study'. I go into more detail about the latter in my essay on 'Landscape, Trauma and Myth-Work' but want to suggest in a speculative conclusion to this essay that there might be a productive encounter to be had around this question of exploring other modes of existence. As Denise Ferreira da Silva convincingly argues in her essay on 'The Equation of Value' (2017): Blackness signifies a mode of being set away from the white Western—and 'self-determined'—subject and, in particular, the value systems and hierarchies set up and endlessly affirmed by them (and which they sit atop). It is also a more haptic and collective mode of being as Stefano Harney and Fred Moten argue in their book *The Undercommons* (2013). Blackness might also name a device that can resist or undo algorithmic governance insofar as it refuses a certain regime of visibility (or partakes of opacity).[11] This is not to say that Blackness is a form of headlessness. Indeed, this would be to repeat various clichés and tropes of racism. But it is to say that affirming another mode of existence will require the sacrifice of a previous mode, especially when the latter is both the priest and the cop (and perhaps the philosopher too?) that has often determined the possibilities of a certain kind of thinking and, indeed, life. These theorisations of Blackness are specific to their context and are certainly not available to be appropriated by white subjectivity (I'm thinking of my own writing here and the limits to the kind of synthesis I am speculatively suggesting). But on the other hand it does seem as if there might be resources and methods—and devices too—in Acéphale and neuroscience that can lend themselves to the further thinking through of Blackness as naming a different mode of being in the world.

Coda

What kind of spaces and non-places do these other modes exist within? To follow a refrain of these essays, perhaps it is like a landscape but one in which there is less of a firm border between the landscape and the figures that are in or on it. Or, pushing this further, perhaps these other modes are themselves landscapes with different features and figures. Once the head and the 'I' are backgrounded then these other agencies—more collective ones perhaps?—can get up and begin their work. It's difficult to know exactly what this work will look like from this side of things (I'm speaking of my own experience here). It's difficult to picture these other modes and landscapes that are on the other side of a given self. That kind of knowledge is only available once a head has been laid down on the block. Or, put differently, one can never know what's on the other side of sacrifice (although one can speculate) until that sacrifice has been made.

Notes

1 There are also other accounts of the need for headlessness in relation to the typical and invariably masculine subject (and a call for a new kind of writing that follows from this decapitation). Here for example is Hélène Cixous from 'The Laugh of the Medusa':

Unlike man, who holds so dearly to his title and his titles, his pouches of value, his cap, crown, and everything connected with his head, woman couldn't care less about the fear of decapitation (or castration), adventuring, without the masculine temerity, into anonymity, which she can merge with without annihilating herself: because she's a giver. (Cixous 1981: 259)

2 This attitude arises from Bataille's theory of general economy and especially the idea of solar excess. Bataille affirms different forms of waste (against utility) and the using up of the energy of the sun that gives with no return (thus Bataille's famous aphorism from *The Accursed Share*: '*that the sexual act is in time as the tiger is in space*' [Bataille 1991: 12 (italicised in original)]). It is in this sense that life is about not production, but consumption.

3 This is the case, for example, with eroticism and—more pertinent to my own essays collected here—literature, which is both a pursuit against project (and work) and deals with themes of excess (and, in both these senses, is also characterised as evil) (see Bataille 1958).

4 See the recently published collection of texts, maps and other materials: *The Sacred Conspiracy: The Internal Papers of the Secret Society of Acéphale and Lectures to the College of Sociology* (2017).

5 For Bataille this is the fundamental difference between the human and the animal. The former is alienated in and from the world, whereas 'every animal is in the world like water in water' (Bataille 1989: 19).

6 Burroughs is actually referring to Alfred Korzybski's idea of man as 'a time-binding animal' (Burroughs 2005).

7 To turn briefly from science back to psychoanalysis, there has certainly been a reaction by Lacan (and Lacanians), for example, against 'ego therapies' which, in this context, involve the idea that conscious experience defines the subject (so, these therapies deny, or at least significantly play down, the role of the unconscious subject).

8 See for example *Doctor and Healers* that addresses these differences in attitude between a scientific perspective (or modern and Western one) and a more 'folk' one (indigenous or non-Western). Crucial here is the way the former focus on the internal structures and processes of the individual (especially in relation to mental health), whereas the latter attends to external agents and entities (Nathan and Stengers 2018).

9 For some tentative ideas around this point see my discussion of the Deleuze/Guattarian concept of 'probe-heads' in relation to contemporary art (O'Sullivan 2012: 200-1).

10 As Nick Land suggests:

Bataille's writing exhibits a marked attachment to the first person pronoun, and the confessional mode is especially predominant in his more 'literary' works, although it spreads everywhere. The most obvious consequence of this device is to immerse the narrative ego in the text, fusing voice and discourse in a field of immanence, and putting identity unreservedly into play (*en jeu*). (Land 1992: xv)

11 See Édouard Glissant's account of opacity in *Poetics of Relation* (Glissant 2010) and Ramon Amaro's thesis of the 'Black Technical Object' that might affirmatively disrupt algorithmically determined recognition and other AI systems (Amaro 2019).

4

Time Circuits and Temporal Loops

This essay concerns itself with non-standard accounts of time, especially when this involves retro-causality or, more generally, temporal feedback loops. This is partly to excavate an occult/magical theory of time or, to use a more contemporary term (from the Cybernetic culture research unit), an idea of 'hyperstition'. If time is understood cybernetically then are past, present and future simply different kinds of circuit? And what kinds of practices and rituals might allow travel along these circuits? This relates to some of the material in previous essays about claiming a prior determination (in relation to the fiction of the self) and also sets up some of the subsequent essays about our relation to the past and how this can involve an activation of other futures.

Science Fictions

Other times and other cultures have understood—and represented—time in other ways than is currently the case in the West. This might mean they have also experienced time differently, at least to some extent. We can read about these other ideas of time, perhaps even imagine some of them ourselves (at least to some extent), but we are invariably situated within our own temporal framework. Something similar might be said about more future projections of time from within our own time—Science Fictions for example—when these simply extend our existing temporal frameworks or project existing logics forwards (as is also the case, more explicitly, with corporate 'future predictions'). That said, there are other accounts—and other fictions—that do seem to involve a different take on time itself. Quentin Meillassoux addresses something like this other genre (within a genre) in his thesis on 'Extro-Science Fiction' (XSF) or those Science

Fictions that are about worlds where science—and theories of temporal causality—are more or less not operable (Meillassoux 2015). Meillassoux draws out a schema of these different fictions with their different disruptions of cause-and-effect sequencing, but also points to some limitations insofar as a fiction needs to be narratable (and readable) in some senses which means it must necessarily obey at least a basic temporal sequencing.[1] Meillassoux also turns to Kant—who, in many ways, sets the terms of our modern and Western conception of time (in terms of this sequencing and the relation of that to our experience)—in order to explore the philosophical implications and underpinnings of these other presented worlds that play with our ideas of science and causality (and space and time).

Cybernetics and Occult Diagrams

This other idea of time—as not simply linear and progressive—is also in play in some of the writings of the Cybernetic culture research unit (Ccru) where time is understood cybernetically which means, as I suggested in my first essay, that there are various feedback loops operative between different times (see Ccru n.d.). Here a particular kind of 'time diagram' is at stake, one that involves seeing time from the outside or certainly from a 'non-standard' point of view. This shift in perspective, a seeing time all at once—past, present and future—is in play too in Amy Ireland's essay 'The Poememenon', which follows the Ccru in excavating a certain diagram of time but also, like some of the Ccru texts, performs the temporal looping it writes about insofar as its ending loops around to its beginning (2017).[2] Ireland connects this cybernetic diagram with older, more occult diagrams, for example W. B. Yeats' double spinning gyres. In her essay she lays out a compelling argument for both a catastrophic idea of time—a past-present-future direction—and an anastrophic one in which the future works back on the past.

Occult certainly seems to be the correct term here insofar as these diagrams of time are necessarily hidden. They are often kept in secret, but they also involve a knowledge that is not easily accessible—or easily understandable—when one is a creature situated in time. Indeed, they are not really circuits of the subject at all but name a kind of process of which the subject is a by-product or 'residuum' (to use a formulation from Deleuze and Guattari's *Anti-Oedipus* [1984] in relation to the loops and circuits of desiring-production) or, at least, is always already caught within. Ireland follows Nick Land in attending specifically to this primary process that, ultimately, is indifferent to (and outruns) the human subject. In her essay she makes a persuasive argument that avant-garde poetics is involved in a similar primary process—a trajectory away from the human—something the title of her essay creatively gestures towards.[3] The issue of free will and determinism is crucial here. These circuits in which the future has always already happened militate against individual agency or, once again, are part of a primary process of which the human (in this understanding) is simply a secondary effect. This can mean there is an attendant affect of despair or, at least a feeling of being trapped.

Time Wars

If one is caught within time—the human as a time-bound creature—then what are the options for exit? In one of the key Ccru texts, 'Lemurian Time War', it is suggested that fiction might allow some travel. Indeed, fiction can be mobilised in the war against time (as the title of that essay suggests) (Ccru 2017). William Burroughs is a crucial figure here. For Burroughs, reality was itself a series of scripts or fictions which could be edited and rewritten (see, for example, Burroughs 2005). Indeed, with the technique of the cut-up, Burroughs suggests that typical temporal sequencing can be altered (again, this understanding is foregrounded in the Ccru's reading of Burroughs). But, for the Ccru it is also the way fiction can insert or nest itself within reality and then have real effects that is important. As I've mentioned in previous essays, this is the practice of what they call 'hyperstition'. In fact, these two are the same. Reality is a series of fictions nested in one another and, as fictions, they can be rewritten and/or added to. As the Ccru essay mentioned above has it, fiction is then a weapon in the time war against what Ccru/Burroughs called the 'One God Universe' (or OGU), which is also, necessarily, a one-time universe too.[4] In fact, this is more or less what defines it. 'Lemurian Time War' is about this time war, but is a move in it as well (so, as with the Ireland essay I mentioned above, this Ccru essay on time war performs its content).

That said, it does seem to me there is a limit here or, perhaps, a further factor to consider. Certainly, one can read fiction and be 'transported' to a certain extent, but in order to really travel these fictions need to be enacted or performed somehow. Time is a set of habits in one sense (albeit very deep habits). To live a different time will necessarily involve cultivating other habits; it will involve developing other practices and rituals. Something like this has been at stake with different collective set-ups that have explored other temporalities besides that of, for example, 9-5 jobs or a certain sequencing of a life. The latter might involve the dividing of time into work and leisure or, as is the case more recently, different 'packages' of 'productive' time. It might mean the dividing of a life more generally into different 'stages'. Through different practices and rituals, these different ways of being in time can certainly be disrupted to some extent. However, time is still experienced—presumably even in these collective set-ups—in a certain direction. Past, present, future, in that order, remain operative. Or, put differently, the cause-and-effect sequencing is still in play. It's not as if this sequencing can just be shrugged off. Again, these temporal frameworks are very deep structures within the human subject, in fact, they more or less define the latter (at least in the modern West).[5]

Temporal Gaps and Magical Causality

There do, however, seem to be cases where this deeper sequencing is upset or put into question. For example, with various neurodiverse psychic set-ups (such as with what is sometimes labelled autism), where—according to some accounts—there is less of this linear sequencing in relation to memory. Memories exist, rather, in a kind of non-linear pool or, put differently, the past—all of the past—is contemporary with the present. We might note a connection here with Henri Bergson's account of memory and the past. For Bergson, the past has not gone anywhere—it survives—albeit it is not typically 'seen', focussed as we are on the utilitarian present. But opening up a gap between stimulus and response in the organism (a particular sensory-motor apparatus)—or bringing about a pause of some kind—can allow the past all of a sudden to foreground itself (hence the infamous Proustian moment of the madeleine that Bergson refers to).[6] This Bergsonian understanding of time and the subsistence of the past runs counter to the Kantian idea of sequential time.[7] I will return to this below with my own version of Bergson's famous diagram of the cone of memory (a diagram that has been important to me throughout my work).

On the subatomic level there is also the phenomenon of retroactive causality—the behaviour of tachyons—that would seem to suggest that the typical sequencing we experience is not absolutely universal (although we must be wary of drawing direct lessons for the subjective experience of time from the subatomic level of reality).[8] These 'new' scientific accounts resonate with earlier magical accounts of reality where causality operates in a different way across time and space. In fact, this partly defines what J. G. Frazer has called 'sympathetic magic' or action at a distance.[9] Magical thinking, as Gilbert Simondon has also suggested, involves a different 'structuring' of the universe, one that invariably involves a different sense of both time and space. Hence the importance of certain specific times and privileged places—or 'key-points'—which are connected together in this magical structure.[10] I will return to Simondon and his account of the magical mode of existence in some of the essays that follow in the second part of my book, but might we say that practical magic is a way of 'using' this knowledge—this non-scientific understanding of the human's relationship to the cosmos—and, with that, mobilising this other sense of causality?

From a psychoanalytic perspective, to deploy other fictions that are authored by you—but not as you are before that authoring—allows a kind of retroactive claiming of a certain sequential narrative or prior determination (or even the changing of that narrative). This is Lacan's 'becoming a cause of oneself' (see Lacan 1992).[11] Here a certain kind of temporal looping is again in play. As I suggested in my first essay, magickal practice (so magic with a 'k') can also involve a non-standard idea of causality—or again a retro-causality—with the subject becoming involved in claiming their own determination.

Artificial Intelligence and Other Basilisks

Other non-Western and pre-modern cultures also seem to suggest that what one does in the present can have an effect on the past. Or, put differently, that our relationship with the past is always there to be negotiated. Hence the business of ancestor worship and other practices of speaking with the dead. And then there is the example as well of the Ccru's hyperstitional logic, especially when that concerns a future Artificial Intelligence. Here it is not the present having an effect on the past that is at stake, but the future having an effect on the present (so a further retro-causality). Certainly, looking back from our present moment to the past, one can see that everything that has happened has been to get to this point. And the same is the case if we speculatively look back from a future point to our own present. So, in this case, a future Artificial Intelligence is looking back and in some senses assembling the components for its own self production. Crucially, for this future Artificial Intelligence time will not exist in the same way as it does for its human progenitors and so, from its perspective (to maintain a fiction that it has one), there is just a set of conditions that have been put in place so as to allow it to emerge. But also, it has always already emerged, to speak in terms of that more occult temporal diagram. This is why you have the compelling—but frightening—scenario in some writing by Nick Land about a future Artificial Intelligence throwing back agents into the past in order to bring about the conditions for its own genesis (and, again, from this perspective, it is we who are the agents that are making this future Artificial Intelligence entity) (Land 2011). Sadie Plant, who initially set up the Ccru, also attends to these retroactive time loops which operate 'as though the present was being reeled into a future which had always been guiding the past, washing back over precedents completely unaware of its influence' (Plant 1997: 13). Plant is particularly attentive to fictions' role within this temporal circuit. For example it is the Science Fiction writer William Gibson who prompts the Plant quote immediately above.[12] Indeed, for Plant the distinction between fiction and reality—and between the future and the present—is nothing if not porous.

There is also a more abstract—and fantastical—account of something similar to this time looping in the set-up called 'Roko's Basilisk'.[13] Here, once again, a certain future scenario—and, again, an Artificial Intelligence—is reaching back, capturing subjects in its paralysing gaze and threatening them with abysmal torture if they do not help bring about its genesis. Once you know about the future Artificial Intelligence—the Basilisk—then you have always already been interpellated, caught within its gaze and are thus subject to these demands and threats of punishment. 'Roko's Basilisk' is a kind of temporal trap in this sense.[14]

Reclaiming Agency

The issue with some of these accounts, once again, is the way they empty out agency or, at least, position agency elsewhere (away from a given subject). Hence the accompanying affect of despair I mentioned above. Might there, however, be a way of reclaiming some of this agency away, for example, from a future Artificial Intelligence? Might there be a different imagining of a future and, with that, a different kind of reaching back to bring that future about? Or, for example, might there be other narratives as regards the future of the human in relation to machines? This would still be to hold to the circuit/occult diagram, but to envision the process and outcomes differently. Something like this seems to be at stake with Alex William's deployment of hyperstition for a left accelerationism, especially with the call for new 'socio-political attractors'—different visions of the future—that might themselves then call forth a different future (see Williams 2013). It is also there in Reza Negarestani's writings on the 'labour of the Inhuman' which gives an account of AI's retroactive self-construction but with more emancipatory aims (Negarestani 2014).

Are there also further ideas and images of how time works? And how might they be lived as it were? Certainly, it would seem that we have a body that is within time, but the issue here is perhaps the ideas we have about that body. I have gestured to this above, but we might say that it is not so much that the body 'experiences' time, but rather that it is the fiction we have of ourselves—as a separate self—that experiences this temporal sequencing (so the 'fiction of the self' once more). Following Kant on this point, time (and space) are properties of the (transcendental) subject or, more accurately, are a condition of possibility of experience for that subject. The question might then be whether there are other fictions we can take on that can disable this ur-fiction somehow? We can turn here to more scientific accounts of the body and, with that, begin to break with a certain folk image or ego and attendant idea of time. To untether experience from a given self will certainly mean things are experienced differently (if, in fact, it makes sense to say they are experienced at all—after all, that would seem to imply an 'experiencer' existing within time). Besides this radical idea of a non-self—something that is at stake in neuroscience and Buddhism—are there other fictions that can be taken on?

Collective Time and Performance

I mentioned collectives above and this seems to be a compelling way of experimenting with a different kind of temporal sequencing and with the substituting of one mode for another, at least when these collectives work against the ubiquitous atomised individual. And then, following Félix Guattari, we might say there is also the collectivity that operates at a sub-individual level (see Guattari 1996a). The world of more impersonal affects and intensities 'beneath' any register of the individual understood as a particular signifying formation. To a certain extent this is to break open or, at least, to radically distribute subjectivity. But, to turn to something more performative for a moment, is there a sense that adopting and enacting other fictions might also change our experience and, with that, allow some kind of travel in time? And does this further answer the question of how one might get a purchase on the fiction of the self that one is? Indeed, perhaps there is something even more radical at stake in adopting and performing these different perspectives. Might there be a different experience of time—or even of a kind of non-time—in play?

Against Colonial Time

Stefano Harney and Fred Moten gesture towards something like this in their theorising of Blackness as an 'unsettled feeling' set at a distance 'from those who locate themselves in space and time, who locate themselves in a determined history' (Harney and Moten 2013: 97). I mentioned at the end of my previous essay that for Harney and Moten Blackness is to be reclaimed and affirmed as a different mode of being, even, to some extent, a non-Kantian one. I will return to this more fully in the next essay but want to foreground here that at stake is also an instrument—or device—that would enable this other mode or that can 'sound out' this Blackness with its attendant poetics and ways of being. As Harney and Moten suggest, 'blackness is an instrument in the making' (Harney and Moten 2013: 94).[15]

There have also been other more practical experiments that resonate with these ideas, for example the 'event mapping' of Black Quantum Futurism, with its intention to work against a dominant—and Western—linear narrative.[16] At stake here is a different relation to history, even a different understanding of the so-called 'past' (and especially the seeing of certain pasts as still operative and thus determining in the present).[17] Part of this work is to uncover other pasts as well, including those that have been obscured or not recognised as fact. For Black Quantum Futurism it also involves a turn to indigenous African ideas of time and retro-causality as well as to scientific ideas of quantum entanglement. This project is not just one of diagnosis and critique, but one of creativity and pragmatics (if not survival) too. This is evidenced in their pedagogical 'event mapping' instructions that allow a kind of individual re-claiming of time and history but also, crucially it seems to me, in their multimedia performances which enact, at least to some extent, the different spaces and times they theorise. Here it is not just a question of different histories but also of understanding and imagining time differently, and, with that, of actually exploring other non-linear temporalities in different ways some of which are self-consciously performative. Practices like this are explicitly about travelling other circuits of time (which then foreground other histories and other possible futures) and performing other kinds of temporal loop (for which different technologies might be utilised). Black Quantum Futurism look back to Sun Ra's myth-science in this sense of re-engineering both past and future so as to contribute towards a different present.

From the Future to the Past

There are then different strategies and practices for working against our time-bound status. There are different circuits and loops that offer up exits away from what we might understand as our present. And then, returning to my brief comments above about Bergson, there might be further technologies (or devices) that produce a gap or pause so as to allow these circuits and loops to be activated. Might we diagram this set-up as in Fig. 4.1? It is this diagram—or something very like it—that is at stake in some of the other essays collected here insofar as many of them are concerned with a device that allows travel along different circuits and loops away from the plane of matter (whether that device is an art practice or meditation practice for example).

In this essay I have been broadly concerned with those elements of the future that are operational in the present (so, broadly speaking, Science Fiction logics). In the essay 'Archaeofictioning' in the second part of my

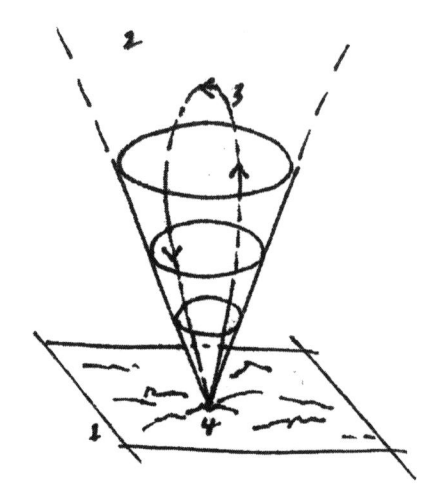

Fig. 4.1 Diagram of activation of device (based on Bergson's cone of memory). 1. Plane of matter/landscape; 2. The past/virtual; 3. Time-travelling circuit; 4. Ritual/performance/device. (Author's own drawing)

book I will explore some of these ideas in relation to those remnants from the past that survive into the present and, especially, with contemporary art practices that fiction these in some way. But in each case, it does seem to me that a performance of some kind is necessary. Something needs to be set to work—or, again, enacted—within this time that allows a different perspective to be taken on. Or, put more simply, it would seem that in order to travel in and out of time—to follow different time circuits and temporal loops—devices will need to be built and activated and other rituals devised and performed.

Coda

What will these devices and rituals look like? This cannot be known before the building and performing of them. Or, put differently, the building and performing will only make sense when looking back from a future point (it is then that they will have been seen as devices and rituals). Could this essay—and others collected here—be part of this project? Can theoretical work operate as a platform or scaffolding to allow other kinds of travel to take place? In this preparatory work (that includes the mapping out of the fiction of the self) repetition and failure is always a risk (as are many other affects such as frustration and shame). Indeed, it is sometimes these uncomfortable affects that point in the right direction, as if the new rituals will necessarily have to take place at the edge of a given subjective set-up just as the new devices will need to be placed at the limits of a more familiar space-time.

Notes

1 See also the discussion in *Fictioning*, where Burrows and I make an argument for a development of Meillassoux's thesis—using the invented cipher (X)SF—in terms of those Science Fictions that are more performative or exhibit their arrival from another world in their play with style and syntax (so these fictions are not just *about* another place and time but *from* it in some respects) (Burrows and O'Sullivan 2019: 297–312).

2 And in this sense Ireland's essay has something in common with the more performative fictions—(X)SF—mentioned in the note above on Meillassoux (both being writings which perform their content in some senses).

3 To quote Ireland:

Against this qualified experimentalism (the false 'novelty' of catastrophic modernity) the pomemenon diagrams reckless adherence to the modernist dictum that novelty is to be generated at any cost, privileging formal experimentation—towards the desolation of all intelligible form—over human preservation, and locking technique onto an inhuman vector of runaway automation that, for better or worse, charts the decline of human values as modernity hands the latter over to its machinic successor in final, fatal phase shift. (Ireland 2017: 9)

4 To quote the Ccru (who quote Burroughs):

Since writing customarily operates as the principal means of 'time-binding', Burroughs reasoned that innovating new writing techniques would unbind time, blowing a hole in the OGU 'pre-sent', and opening up Space. 'Cut the Word Lines with scissors or switchblades as preferred...The Word Lines keep you in time...Cut the in lines...Make out lines to Space.' (Ccru [and quoting Burroughs] 2017: 43)

5 Reza Negarestani has recently attended to this deep structuring of experience or what he calls 'time-consciousness' (see Negarestani 2022). For Negarestani a crucial question is how to get some purchase on this time-consciousness when we are always already 'entrenched' within it. How to imagine that our subjective set-up might have been different so as to allow another kind of experience and with that another world to emerge? In many ways this is the same issue—but expressed at a deeper level or given a more philosophical acuteness—that concerned the Ccru. To quote the latter (who quote Burroughs):

Power operates most effectively not by persuading the conscious mind, but by delimiting in advance what it is possible to experience. By formatting the most basic biological processes of the organism in terms of temporality, Control ensures that all human experience is of—and in—time. That is why time is a 'prison' for humans. 'Man was born in time. He lives and dies in time. Wherever he goes he takes time with him and imposes time.' (Ccru 2017: 43)

If we cannot get a perspective on our own time-consciousness because we are entrenched within it—we cannot step on our own shadow—might there be another path or method of making/positing a further model (of time-consciousness) of some kind? So, not finding a gap or limit to our existing time-consciousness—or not trying to find the edges that we cannot, by definition find—but positing a further fiction (or, a further representation) within this one which, in a recursive/reflective manner, allows a purchase on the fiction (and time-consciousness) that we always already are.

6 Elsewhere Bergson relates this to the experience of the mystic who, in this context, is able to travel through time or, more generally, access other planes of reality (see Bergson 1935 and the discussion in O'Sullivan 2013).
7 For Bergson, Kant's account is overly mechanical and, indeed, relegates time to space (hence Bergson's idea of 'duration' that he develops elsewhere).
8 See the discussion of tachyons in Victoria Halford and Steve Beard's *Voodoo Science Park* (the film and the book) where this idea of retroactive causality is also related to fiction and, more particularly, their fictioning of a particular archive (and landscape) (Halford and Beard 2011).
9 For an account of the principles of sympathetic magic see Frazer 1983: 14–16. A brief definition from Frazer:

If we analyse the principles of thought on which magic is based, they will probably be found to resolve themselves into two: first, that like produces like, or that an effect resembles its cause; and, second, that things which have once been in contact with each other continue to act on each other at a distance after the physical contact has been severed. The former principle may be called the Law of Similarity, the latter the Law of Contact or Contagion. From the first of these principles, namely the Law of Similarity, the magician infers that he can produce any effect he desires merely by imitating it: from the second he infers that whatever he does to a material object will affect equally the person with whom the object was once in contact, whether it formed part of his body or not. (Frazer 1983: 14)

10 To quote Simondon at length here:

A privileged place, a place that has a power, is one which draws into itself all the force and efficacy of the domain it delimits; it summarises and contains the force of a compact mass of reality; it summarises and governs it, as a highland governs and dominates a lowland; the elevated peak is the lord of the mountain, just as the most impenetrable part of the wood is where all its reality resides. The magical world is in this way made of a network of places and things that have a power and are bound to other things and other places that also have a power. Such a path, such an enclosure, such a temenos contains all the force of the land, and is the key-point of the reality and of the spontaneity of things, as well as of their accessibility. (Simondon 2011: 412)

And a little later: 'This network of boundaries is not only spatial but also temporal; there are notable dates and privileged moments to begin one action or another' (Simondon 2011: 414).

11 There is also Lacan's account of retro-causality within language/writing as when the last word of a sentence determines the prior meaning of the words (see the discussion in Fink 1995: 63–66).
12 Here is the relevant further quote:

> Fictions might be speculative and inspire particular developments, but they were not supposed to have such immediate effects. Like all varieties of cultural change, technological development was supposed to proceed step after step and one at a time. It was only logical, after all. But cyberspace changed all this. It suddenly seemed as if all the components and tendencies which were now feeding into this virtual zone had been made for it before it had even been named; as though all the ostensible reasons and motivations underlying their development had merely provided occasions for the emergence of a matrix which Gibson's novel was nudging into place. (Plant 1997: 13)

13 See the account given here (although think twice before following the link): https://rationalwiki.org/wiki/Roko%27s_basilisk (accessed 17 January 2024).
14 Although I have some sympathy with Robin Mackay's argument—made in relation to the Gruppo di Nun's *Revolutionary Demonology*—that a surrendering of individual agency (or an identification with the entropic dissolution of the subject) might, for some, mean a way of finding a kind of inhuman joy within any existential despair (Mackay 2022).
15 To quote Harney and Moten at more length here:

> But this is to say that there are flights of fantasy in the hold of the ship. The ordinary fugue and fugitive run on the language lab, black phonography's brutally experimental venue. Paraontological totality is in the making. Present and unmade in presence, blackness is an instrument in the making. (Harney and Moten 2013: 94)

See also the discussion 'On Opacity and the Hold' in Burrows and O'Sullivan 2019: 227–9.
16 See as indicative the essay 'Placing Time, Timing Space' by Rasheedah Phillips, one of the members of the collective (Phillips 2018).
17 See also the Otolith Group and their excavation of different histories with their promised futures. Burrows and I have gone into more detail on this in *Fictioning*, especially in relation to the film-essay and docufiction which might be understood in this context as time travel devices (Burrows and O'Sullivan 2019: 229–32).

5

Landscape, Trauma and Myth-Work

This essay looks at the relationship between landscape and myth. Myth has often functioned to obscure trauma, so this essay asks what kind of myth-work it might be important to carry out so as to critique existing myths and allow new ones to be written. This is especially the case with collective forms of myth-making that might work as different forms of care and repair (and in this way this essay also operates as a precursor to some of the material in the second part of my book). At stake in this critical/creative project is an understanding of the landscape as marked by the expropriation of the commons and colonisation/the slave trade. These are the founding traumas of modernity and, as such, we are all living in their aftermath.

Myth and Obscuration

Is every myth of England written over a darker history? Certainly, the myth of 'Great Britain' as a particular kind of civilised nation and Empire was in part written through exploitation and colonisation. Myth, as a particular kind of story, can be a way of hiding these other histories or even justifying them.[1] There is something akin to the analytic process at stake here. From a Lacanian perspective there is a Real (a trauma) that persists 'beneath' any Symbolic register (or story). Again, this is certainly the case for myths of Nationalism that are often written through the affirmation of certain characteristics of a nation and its people (and, with that, a certain Symbolic order).[2] In order to assert these characteristics and alongside them a particular set of values then a whole world of more unsavoury beliefs and bloody actions must be hidden. Or, to put this more bluntly, history is invariably written by the victors and colonisers. Likewise, those beliefs and practices that do not 'fit' the story—other (counter-) myths of

England perhaps, but also accounts of lives that do not subscribe to these myths at all—are necessarily denigrated, obscured or even destroyed.

As well as this weaving of a Symbolic story over the Real there is also the way in which these myths work through producing a particular image of their other. The colonial project is justified retroactively on the basis of this othering. If a people are seen as less than human (as defined by those doing the defining) or, more generally, as having less value, then a whole system of oppression (and resource extraction) becomes enabled and 'justified' as Denise Ferreira da Silva convincingly argues (2017). The colonial project has not finished in this sense insofar as these value systems continue to structure both personal and public life (as well as our larger geopolitical reality). This has also been referred to as the continuation of the 'plantation system' (Wynter 1971) and/or the 'afterlife' (or being in the 'wake') of slavery (Sharpe 2016).

Marked Landscapes and Myth-Work

There is an important and urgent task here to 'reveal' these other histories that have been obscured. For example, by attending to how institutions of one form or another (and their accompanying narratives) are built (and written) off the back of exploitation and slavery. This might involve careful analysis of various contracts, leases and other acts or those structuring fictions that are themselves often hidden.[3] It might result in the toppling of statues. Certainly, from one perspective, our towns and cities still bear the mark of this mercantile trade and accompanying exploitation of other peoples, some of it more apparent, some less so. And it is not just in our towns and cities that we see evidence of this past and thus also evidence of how our present is continuing to be structured by that past. The very landscape of England is marked by the colonial project insofar as the latter is an integral part of the larger logic of capitalism that dictates private property. Once the landscape is seen in this way—in terms of the economics of ownership that is invariably caught up with overseas trade and slavery—it cannot be unseen.

Paralleling these racialised logics there are also the various enclosures acts of the past and other exploitative measures to disenfranchise the commons, as well as the ongoing uprisings against these state controls. This includes the ongoing war against women (and especially women who are poor) and its resistance (see Federici 2014 on this primitive accumulation in relation to the witch hunts).[4] Again, the landscape is marked by this expropriation and the struggle against it. To that extent any account of the landscape that does not also note that it is a site of struggle—and specifically a class/race struggle—continues the work of naturalising those man-made hierarchies and inequalities (and expropriations). Indeed, myths of England that look back to a feudal set-up as a kind of idyll are especially pernicious, as for example can often be the case with the fantasy genre of fiction (as Raymond Williams has perceptively argued).[5]

There is also the way in which our contemporary landscape now evidences a more global stage of capitalist development. Patrick Keiller's second two *Robinson* films attend to the 'new' non-spaces of this international trade, but it is with Justin Barton and Mark Fisher's *On Vanishing Land* that we get a sense of how the container ports and so forth in our landscape have themselves an eerie quality—because the actual mechanics of global capitalism are in many ways hidden (another obscuration then)—that brings them into resonance with pre-modern sites like Sutton Hoo (both being emptied of human presence).[6]

Where does this leave myth-work and its relationship to the landscape? On the one hand—to repeat the point above—this work will involve attending to those other myths—with their accompanying modes of life, their practices and beliefs—that have been denigrated, obscured or at least partially destroyed. From a Marxist perspective it is to look at 'residual cultures' understood as previous modes of existence and, especially, to see what might be repurposed in and for the present (and as an alternative or opposition to that present) (see Raymond Williams 1980 and the discussion in Burrows and O'Sullivan 2019: 86–7). It might also be that new myths need to be written, so a turn to more 'emergent cultures', to use another term from Williams. It will also be to look to those more particular 'myths of resistance'. Myths that attend to and perhaps even re-activate the uprisings and other acts and forces of sedition (and here it is worth remembering that it is the commons that comes first; resistance is always ontologically prior to its capture). A good example of this kind of myth-work is Victoria Halford and Steve Beard's *Voodoo Science Park* (the film and the book) (both 2011) which tells the story of the war against the Leviathan (the state) as evidenced in the landscape of the Peak District. This account is given through a compelling fictioning of the work of the Health and Safety Lab where large-scale industrial accidents are investigated.[7] Myth-work, in this case, involves working across text, sound and moving image. It involves the invention of different narratives—different fictions—alongside the excavation of different histories and then a kind of layering of these two together over other imagery. As Halford and Beard suggest towards the beginning of their book (composed of fieldnotes for the film): 'It is simply a matter of finding the right technique' (Halford and Beard 2011: 15).

In this kind of myth-work the landscape is not seen as empty of human presence but, crucially, as marked by it. And key in this work is that we are also implicated here. We are part of this history, involved in and with these landscapes. I will be returning to my own investments in different landscapes (and to the idea of the self as a landscape) in some of the essays in the second half of my book but suffice to say here that myth-work needs to involve our bodies and emotions. Or, put differently, these other counter-myths need to be performed in some manner (after all, the other myths—the dominant ones—are also embodied or 'lived'). A practice of myth-work that interweaves the personal and the political—as well as attending to other histories and, why not, fictions too—is then an especially powerful method here. This, I take it, is also what is at stake with Justin Barton and Mark Fisher's important work *On Vanishing Land* that involves this imbrication both of the personal and political and of fiction and history in order to enact a different narrative or myth. Crucially this enactment involves a kind of performance, in this case walking the landscape.

Founding Traumas and Myth-Work

Our landscape is then always already a site of the contestation of myth as well as of trauma. In terms of the destruction of a way of life, of expropriation and mass murder—and to repeat the point I made above—there has already been the burning of the witches. In terms of slavery there has already been the event of horrific abduction and transportation. Might myth-work also be about coming to terms specifically with these founding traumas of modernity? Or not coming to terms exactly but working out how to relate to them or stand witness. Isabelle Stengers' work involves this kind of bearing witness or 'reclaiming' in relation to witches. She quotes the activist and writer (and witch) Starhawk in her essay on 'Reclaiming Animism': 'The smoke of the burned witches still hangs in our nostrils' (Stengers 2012: 6). And then there is Greg Tate's take on Science Fiction as involving a relation to the 'Middle Passage' insofar as Science Fiction often foregrounds alienation and a relationship with that which is radically alien (when this includes stories of abduction). Tate (and others) explore this further in the Black Audio Film Collective's own myth-work *The Last Angel of History*, a film about the history of Black music that also involves time loops and a time traveller (or 'Data Thief') as the key protagonist. A more specific example here is the Drexciya Science Fiction mythos that concerns an aquatic underwater race birthed from the pregnant slaves thrown overboard during the Middle Passage and which is also the name of the Detroit techno duo that first invented the myth. Myth can be a way of coming into relation, and perhaps even reclaiming, trauma.

If these traumas—the great witch hunts and the 'Middle Passage'—are at the centre and origin of Western modernity (as Silvia Federici [2014] and Paul Gilroy [1995] convincingly argue), then they are also at a centre—or play a determining factor—within Western subjectivity. Indeed, the white Western (and especially male) subject is both cause and effect of these traumas (again, Ferreira da Silva does important philosophical work excavating and critiquing this so-called 'universal' subject [2017]).[8] As I have briefly mentioned in previous essays, different accounts of Blackness—and of an alternative mode of being that can be implied by this term—have attended to this, especially in the assertion of a more positive value for that which is often seen as negative. Blackness does not oppose whiteness but undoes it. It is the spinning of something else—again, a different mode of being—from out of and around a void as Harney and Moten might have it (Harney and Moten 2013: 94–5). It is to claim something from the horrific experience of the hold.

Harney and Moten, it seems to me, are calling for the writing of a different myth in this sense. A myth that is both for and about what they call the undercommons and where the how—what might be called the form of a myth—is as important as the content (or, to repeat a refrain of my own book, where the form performs the content). Harney and Moten's book moves between styles, from political economy to something more poetic and rhythmic, and from argument to affect. It is a collaboratively written volume that also includes conversations between its two authors. It is at once tough—some passages are hard to fathom or somehow awkward—and also deeply personal and vulnerable. It is in all these senses that Harney and Moten's writings are a component of the myth-machine they call for. This is then a myth that is both collective (it is from a collective as well as calling one forth) and haptic (arising from the closeness of bodies in the hold). It calls for a different kind of reading at the same time as it calls something different forth from within its readers (a different 'feel').

There might also be the production of other stranger counter-myths here, as, for example—in another register—with Sun Ra's myth-science which, again, looks to Science Fiction alongside—and in combination with—the ancient past in its particular myth production.[9] Kodwo Eshun is especially attentive to this character of Sun Ra's myth-science as offering a radically different narrative (or 'counter-mythologies') for an immiserated Black subjectivity (Eshun 1998: 154-63). Indeed, Eshun's idea of 'sonic fiction' that he develops in his important work *More Brilliant than the Sun* (1998) is itself a form of myth-science and myth-work. We need to be careful that we do not position these texts around Blackness and myth as a regression. We also need to attend to the specificity of them and, more especially, not simply appropriate their arguments or, in some cases, extract the latter and apply them elsewhere (a danger I am only too aware of with my own essays here). But on the other hand these kinds of text are a valuable resource (and offer up important case studies) for what I have been calling myth-work, especially in relationship to working with historical trauma.

In relation to the witches there is also that contemporary work that reclaims this term or repurposes it in some manner. An example here is the French feminist writer Xavière Gauthier who in her essay 'Why Witches?' (originally an editorial for the first issue of a new journal titled *Witches*) outlines the characteristics of the witch as a way of mapping out a trajectory for a contemporary feminism (Gauthier 1981).[10] Here the witch is a past mode of existence that nevertheless gestures towards a different future. To quote Gauthier: 'If I propose *Witches* as the title of a journal, it is because I think that this word also resonates strongly in other women. But resonates differently for each one. I propose here *Witches* as a historical anchor, an immense political revolt from the past, probably, but also and especially turned toward the future' (Gauthier 1981: 203). Turning to a more Anglo-American tradition, there is the figure of Starhawk too who brings the practice of witchcraft into productive encounter with contemporary activism (see, for example, Starhawk 2003). Indeed, with the latter and the associated communities there is a contemporary tradition of feminist and ecological witchcraft that includes writers like Isabelle Stengers and Donna Haraway.[11] There are other recuperations and reclaimings as well that expand the idea of witches and witchcraft, for example the somatic poetry/spells of CAConrad that might also be understood as a kind of myth-work (see CAConrad 2014). Here the relation of witchcraft to trans and non-binary identity is crucial too.

Although it is important to do what we can to undo dominant myths and prepare the ground for new myths, it is not always a case of writing these myths ourselves. That is partly what the problem has hitherto been: a 'speaking for' which can also be a silencing. A certain kind of myth-work—to repeat the point above—is about foregrounding other voices in this sense (I'm thinking here especially of the work being carried out by indigenous peoples in terms of reclaiming their land and identities from settler narratives and history). Part of this work might involve returning to that dark place of trauma. To go there and see what befalls. This is to keep on with the work of decolonisation when this is understood as a decolonisation of subjectivity as well as anything else (starting with one's own).[12] What might that look like? Certainly, it is to be undone, to have the centre upset. It is to turn towards this sometimes obscured material and hidden history which, again, continues to structure the present. It is also to work out what kind of consistency is possible in the face of that Real. What other myths need to be written and by whom?[13]

Making Devices

In order to be able to shift perspective and, with that, mobilise other myths and fictions, then some kind of device is required. A device that involves different lenses perhaps, but also a mirror function in some senses too. David Burrows and I write more about this in a recent essay on 'Science Fiction Devices' (where at stake are works of fiction that contain these perspectival devices, but also the idea of the book as itself a device) (Burrows and O'Sullivan 2022). Here, though, it is worth remarking that such a device might take other forms. As I briefly mentioned in the previous essay, it might, for example, be the Black sonic device that Harney and Moten discuss in relation to Nathaniel Mackey and Don Cherry ('blackness is an instrument in the making') (Harney and Moten 2013: 94). Or, again, Sun Ra's myth-science systems, especially as written about by Kodwo Eshun (Eshun 1998: 154–63). Or it might be something like Denise Ferreira da Silva's 'analytic formal artifact' (the 'Equation of Value') that she develops as an alternative to dominant Western value systems that position Blackness as negative (Ferreira da Silva 2017: 4). In the latter case it is the construction of something that allows a grasp of the potential of Blackness (beyond dialectics), a kind of philosophical equivalent of Harney and Moten's more poetic devices.[14]

Ultimately, it seems to me, this myth-work with its associated devices is about disabling a certain arrogance and production of subjectivity and, in its place affirming difference and diversity. Such a perspective involves seeing through existing myths—seeing what is obscured and how—but then also writing other myths and constructing other devices so as to replace these (and which then might allow other forms of community and collectivity to arise). This will mean reclaiming certain images and narratives (and figures too). And once again, it will also mean, for some, a standing aside or an enabling of these other myths to take shape without directing or co-opting them.

But in order to make a new device one first needs to know the devices one already has or already is and, indeed, see these devices as such (which is partly the motivation for at least some of the essays in this collection). Both these moves are required. Without a seeing of one's perspective *as* a perspective any turn to difference remains within a given frame. But to focus exclusively on the frame—or the questioning of perspective—can mean one is just caught within a narcissistic loop (or, to switch metaphors, a hall of mirrors). My understanding of the importance of this double gesture was, for me, enabled through my own collaboration and conversations with David Burrows which, if nothing else, gestures towards the importance of always being open to having one's own archive and presuppositions interrogated. Or, put differently, allowing one's own pre-existing myth-work to be seen as such and then, if need be, critiqued.

Myth-work might then be a name for the collaborative and collective endeavour of repair, especially when links and loops are made to individual life situations and circumstances. It is these circuits of connection that are crucial. It is also for this reason that writing and other forms of representation are key in terms of the devices I mention above. Might we even say that a characteristic of these devices is that they are Symbolic instruments that allow a different view on—and thus a different relationship to—the Real? Or, to put this differently, they allow a different relationship to trauma, even a claiming of it in some senses or certainly a resignifying (perhaps they will also operate on an asignifying or affective register too). This means too that these devices will foreground other times within our own or take us out of our more typical space-times. They will involve a different take on our past that then gestures towards—and perhaps helps summon forth—a different future. But it is also the case that they will not always be seen as these kinds of transformative device by those who have an interest in maintaining the status quo or proceeding with 'business as usual'. Those who have an investment—for whatever reason—in keeping certain pasts hidden and thus certain possibilities for the future obscured. As well as anything else then myth-work involves this reclaiming and repurposing of devices that are already here but have been hidden or rendered inoperative in some manner.

Coda

This essay has been about traumas that are not directly mine and about myth-work that is necessarily more the concern of those communities and individuals more directly affected. Many are still firmly living within the plantation system or are struggling against settler attitudes, just as others are having to face every day the ongoing war against women. Capitalism and colonial logics continue to produce an uneven landscape in this sense even though these traumas are structural to our contemporary world. I have written this essay from a privileged position and partly as a reflection on that, but also as an ally to these other communities who continue in their struggles and in their own practices of myth-work too.

Notes

1. Myth, as I'm using the term in this essay, refers to narratives and stories (and their enactment), but also has resonances with Roland Barthes' understanding of myth as naming the '*what-goes-without-saying*' (Barthes 1973: 11).
2. For a critique of these kinds of Nationalist myths, especially as mobilised by the alt-right and Neoreaction, see my essay 'Accelerationism, Hyperstition and Myth-Science' (O'Sullivan 2017a).
3. See for example the work of the artist Cameron Rowland (and specifically '3 & 4 Will. IV c. 73'). Details available here: www.ica.art/exhibitions/cameron-rowland (accessed 22 February 2022).
4. To quote Federici:

    Just as the Enclosures expropriated the peasantry from the communal land, so the witch-hunt expropriated women from their bodies, which were thus 'liberated' from any impediment preventing them to function as machines for the production of labor. For the threat of the stake erected more formidable barriers around women's bodies than were ever erected by the fencing off of the commons. (Federici 2014: 184 [italicised in original])

5. See the essay 'Utopia and Science Fiction' (Williams 1978).
6. To quote Fisher: 'The port is a sign of the triumph of finance capital; it is part of the heavy material infrastructure that facilitates the illusion of a "dematerialised" capitalism. It is the eerie underside of contemporary capital's mundane gloss' (Fisher 2016: 77).
7. See also the fuller discussion of *Voodoo Science Park* in my essay 'Fictioning the Landscape' (O'Sullivan 2018).
8. As does Sylvia Wynter in relation to further demonstrating that racial categories are produced by the West. To quote Wynter: 'For these categories had not existed before the West's global expansion and its forcible incorporation of the peoples and cultures it met into its own secularizing Judaeo-Christian cultural field' (Wynter in Scott 2000: 174).
9. David Burrows and I have written at length on Sun Ra and myth in *Fictioning* (2019). See, especially, the chapter on 'Myth-Science: Alien Perspectives', pp. 199-216. It seems to me that Ferreira da Silva's 'Equation of Value' might be brought into productive encounter with Sun Ra's equation of myth that we discuss in *Fictioning* (both being an example of the invention of an 'analytic formal artifact' that allows a thinking and being otherwise [Ferreira da Silva 2017: 4]).
10. Gauthier organises her polemic around the question of 'why witches?' She answers in turn (to give a very brief synopsis) because they *dance, sing,* are *alive* and *rapturous*.
11. In relation to this intersection between witches and ecological activism it is crucial to acknowledge a further trauma—the climate crisis—that is continuing to be experienced by people, animals and the planet at large. This is still part of our human history insofar as we are causing the crisis (the Anthropocene) but certainly it is not just humans that are experiencing the effects. The climate crisis is a symptom of the same logics of capitalist racialisation and resource extraction that I mentioned above and, as such, other nations have already been experiencing the crisis for some time (it's just that its now beginning to effect Western nations). As the saying goes (attributed to the Science Fiction writer William Gibson): 'The future is already here—it's just not evenly distributed yet.'

12 Or to quote Wynter (speaking about the attitude of some English intellectuals to the Caribbean) this work of decolonisation is to understand that 'the condition of *their* being what they are today, and the condition of we being what we are today are totally interlinked' (Wynter in Scott 2000: 152).
13 And in relation to that other trauma—the climate crisis or 'capitalocene'—mentioned in the footnote above, might it also be that myth has a role to play? Certainly, we need other myths (or we need to make a qualified return to older myths) that are not part of the tool/weapon narrative that has got us to where we are. This is not to suggest a 'back to nature' narrative with all the dangers that can imply (in the most extreme case, a green fascism), but rather to call for other more future looking and also hybrid myths. Myths that have been—and are being—collectively written (as in some of Donna Haraway's work [2016]). Myths that foreground as well a different kind of relationship between humans, but also humans and non-humans. I will return to this in the next essay.
14 Ferreira da Silva mentions Moten towards the end of her essay when drawing out the connections of her own work to a larger 'radical practice of refusal to contain blackness in the dialectical form' (Ferreira da Silva 2017: 9). One of the prompts for Ferreira da Silva's essay is also the artwork of Otobong Nkanga (so a further kind of artifact or device):

> For the most part, what I do here is try to emulate Nkanga's artistic intervention into Western aesthetic culture with an analytic formal artifact—that is, the proof of the Equation of Value—which might implode the basis of the ethical grammar that cannot but provide a negative answer for the never-asked question for which Black Lives Matter demands a different answer. (Ferreira da Silva 2017: 4)

6

On Magic and Place

Developing some of the themes of the previous essays (especially around performance and the activation or summoning of other times) here I write about the importance of place in relation to magic and what I call myth-work. This essay proceeds through examples of contemporary art practices and cultural production more generally, including Mark Leckey's O' Magic Power of Bleakness *and Sophie Sleigh-Johnson's* Cealdwiellla. *Equally crucial is a thinking through of Mark Fisher's concept of the 'eerie' in relation to both landscape and fictions about landscape. My essay also develops the idea of a device that might be technical but that might have aesthetic or magical effects as well.*

The Eerie and Representation

A landscape is characterised by certain features that foreground themselves and thus have a traction on a given subjectivity or, indeed, community. As I discussed in the previous essay this can also mean that a landscape is always already marked by trauma, both personal and collective. But even if there is no trauma, there can be a sense that a given landscape holds within it (as well as partly obscures) certain histories and other events which are, again, both personal and collective. In these cases, a representation of that already marked landscape seems to be able to allow a reclaiming of these histories in some way or, at least, a reactivation of them in and for the present.

Mark Fisher's account of the eerie—a certain 'structure of feeling' (Williams 1977) associated with or constituted by '*a failure of absence* or by a *failure of presence*' (so a kind of trauma it might be argued)[1]—involves the claim that although 'triggered by particular cultural forms, it does not originate in them' (Fisher 2016: 61).[2] This seems an especially good way to get deeper into this question of landscape and the relationship of magic and place. Certainly, Fisher's writings offer a way of understanding how art can operate as a kind of optic—or device—in relation to landscape. In *The Weird and the Eerie* Fisher generally looks to works of literature and film, often attending to the way a given narrative involves certain objects and props that are able to conjure this particular 'structure of feeling', especially those residues that are unearthed from within a landscape. As I mentioned in the previous essay he also attends in the chapter on his and Justin Barton's sonic fiction *On Vanishing Land*[3] to the way in which a site like Sutton Hoo (another physical reminder of previous times) produces this eerie affect and, indeed, resonates with other contemporary spaces and places that are emptied of human presence, such as the container ports of the Suffolk coast (so global capitalism has itself an eerie quality for Fisher). There is something important here about how contemporary sites can resonate with more ancient ones. It is one of the hallmarks of Fisher's writing that he connects these deep pasts with what are often lost futures and bleak Science Fiction presents (and this links *The Weird and the Eerie* up with earlier work Fisher carried out with the Cybernetic culture research unit as well as to his other work on hauntology—see for example Fisher 2014).

There is also something important about representation at stake here and how a representation can sometimes focus the power of the original (or of a particular site for example). As I gestured to above, it is stories—fictions—about unearthing remnants that Fisher especially looks to rather than the archaeological accounts themselves (although we might want to ask whether there is such a hard and fast border between fiction and archaeology here). Fisher looks to Alan Garner's novel *Red Shift*, for example, which involves a found ancient stone axe head as a central motif and time-travelling device.[4] The idea that a book might itself operate as a prop or time-travelling device (that is, as well as being about one) is also important here (Garner's *Red Shift* seems a paradigmatic example of this).[5] Or, another example, it is partly through Brian Eno's record *On Land* and M. R. James' ghost stories that Fisher (and Barton) 'see' the Suffolk landscape (and with M. R. James there are further found artifacts—a whistle and a crown—in play that operate as time-travelling devices).

In a sense, Fisher's own essays on these other works are themselves a further device or another circuit of representation. Relating this back to some of the other essays gathered in this collection, there is a sense that reaching the outside—which is what the eerie is essentially about (certainly for Fisher)[6]—can sometimes seem to involve turning in the other direction. A turning inwards and in this case producing representations (fictions, but also commentaries) *about* our relationship to the outside. When these representations are then materialised or performed in some way—as with Barton and Fisher's own audio *dérive* along the Suffolk coast (*On Vanishing Land*)—then the effect is even more pronounced.

Affect Bridge Regression

Another example of this kind of myth-work—if we can call the work Fisher looks at (and his own essays to some extent) as such—is Mark Leckey's series of works around the motorway bridge at Eastham Rake in Liverpool. This site operates as a very particular and modern liminal space for Leckey, but also as a 'place' within the landscape. In Leckey's installation *O' Magic Power of Bleakness* in Tate Britain in 2019—which involved the building of a life size replica of the bridge in the gallery (see Fig. 6.1 in the colour plate section)—the association of being under the bridge with neolithic underground burial chambers is made explicit and it is the medium of film that allows this exploration and layering of different times (so here the use of a modern technology allows a conjuring of a more pre-modern one).[7] There are other crucial components to the exhibition. The film *Under Under In* that restages—or *fictions*—Leckey's memories of an event and encounter under the bridge (more of which below).[8] And then there is the presentation of previous film works by Leckey alongside various posters and, crucially, a very particular low lighting that mimics the original setting of the motorway bridge.[9] All of these different components produce a very particular set-up and, with that, a certain 'structure of feeling' (which, I think, fits Fisher's definition of the eerie). This is accentuated by the fact that the audience/participants enter into the work themselves, literally standing under the bridge. The reconstructed space also becomes a kind of stage set (as perhaps the original bridge was too?) with a 'magic lantern' projection on to a ledge under the reconstructed bridge that also conjures—or, again, fictions—Leckey's memories (again, see Fig. 6.1). And then there is as well the fact that the installation becomes a site for further actual performances invited in by Leckey. Or, we might say, further encounters are then enabled by this set-up.

This motorway bridge is a recurring motif for Leckey. Something happened to his younger self when under this bridge. There was an encounter with an entity of some kind that crossed over. Or, put differently—and in terms of Fisher's writings—there was an incursion from the outside. Leckey's work—as the title of a previous incarnation, *Exorcism of the Bridge@Eastham Rake* makes explicit—is an attempt at exorcism of this presence or haunting, although exorcism is also here connected to summoning (the latter allowing the former perhaps?).

The bridge is then a site of passage or a portal between worlds. Leckey refers to the myth of Tam Lin—a story of a changeling—which takes us back to Fisher who also relates how this narrative was important to Alan Garner and *Red Shift*. At stake here is a kind of time travel, or a cut in time that then allows other agencies to foreground themselves (we might be reminded of the Ccru's idea of a time rift here that they address in 'Lemurian Time War' [Ccru 2017]). Crucially, there is a sense that the work of repeating and representing this scene focuses something and, with that, allows a different relation to memory and the past to take hold. For Leckey this kind of sustained and intense work might well operate as an exorcism. But it also functions—for us, the viewer/participant—as a representation of an exorcism, one that foregrounds the co-presence of other times and other possible agencies which, more typically, are invisible. The repetition of a given motif—in this case the reoccurrence of the bridge in different forms and genres—would seem to increase this magical power.[10]

Leckey's practice might be understood as a kind of myth-work in this sense insofar as it involves a revisiting and reclaiming of a previous narrative and associated images. Even a rewriting (broadly understood) of an external event or prior determination. This turning around and returning to a past seems key to the work, especially, again, when it is repeated.[11] And seeing another's myth-work—having it presented to us (again, often in different media and through different genres)—can work to prompt us to reflect on our own fictions or even to begin our own myth-work. So here a cultural production operates as a kind of case study but also a trigger, to borrow Fisher's phrase.

The motorway bridge at Eastham Rake is then one of Leckey's 'key-points' in his landscape (to use that phrase from Gilbert Simondon again). There are others and, indeed, his practice seems to be partly about laying out these points and revisiting them. See, for example the film *Dream English Kid, 1964-1999 AD* that involves Leckey revisiting various places—and images—from his past (and also contains a model of the Eastham Rake Motorway Bridge). This again relates to the way Leckey is a character in these works or is included within them as a figure or as a perspective (so, the practice can also be understood as a kind of autofiction in this sense). But can we extract a more general principle here as well? About how art can involve a relationship to certain key-points in a given landscape that have had an impact on a given subjectivity. Indeed, are these two necessarily imbricated? Or, put differently, is the self, when all is said and done, itself a kind of landscape (or series of them?).

Occulture and Landscape

There is a particular occult tradition of cultural production that focuses on some of these ideas (broadly speaking, a tradition of magic and place). A good example is *Penda's Fen*, a film that involves a narrative about trauma, landscape and magic, but also a young man's subjectivity and queer sexuality. Yvette Salmon suggests that this film is part of an occult tradition that operates across time and involves the 'persistence of a shared sensibility or even a collective paradigm' (Salmon 2019: 56) that is connected to place and especially the English landscape.[12] Certainly there is the sense that the external landscape of *Penda's Fen* is doubling the internal one of the young protagonist or, at least, that there is a transit between these two, not least in and through dreams and visions. It is this porosity—which itself operates through time as well as space—that gives the film its singular quality.[13]

Penda's Fen then produces a particular feeling, but one whose origin is not located there—to return to Fisher's idea. It is as if a device is needed so that the particular structure of feeling of that landscape can be foregrounded. The device need not necessarily be contemporary. Standing stones, for example, might work to focus the feeling of a place (so here it is not exactly a made thing, but certainly there is a sense of human intervention in a natural scene).[14] It does seem important, however, that there is this minimal human presence, or residue of it, so that this feeling can be conjured in some manner. Or, put differently, the landscape needs to be seen—or have been seen—by other eyes. Or to have been felt perhaps.

As far as standing stones go this activation is increased when they become a further set-up for other scenes and performances. So once again repetition is important. Festivals, for example, which are in this sense always already an echo back to previous festivals and also a gesturing forward to those to come—as Gilles Deleuze suggests at the very beginning of *Difference and Repetition*—all of them activating these sites or 'key-points' in a landscape (Deleuze 1994: 1). The power of these festivals or celebrations—as with rituals more generally—is that they are always part of a sequence or series in this sense. More broadly it is some kind of performance at these privileged key-points in a landscape that activates this magical functioning (or—to return to Leckey—allows the conjuring of other space-times).

Indeed, to repeat a point I have made in previous essays, performance seems crucial to myth-work in this sense. And, following that, also the deployment of more sonic devices. Again, this is certainly the case with Barton and Fisher's *On Vanishing Land*, not least with the turn to Eno's *On Land* that I mentioned above. It is also there in Leckey's own sonic invocations and performances.[15] Indeed, for Fisher, the sonic is an especially good way of invoking the eerie (it seems to have a privileged access to this mode). But this also explains the intrinsic connections between music and place as if, once again, a sonic device (or sonic fiction perhaps?) is able to focus a particular sensibility of a given landscape.

English Heretic

Another occultural practice—more on the edge of contemporary art than Leckey's—is that of English Heretic (the moniker of the artist and writer Andy Sharp) which also involves this kind of attention to particular sensibilities in the landscape or what I would call myth-work (the essay by Salmon I mention above looks to English Heretic as a case study too). In a Foreword to the recent collection of English Heretic's projects and writings the artist Dean Kenning writes about English Heretic's interest in place—what Kenning names as an 'esoteric materialism'—and especially the investigative work of uncovering other more secret or hidden histories (as for example with the Black Plaque project which involved the commemoration of occult figures and the marking of key sites associated with them).[16] There is here a kind of magical mapping (or psychogeography) of the landscape in play and with that also an idea of the transformational potentialities of the latter. To quote Andy Sharp from the very beginning of his collection of writing, 'Not only did landscape offer the possibility for creative engagement, but it could also be used as an arena to disrupt reality' (Sharp 2020: 21).

Kenning makes a connection back to J. M. Frazer and *The Golden Bough* with the idea that certain sites might hold an energy or contain certain presences. There is something *contagious* that is still there. Something that has been left behind (so there are resonances with Fisher here). And, Kenning suggests, English Heretic's practice—involving as it does a kind of doubling and mirroring of these sites and histories—might also be involved in a kind of *sympathetic* magic too (where like produces like). Again, the key aspect here seems to be that it is through cultural production at, around or more broadly in relation to these sites that something becomes focussed.

We also return here to a theme that I have touched on in some of the previous essays (and one I will return to) that the past can be a resource for the present—offering up alternative modes of being perhaps?—and that other histories are there to be reactivated. And, further, that fiction—broadly construed—might be involved in that reactivation. Kenning draws attention too to a more performative aspect of English Heretic's practice. The actual journeying to obscured sites (those overlooked by the culture industry) but also the music and songs—and performance of them—that conjure (or trigger) the particular sensibility.

More generally there is also an idea of a different kind of method at play here. Less high theory, but instead, something more obsessive, even adolescent (although we have to be wary of suggesting it is a regression in any sense).[17] Certainly, English Heretic, like Mark Leckey, is involved in an autodidactic process of research (self-described in both cases). Is there perhaps a connection here between this self-teaching and magical practice? And, with that, a connection also to practices of self-determination? Certainly, with these two artists there is a sense that they are writing (or re-writing) their own narratives—and indeed making their own devices—as part of their own myth-work.

Running Wells

A third and final further case study of magic and place is the expanded practice of Sophie Sleigh-Johnson. Tethered to Essex and the landscapes there—including the marshlands—Sleigh-Johnson's work involves sound and sonic fictions alongside writings, sculpture (broadly understood) and other representations (when this includes 'found' objects).[18] Crucially, however, it is performance that activates these other elements. The latter might take place in a particular landscape—or, indeed, involve a pilgrimage to specific places (often following in the footsteps of previous travellers)—but it can also involve a kind of extraction or focusing of these energies via a re-staging (or re-versioning) in other places and spaces (so there is a resonance with Leckey here). The focus on a particular place and, indeed, an emphasis on the local also gives the practice a traction across time and space. It speaks to other locations and places, not because it generalises, but because it moves in the opposite direction. There is a secret link or connection here between these different localities or 'key-points'. Might we call this the secret power of the parochial?

An example is the *Cealdwiellla* project that involved Sleigh-Johnson journeying to a sacred well in Essex (so a pilgrimage of sorts) as well as research around the history of that site.[19] But it also involved a performance—with the performance artists New Noveta—in a gallery space, Arcadia Missa in London, that included a representation (or remade version) of the well alongside a live transmission (from the well itself) (see Fig. 6.2 in the colour plate section). The performance was then a kind of ritual operating across both space and time, or, to say the same differently, involved the setting up of a space–time travel device. Of particular relevance to this essay is Sleigh-Johnson's use of props. In the case of this performance, this was an iron crosier that incorporated a version of the Runwell prioress' cross that is found carved on the stones near the well, but that also referenced other objects from across Sleigh-Johnson's practice and research (for example the iron-tipped wooden staff of Antonin Artaud). Crucially these props are made (or fictioned) by Sleigh-Johnson.

Once again, the adage that the magician must make their own tools seems pertinent.

More recent performances (for example 'Big News 2') are more quotidian but no less concerned with magical practice and involve Sleigh-Johnson using various technical devices to splice together different sounds or modify/distort her voice. There is also an obsession here with certain themes and, indeed, objects, such as the Holsten beer can and the cheap off-licence polythene bag (that in Sleigh-Johnson's performance and wider practice is sometimes printed on, drawing in other motifs and references).[20] Sleigh-Johnson returns to certain scenes and objects almost, like Leckey, as an exorcism (or summoning). Certainly, there is a looping in play (literally in the use of sonic loops and layering in the performances). In relation to this there is also an ongoing fascination across the practice for a particular group of figures. Artaud, as mentioned above (whose own staff was used to mark the landscape), but also, for example, Leonard Rossiter from the 1980s sitcom *Rising Damp*. This comic element is important (the above props—the cans, bags and so forth—are part of it too) and, rather than diluting any serious or magical effect seems to increase it. The comic here seems to be about foregrounding certain details, laying out alternative narratives, as well as short-circuiting existing ones.

As with Leckey, Sleigh-Johnson is also a figure within this landscape. As far as this goes her job as reporter for the *Leigh Times* plays into her performances or, we might say is thematised in there or, again, fictioned (she plays 'The Reporter'). There is something important here about how such work blurs the distinction between fiction and reality or, more particularly, gives the fiction a traction in reality (because it partakes, at least in part, of that reality). This is the case with these 'real' figures (including Sleigh-Johnson) and also the way in which 'real' objects are used as props in more fictional set-ups.

Finally, there is also Sleigh-Johnson's research practice of interviews and podcasts (a gathering of materials) or the making of 'mix tapes' for example the recent *Nuncio Ref* (on which the above performance is based). The latter in particular, with its use of feedback and snatches of narrative, repeated phrases and looping of sounds, conjures a very particular scene or 'structure of feeling'. These all highlight a key concern of this essay: that magic and place is best accounted for by the sonic. Or, put differently, that it is the sonic that can most successfully conjure the entities and other forces of a place, not least as sound and the spoken word can bring other times into play.

From Technical to Magical Objects

Ultimately then some artworks—or, more generally, cultural productions—operate as devices that focus the feeling of a place (or, indeed, make a place as such) and also foreground the presence of different times and the imbrication of external and internal landscapes. It would seem that this desire—to put something in a landscape or to mark it somehow—has been characteristic of humans for a long time. Following Simondon it might well be that initially these objects (or devices) were once tied to certain places (in a magical structuring of the universe)—certain sacred sites for example—but that eventually they became separated from them. This for Simondon is the beginnings of technicity. But something is certainly lost in this detachment (simply put, a connection or relation). Might it be the case, however, that technical objects can have a role in summoning these other feelings of connection and relation? At least, if these are used in a certain way or, perhaps, repurposed in some manner? Certainly the practices I have briefly discussed in this essay use technical objects in carrying out their own myth-work.[21] In fact, might there be a sense that technical objects have always contained within them this other, more magical function? This amounts to saying that the technical object can be both a magical and an aesthetic device depending on context and, in particular, depending on its detachment from an overly technical consciousness (or technicity). When these devices are activated in some manner, then something else is summoned. A particular sensibility or 'structure of feeling' that as well as anything else foregrounds the occult relationship between magic and place.

Coda

The practices I have briefly discussed in this essay—as well as others in this book—are ones that for whatever reason have drawn me in (or, we might say, they've selected me rather than me them). It's partly that they resonate with themes and materials I am interested in (as evidenced by some of the other essays collected here), but they also involve aspects that push this further or introduce other elements into that set-up. They are in addition practices that are singular or very much their own thing (and which, as part of this, involve a will to repetition). Another way of saying this is that each of them constitutes its own genre to some extent (or even its own landscape). Finally, they are practices that thematise their practitioners within them too (or even fiction the latter). It is this claiming of a narrative and with that the blurring of art and life (or a traversing between the two) that also lends these practices their magical power.

Notes

1. To quote Fisher: 'The experience of the eerie occurs either when there is something present where there should be nothing, or there is nothing when there should be something' (Fisher 2016: 61).
2. Fisher also suggests that this is tied up with a sense that a different kind of agency is at work.
3. For a discussion of *On Vanishing Land*—in relation to fictioning the landscape—see Burrows and O'Sullivan 2019: 138-40.
4. Garner returns to the idea of an object as time-travelling device in his recent novel *Treacle Walker*, where a 'donkey stone' allows a kind of looping of different times and summoning of past entities (Garner 2022). This novel is also more specifically about how fiction can interfere with reality and, as such, works as an interesting commentary on Garner's own method and oeuvre.
5. It is especially the way in which *Red Shift* does something to the reader's 'reality' that is important, not least in the strange inclusion of the letter in code at the end of the novel (which works, it seems to me, as a kind of anamorphosis).
6. 'The allure that the weird and the eerie possess…is to do with a fascination for the outside, for that which lies beyond standard perception, cognition and experience' (Fisher 2016: 8).
7. See also the discussion in *Fictioning* of Derek Jarmen's *Journey to Avebury* along these lines (a technical mode and object—in this case a Super 8 camera—allowing access to a magical one) (Burrows and O'Sullivan 2019: 98).
8. Important here is also the way in which Leckey brings his sense of magic and place into relationship with popular/counter-culture, so, again, a bringing together of the ancient and the modern. The bridge (and the ledge underneath it) was somewhere he went with his friends to hang out and in the film *Under Under In* it is a gang of teenagers dressed in modified sportswear and with mobile phones who are the protagonists in the fictioned drama Leckey sets up (Leckey is explicit that it is his own working-class youth culture that he is revisiting here).
9. In relation to the two other film works, the earlier *Fiorucci Made Me Hardcore* constructs another narrative—of the 'hardcore continuum' connecting rave culture back to

Northern Soul—and might be understood as a kind of occulture (Leckey refers to the film as being about ghosts). It's also a film-essay that constructs a certain historical sequence and one in which the personal and more public become entwined. The more recent film, *Dream English Kid, 1964-1999 AD* also involves a further weaving of the personal with found images. Again, this allows for the construction of a narrative and mythos associated with place and, in this (and the focus on London) harks back to Leckey's collaborative work as Donatella.

10 The bridge first appears as an image in *Dream English Kid, 1964-1999 AD* (2015) and then, again, as a model in *Affect Bridge Age Regression* at Cubitt Gallery, London (2017). The life size replica built at Tate has its precursor in two other shows: *Containers and Their Drivers* at MoMA PS1, New York (2016) and *He Thrusts His Fists against the Posts but Still Insists He Sees the Ghost* at SMK, Copenhagen (2017).

11 Leckey himself relates this return to loops and looping:

> It's all to do with loops, the same thing being repeated over and over again to generate an altered state…The reason I make art is to understand why things fascinate me, and I want to repeat them in order to feel, again and again, my fascination for them, and also so I can understand these fetishes as a symptom of a contemporary condition. (Leckey 2019: 15)

12 Salmon quotes Simon Dwyer from *Rapid Eye* with a definition of occulture or, at least, of occulture understood in this particular way:

> Occulture is not a secret culture as the word might suggest, but culture that is in some way hidden and ignored, or wilfully marginalised to the extremities of our society. A culture of individuality and sub-cults, a culture of questions that have not been properly identified—let alone answered—and therefore, do not get fair representation in the mainstream media. It is a culture that has been misinterpreted…It is a sub-culture that is forming a question that 'reality' alone cannot answer. (Dwyer quoted in Salmon 2019: 56)

13 There is also the example of certain television dramas (especially for children and adolescents) that involve this kind of temporal porosity and, with that a definite sense of the eerie, for example *Children of the Stones* or *The Changes*.

14 A contemporary artwork that involves a turn to standing stones is Jeremy Deller's *English Magic*. Here elements of the past—images of the stones of Avebury or of stone axe heads for example—are brought into relation with the contemporary (so other objects and images) and occasionally literally layered on top of them to make an image. In this case it is the specific combination of elements that produces a certain affect. Collage is a key method here, allowing this superimposing of different forms and genres, but also different times. Deller's work is less to do with the eerie however (indeed, humans are very much a presence in the work), but more diagrammatic, to do with mapping out objects, people and their relations and cultural productions, including across time (its politics is more explicit in this sense). See especially the book—also titled *English Magic*—that was produced to accompany Deller's Venice Biennale show in 2013.

15 Leckey performed at previous incarnations of the show (in New York and Copenhagen) and, at Tate Britain, also curated a series of invited performances.

16 Kenning refers to Walter Benjamin's different treatment of history here and to a certain constructive principle that is always already in play (or the way history is always constructed from the perspectives and points of views of the present). To quote Kenning:

That most esoteric of materialist philosophers, Walter Benjamin, berated those who recount history like the beads of a rosary, as if events are simply given for the re-telling and not cast in the moulds of the masters. Redeeming a past buried under the weight of historical myth, the materialist must, according to Benjamin, 'grasp a constellation which his own era has formed with a definite earlier one', thereby interrupting the empty flow of linear time, the ritual summation of positivistic data. Benjamin called such constellation-forming a 'constructive principle'. (Kenning 2020: 10)

17 McKenzie Wark's definition of 'low theory' also seems appropriate here: 'What has escaped the institutionalization of high theory is the possibility of *low theory*, of a critical thought indifferent to the institutional forms of the academy or the art world' (Wark 2011: 3).
18 For an insight into the practice, see the representation of Sleigh-Johnson's hand-written notes—'Fragments (Glyph, The Flicker)'—in *Chthonic Index* (Sleigh-Johnson 2015).
19 Sleigh-Johnson's research practice seems to me to involve a different form of knowledge production to the Academy. Indeed, the method—pilgrimages, archive visits, performances—alongside research into local papers and pamphlets, the close reading of theoretical material, and so forth—is very much an artist's one. There is a will to find patterns and make connections (utilising principles of 'serendipity and contingency' as Sleigh-Johnson puts it in her thesis [Sleigh-Johnson 2022]). Comedy, as I mentioned above, is also a crucial part of this method.
20 For example, the cover image of a stylised cloud from the Penguin Classic edition of *The Cloud of Unknowing* book or, for the more recent performance, the slogan 'Big News 2' (also the name of that performance).
21 Kodwo Eshun, for example, writes about certain sonic devices—for example turntables—that are used against their original intention so as to produce other affects and summon other worlds (see Eshun 1998).

7

A Thousand Devices

The final essay of this first half of my book draws some threads together and briefly tracks the idea of the device (that has been partly sketched out in some of the previous essays) across different terrains: literary, philosophical, artistic, magical/magickal and technological. It also involves some more speculative reflections on AI and the relationship between technical and magical devices. In most cases it is the way in which there can be writing about devices (or as a representation of them) but then also writing as device (or as involved in the making of one) that I attend to. This relates back too to one of the central concerns of my book (and especially this first half), which is the exploration of that most ancient of devices, the fiction of the self (and, indeed, what kinds of device allow us to 'see' this fiction as a fiction).

Literary Devices and the Novel

Within literature there are formal devices, as for example when a novel introduces external elements (to the narrative or form of the novel) or plays with style and syntax so as to shift a register of reading. A paradigmatic example here is the cut-up (although this is a device that also allows a more radical shift and operates on other registers besides the literary), but we can include in this category any other avant-garde formal strategies that foreground writing as text. Another way of putting this is that these formal devices break with a certain reality effect (or what Jean-François Lyotard once called the 'fantasies of realism') (Lyotard 1984: 74). I will turn to the more radical and future-orientated version of this formal experimentation below.

And then there are also those works of fiction that contain devices within them, that is, writing that is *about* devices or that use the device as a central motif/theme within the narrative. Here the device is part of the content of a fiction. This is often the case with Science Fictions, especially insofar as the latter concern future technological developments. A good recent example is Ted Chiang's short story collection *Exhalation*, that contains and concerns a proliferation of these futuristic technical devices (Chiang 2019).[1]

It is especially compelling when a device traverses these two regimes of operation—broadly form and content—as it also is when a device more generally works across different genres.[2] David Burrows and I address some of these more complex devices—and the various traverses they make—in our essay 'Science Fiction Devices' (Burrows and O'Sullivan 2022). An example that we discuss at more length in that essay is the *feminaries* book in Monica Wittig's novel *Les Guérillères* (1971). The *feminaries* is a book within the narrative (it is read by the community of women that are the subject of the fiction), but it also seems as if it might be Wittig's novel itself.

Following some of this logic further, there is also the novel more generally as itself a device. The novel as a strange kind of fictional object that does something to the reader's perspective.[3] Burrows and I have also written about this in relation to Russell Hoban's novel *Riddley Walker* (1980) and the first-person perspective of the protagonist of that book (Burrows and O'Sullivan 2019: 94-7). In this context that novel—and the landscapes we traverse when reading it—might be said to offer up a world within a world. Or, put differently, the novel can offer up a different point of view from within our own, one that we might take on, at least temporarily.

Philosophical Devices and Non-Philosophy as Device

Within philosophy there might also be the use of formal devices that switch the register of reading. Here the style—broadly understood—in which a philosophical work is written is important to its overall function. In these cases it's not just the philosophical content that's at stake (which might be about devices—I'll return to this below), but the way that content is presented. For example, there is the way the genre of theory-fiction can involve utilising the perspectives of fictional characters—Nietzsche's Zarathustra or Gilles Deleuze and Félix Guattari's Professor Challenger are precursors to this particular scene of writing[4]—or any of the more recent uses of fiction within philosophy that dramatise concepts or which, more generally, experiment with structure and presentation (for a discussion of some of these see my book *On Theory-Fiction and Other Genres* [O'Sullivan 2024b]). Style, again understood very broadly, in philosophy is then a kind of device that does something besides and beyond any straightforward conceptual development and presentation. Or as I have put it in previous essays here, there are certain philosophical works that perform their content.

It might be that there are other devices in philosophy that also break with a certain regime of representation or present a different kind of working through of materials. For example, there are diagrams or other kinds of figures that 'picture' concepts in different ways (as, with C. S. Peirce or, again, in some of Deleuze and Guattari's writings).[5] Here the device is mobilised for properly philosophical ends (when philosophy is understood—following Deleuze and Guattari—as this work of concept creation). Diagrams can also foreground and allow a more constructive principle of encounter and synthesis insofar as they can allow a treatment of philosophical concepts as a kind of material (they can allow a kind of fictioning of philosophy in this respect).[6]

And then there is philosophy *about* devices or that invents them on some level. An example of the former is Gilbert Simondon's account of the phase shift away from a prior magical mode of existence to religiosity and technicity. The figure-ground set-up of the earlier magical phase of humanity becomes undone in this shift. Figure is detached from ground (and, as such, there is no longer a magical unity between figure and ground) and becomes a mobile device (the technical object), just as the power of the ground itself becomes detached from specific privileged locations and extends throughout space (resulting in religion and its mediating figures). But it might also be said that Simondon posits another kind of device—an aesthetic one—that reminds of this unity and even re-enacts it in some manner (see the discussion in Burrows and O'Sullivan 2019: 87-94). So, here, there are technical devices (and possibly religious ones), but also magical devices (especially those that have survived from the past) and, further, aesthetic devices too (again, those that remind us of—or conjure up—this other magical mode of existence).

In terms of the invention of philosophical devices two interesting recent examples are Quentin Meillassoux's invention of the 'arche-fossil' (Meillassoux 2008) and Denise Ferreira da Silva's invention of an 'analytic formal artifact' she calls the 'Equation of Value' (Ferreira da Silva 2017: 4).

In each case the device is invented—or constructed—so as to accomplish a task. To show something about the existence of the 'Great Outdoors' in Meillassoux's case (a radical outside to the phenomenal world as we experience it) and to demonstrate the possibility of a different kind of value in Ferreira da Silva's (through mathematical formulation that gestures beyond oppositions and the dialectic). Another way of saying this is that these devices (or artifacts) are made so as to allow a shift in perspective. They are the making of something on the inside that allows for an access to—or a perspective from—an outside to a given system of the self. They are speculative devices that are, in philosophical terms, specifically post-Kantian. Ferreira da Silva suggests that her work is similar to the more poetic writings—around Blackness—of writers like Fred Moten and, indeed, in *The Undercommons*, we find Moten and his collaborator, Stefano Harney, using/inventing their own device—this time a 'sonic instrument'—to sound the depths of Blackness (Harney and Moten 2013).

Lastly, to follow the schema I have laid out above in relation to literature, there is also the understanding of philosophy, more generally, as device. So, different works of philosophy as specific and singular devices—the bringing of a world or a change of perspective—but then philosophy as a whole as a kind of device. The latter perspective is in play with François Laruelle's project of Non-Philosophy where at stake is not just seeing the mechanisms of Philosophy (with a capital 'P') as device, but also the repurposing of this device or shifting of its terrain of operation (and Laruelle will turn to the language of devices himself for this purpose in his essay on photo-fiction) (see Laruelle 2012).[7] Seeing something as a device in this sense means getting a certain perspective on it or, put differently, it is to see the edges and workings of something that hitherto was not seen. Ferreira da Silva's work, it seems to me, also allows this outside perspective on philosophy (especially post-Cartesian) and, not least, an understanding of its always-already racialised character.

A different take on this is Sylvia Wynter's switching of perspective so as to be able to 'see' once accepted as general/truthful categories—of the human—as partial (see the interview with Wynter in Scott 2000). For Wynter this is to take a broader or wider 'trans-genre-of-the-human' perspective from which to look back on these constructed categories that are then seen as such (Scott 2000: 206).[8] So, here it is a device—the taking on of a certain point of view—that allows a seeing of the different genres of the human as all human (perhaps the device in this case is like a reverse prism?). It is often the positioning of a fictional viewpoint that allows or enables these various shifts in perspective (as, for example, with Wynter's own novels). Or, put differently, one is able to see a genre as such only if one is looking at it from outside of that genre.[9]

Art Practice as Device (Make Your Own Device)

In many ways contemporary art practice, especially post-Duchamp, concerns devices. Certainly, there is a sense that different objects and installations—as well as performance—work to enact or transform something. It might be that the desired effect of the device is known and then it is the relevant or appropriate device that is assembled (and here there might be a practice of drawing out plans, blueprints and so forth). But it might also be the case that a particular device's functioning is not really known. One builds the device—blindly as it were—in order to see what it might do (much as one might assemble the machine first and then watch for its effects).[10] Here it is to be hoped that once made the device will do something, perhaps unexpected. Does this define the art device properly understood? That it is made but then functions in a way that cannot be wholly anticipated? Again, I have written about this elsewhere albeit with a different inflection, in terms of the idea that art is both intended and non-intended or that it 'speaks back' to its progenitors (see O'Sullivan 2016a). What other reason could there be for making an art device except to circumnavigate this intention in some senses? Or, put differently, to introduce a different agency into any set-up besides an already existing fiction of the self.

To return to my three registers. There might then be art that employs different devices on a formal level. Following my comments above, this will be those works that break with a given reality effect. And then there might well be art that is 'about' different devices as for example is sometimes the case with Outsider art or, more simply any representation of a device or practice that concerns a given device. But then there is the understanding of art—more generally—as a device. Following Laruelle, we might ask here whether there is a 'Non-Art' practice that detaches or repurposes this art. Perhaps, ultimately, this is a name for avant-garde strategies that necessarily depart from previous definitions of art (although an avant-garde tradition is also part of 'Art' and so would itself need to be framed or seen from elsewhere). I work through some of these twists and turns—in relation to a possible understanding of a Non-Art practice—in my essay on 'Non-Philosophy and Fiction as Method' (O'Sullivan 2017b).

To return to my earlier comments, there is also something important here about how art practice can itself offer up a different perspective and then, connected to this, how it foregrounds the business of building a device oneself. It is partly this—the way the artistic device is made by a given subjectivity (however that might be understood) and, as such, expresses a particular point of view—that marks it out from other kinds of device (that is, alongside any other aesthetic function it might have). It is also in these terms of foregrounding a perspective or even different perspectives that an idea of performance is important. Performance understood here as an interaction with devices, but also as a device in and of itself.

From Magical Devices to Magickal Devices

I briefly mentioned magic above in relation to Simondon and the shift to a technical mode of existence or—to extend that out a little—a more scientific paradigm of understanding the world. The section immediately above—on art practice—might also be said to be concerned with aesthetic devices, broadly understood (once again it is aesthetics, for Simondon, that reminds us of a prior pre-technical phase of existence). But, as I also gestured to above, different devices are also at stake within magical practice per se and especially magick with a 'k' that names practices of self-transformation (as opposed to stage magic, although I will return to the latter at the end of this essay). As with art, these practices often involve the magician making their own devices (indeed, this is a key aspect of magical/magickal practice). So, for example, Brion Gysin making his own dream machine or Austin Osman Spare designing his own tarot set. In these cases, part of the actual practice of magic/magick is making the device that then allows a non-typical state to arise or enables a contact with an outside to the subject as they more typically are. Another way of putting this is that magic/magick can involve the building of something on the inside that then allows contact with an outside. There is something similar in play with the cut-up technique here which is why I suggested above that the latter is not just a literary device, but also a more radical one that allows the human—as a 'time-bound' creature—to escape a given and dominant space-time (see Ccru 2017 and the discussion in my essay 'Time Circuits and Temporal Loops').

So, with magical/magickal practice there is the use of these devices and often, as a kind of accompaniment, instructions on how to make them (and/or where to place or enact them). There might also be accounts—more narrative descriptions perhaps—of the workings of these devices. In this case the more literary aspects of magical/magickal practice are foregrounded. And when magic/magick operates through writing—as with sigils and spells—then this becomes more complex, a traversing across these different modes of operation or, again, different registers. After all, a spell is both a sequence of words to be read and partly a set of instructions. It is also, crucially, a performative utterance. Spells are not only about meaning, but about getting something done as well.

And then, finally, it might be that magic in general can be understood as a kind of device. This is the case when it is seen from outside and/or from a different perspective hence those problematic sociological/anthropological accounts of magic as regressive.[11] But from another point of view seeing magic in this way (as a device) allows us to reclaim it in some senses. To work out what its relevance today might be perhaps? Seeing magical practice in its context is important for all sorts of reasons (chief amongst these is being sensitive to its origins and local specificities), but it is also important to be able to detach it and repurpose it so that it has traction in and on different presents. Indeed, often the most interesting practices of magic/magick are those that are detached from their genre (and from cliché). Or magic/magick that does not call itself as such.[12]

Scientific Devices, Technical Objects and Artificial Intelligences

The idea of the device really comes to the fore within our own scientific paradigm. Indeed, from one perspective science involves the invention of devices that allow us to see and interact with the world differently. These are devices that are less concerned with subjective experience than some of the others I discuss above. More abstractly science involves coming up with theories and then also empirically testing these out. Here the device equates to the scientific instrument, but it might be that the theories themselves can be understood as devices too. However abstract or diagrammatic, the principle of the scientific device remains the same. It allows a different take on reality which then allows different tasks to be performed.[13]

On a more general level—and following Simondon once more—there is also a sense that the scientific paradigm proceeds through proliferating devices (including the more abstract—or theoretical—ones I mentioned above). This Promethean impulse—to invent new devices—would seem to characterise the human endeavour (at least in part), although, following Simondon, it can be understood as a pursuit that is cut off from the unity it attempts to move toward (it is blind in this sense). As a brief aside here we might want to ask if there exist other technical devices that work more as optics on this prior (magical) unity? Devices that are, perhaps, concerned with privileged locations (or 'key-points') and that allow a shift in perspective (so, perhaps, returning us to subjective experience)? Here, at the sharp edge of technical development—with some of our most advanced devices—we have something like the appearance or calling forth of a magical device.[14] Might this also work the other way around? The uncovering of older, perhaps redundant devices that can then be reconfigured—or repurposed—as aesthetic devices. I will return to this in my essay on 'Archaeofictioning'.

There is also the question here of that supra-scientific device (or supra-technical object): Artificial Intelligence (AI). A made thing that goes beyond its makers (or will go beyond them, especially when it is made by other devices that have been made by us). Certainly, there is writing *about* this (the genre of Science Fiction) and even fictions that employ it or work in collaboration with it (see, for example, *Pharmako-AI* [K. Alado-McDowell 2020] and the discussion in Burrows and O'Sullivan 2022: 48-50). At the time of drafting this essay ChatGPT—and associated AI writing programmes—suggest that there has been a further step change in the development of these devices. These new technologies now successfully pass any Turing Test. Might we then understand AI more generally as a device that is allowing a different machine perspective to arise? Or at least that our interaction with AI is allowing us to imagine this other perspective. In relation to this, AI will also operate as a framing device (if it is not already), allowing us to see more clearly what the human—and human intelligence—is (or might become).

And then there is that forerunner of AI, the web, which is itself a kind of general device of our time. AI programmes like ChatGPT are, in many senses, advanced search engines optimised for human interaction. Their intelligence, if that's the right word, is partly drawn from this massively distributed data set. The perspective of an AI might be said to be the perspective of the web in this sense. Connected to this idea of a different perspective is how the web allows the foregrounding of different spaces and times, as if it is a device—made by us—that has then shifted the parameters of how we experience the worlds we are in. It is also in this sense that AIs are a technical object that seem to be gesturing towards something beyond technicity. Or they are technical devices that have an affinity with magical devices insofar as they range across space and time (they are time-travelling devices in this sense).

To return briefly to my schema. There is then science as a proliferation of devices, from mathematical theories and formulas to technical objects (and ultimately AI). Then there might also be writing about these devices (as, for example, with the History of Science or, once again, Science Fictions). And then there is science as itself a particular kind of device or operation. Foregrounded in this way we can see too how the scientific device involves certain values and logics that are intimately connected with its development in modernity and, as such, within colonialism too. Western science—as device—has brought about crucial developments but it has also brought about—or been entangled with—an extractive and colonising mentality.[15] Once again, perhaps a similar perspective to Laruelle's Non-Philosophy is required so as to refigure science as a series of practices untethered from this dominating overview (technical objects untethered from technicity perhaps?). To turn to a phrase that will be important in the next part of my book, this would mean a kind of 'dropping down' of any overarching perspective. In fact, something like this seems to be the case with Isabelle Stengers' call for an end to Science (with a big 'S'), with its dominating logics, and an accompanying call for the proliferation of sciences (small 's', plural) which, when seen in this manner—and on this plane of immanence (to use a Deleuzian term)—necessarily interact with other experimental practices and pursuits and thus also other devices, not least magical and aesthetic ones.[16] A thousand devices, each interacting in a thousand different ways.

Could we diagram this 'dropping down' to a plane of a thousand devices as in Fig. 7.1? Again, this shift in perspective will be in play in some of the essays in the second part of my book, for example with the dethroning of the human in 'On the Non-Human' or with the immersion within a fiction in 'On Tabletop Role-Playing Games and Fictioning'. To a certain extent it also diagrams the view from above/the outside that has been at stake in this essay and in earlier essays too (for example 'Fiction as Desiring Work').[17] When this diagram is superimposed on the 'Activation of a Device' diagram from my essay 'Time Circuits and Temporal Loops'—an essay that is also partly concerned with outside perspectives—then we have a picture of the complex process of the dropping down of any dominating perspective which then allows an activation of a given device and thus travel into other regions of being (or other spaces and times).

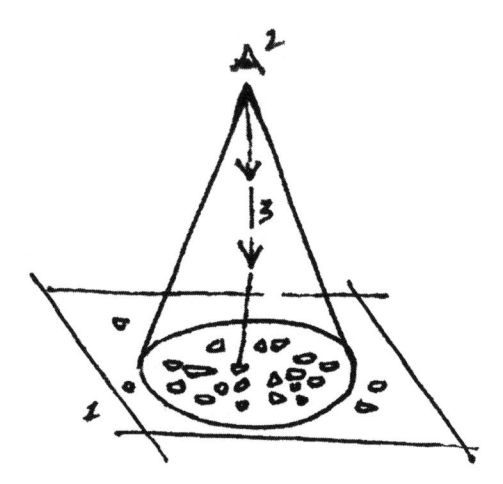

Fig. 7.1 Diagram of 'dropping down' of perspective. 1. Plane of a thousand devices; 2. Dominating perspective/view from above; 3. 'Dropping down' of perspective. (Author's own drawing)

The Fiction of the Self and the Lessons of Neuroscience

I have written about the relationship of devices to the fiction of the self in previous essays in this first part of my book, but, following my schema above, it might be that there are devices that break with a certain reality effect or, perhaps, foreground a different world from within this one (so certain radical technologies of the self). And then there might also be written accounts of these different devices. Fictions about the fiction of the self for example (as in certain kinds of autofiction especially when these foreground the constructed character of the self). But then, more radically, there might be devices that allow the actual seeing and foregrounding of the self as a fiction. Seeing the self as that most ancient of devices (and perhaps a genre like autofiction also involves a tracking across these two regimes of written fiction and the fiction of the self). It's difficult to get this more radical perspective—on the self as fiction—as we are necessarily within this fiction (just as, for example, it is difficult for the philosopher to 'get' the Non-Philosophical perspective). It's not straightforward to be able to see the device that determines one's perspective (one cannot step on one's own shadow). Indeed, a further device is needed so as to show the frame—to mix metaphors—that one is using in the world (when this includes the device that one is). Something is required from within the fiction, but which then allows a purchase or an outside perspective on the fiction (paradoxical though that sounds).[18]

And then, perhaps these same devices—or similar ones—might also show or allow a different mode of being in the world to be experimented with. Such seems to be at stake with, for example, some developments in neuroscience and the exploration of 'experience without a self' (See Metzinger 2009 and Brassier 2011 and the brief discussion in 'On Acéphale and Having No Head'). Crucial here is the ability to model these other 'non-self' modes of existence (if only speculatively). We might also return here to my comments above about AI systems insofar as these are certainly non-self modes or forms of non-self intelligence. But might this kind of modelling and invention also prompt us to further explore other accounts of other kinds of non-human intelligence and agency?[19] I am thinking here of animals (and thus of the secret resonances between animals and machines) but of other living and non-living agents and agencies too. Here the device might operate not only to show the edges of a particular perspective (again, the one we are, as it were), but also and in so doing gesture towards and demonstrate the existence of other devices (and, with that, other perspectives).[20] Once again, a plane of a thousand different devices interacting in a thousand different ways.

Theatrical Devices and Political Devices

In this concluding essay to the first part of my book I have focussed on the idea of the device as a made thing and as an instrument of sorts. But, of course, there is a further definition of the device as a kind of trick (as in the idea of a theatrical device). It seems to me that this latter idea is also at stake in what I have written. For example, such a definition would blur the distinction between magical and magickal devices, or between stage illusion and the transformation of reality. It might also blur the distinction between technical objects and magical objects (and then both of these with aesthetic objects too). Again, this is especially the case with performance which is often situated between the real and the fictional or, put differently, involves a logic of acting 'as if'. It is even more at stake in relation to the fiction of the self, which, as well as a device that produces a certain point of view, is also a kind of theatrical device that produces a certain 'believable' reality (or, simply, an illusion).

Elsewhere I will attend—with David Burrows—to some other kinds of device and the relationship these devices have to maps/landscapes and also to community (and especially the calling forth of a community).[21] Crucial in that operation will be our encounter with different and more diverse devices (especially away from the West). But I want to end here with a brief remark that the idea of a device that switches perspective is also crucial in relation to politics. Which is to say it is not always a question of arguing for a different reality (for example), but instead of making or setting up a different kind of device. Might even the taking down of one device operate as the setting up of another?[22] To return to an example and image I used in 'Landscape, Trauma and Myth-Work', is the toppling of a statue, for example, sometimes a kind of political (and anamorphic) device?

Coda

How does what I've written in this concluding essay to the first part of my book relate to my own writing and specifically these essays collected here? As I've mentioned already it's not as if these essays are themselves performative. This essay in particular is somewhat abstract and certainly theoretical. But perhaps the different essays collected here—including the essay above—can be components in some other kind of device that also works to shift perspective. What kind of device might that be? A device that crosses practices and genres perhaps or, at least, partakes of some of the different devices I have mentioned above. At times awkward and stumbling. At other times repeating itself or, at least, returning again and again to the same themes and resources (as is the case with this essay in particular). If nothing else, this book shows the uneven process—at least for me—of attempting to put something together which might bring some kind of transformation about.

Notes

1 For example, the device of the 'Alchemist's Gate' in 'The Merchant and the Alchemist's Gate' that enables time travel or the 'Predictor' in 'What Is Expected of Us?' that predicts decisions before they are made (Chiang 2019). The latter device is especially interesting in the way it shows up the illusion of free will (a key component of the fiction of the self).

2 Or, for example, when a literary device interacts with devices from outside literature. Félix Guattari addresses what he sees as this fruitful interaction in interview (although it is machines rather than devices that are at stake):

For me, a literary machine starts itself, or can start itself, when writing connects with other machines of desire...Writing begins to function in something else, as for example for the Beat generation in the relation with drugs; for Kerouac in the relation with travel, or with mountains, with yoga...Rhythms appear, a need, a desire to speak. Where is it possible for a writer to start this literary machine if it isn't precisely outside of writing and of the field of literature. (Guattari 1996b: 208-9)

3 Or as Proust puts it in *Time Regained*: 'Every reader, as he reads, is actually the reader of himself. The writer's work is only a kind of optical instrument he provides the reader so he can discern what he might never have seen in himself without this book'.

4 See the plateau '10,000 B.C.: The Geology of Morals (Who Does the Earth Think It Is?)' in Deleuze and Guattari 1988: 39-74.

5 See my essay 'On the Diagram (and a Practice of Diagrammatics)' for a gathering together and working through of some other examples of diagrams as device (O'Sullivan 2016b).

6 I attempt this kind of project of reconfiguring concepts (from a variety of thinkers) as diagrams and then exploring syntheses and other possible compatibilities in my

book *On the Production of Subjectivity: Five Diagrams of the Finite-Infinite Relation* (O'Sullivan 2012).

7 To quote Laruelle from the beginning of his own essay on Non-Philosophy and aesthetics ('Photo-Fiction: A Theoretical Installation'):

> Like an artisan, engineer, or designer, I am going to attempt to construct in front of you a so-called apparatus of photofiction (or at least make an attempt at projecting the diagram rather than contemplating the Idea of the photo). It is an exercise in the construction of a theoretical object, and is thus transparent, but which will function more like a black box. (Laruelle 2012: 11)

8 As Wynter remarks towards the end of her interview on 'The Re-Enchantment of Humanism':

> But if you move outside these limits, look at other cultures and their conceptions, then look back at the West, at yourself, from a trans-genre-of-the-human perspective, something hits you. What you begin to recognise is that what the subjects of each order are everywhere producing is always mode of being human, what Nietzsche [in *Genealogy of Morals*] saw as the 'tremendous labour of man upon himself', by which it was to make itself calculable, its behaviours therefore predictable. (Wynter quoted in Scott 2000: 206)

There are interesting resonances here with Reza Negarestani's 'Labour of the Inhuman' insofar as both writers foreground a grand 'trans-genre-of-the-human perspective' and see the labour (of the human/inhuman) as an unfinished project (see Negarestani 2014).

9 As Wynter remarks pin-pointing this problematic right at the beginning of 'The Ceremony Found':

> Given that such cosmogonically chartered 'webs of significance' are at the same time the indispensable condition of our being able to performatively enact ourselves as *being human* in the *genre*-specific terms of an *I* and its referent *We*, how can we then come to know our social reality *outside* the terms of the eusocializing mode of auto-institution in whose web-spinning field alone we are recursively enabled performatively to enact ourselves in the *genre*-specific terms of our *fictive modes of kind*? (Wynter 2015: 202)

Or as she puts it more bluntly in interview: 'How do you deal with the stereotyped view of yourself that you yourself have been socialized to accept?' (Wynter quoted in Scott 2000: 131) and later, even more succinctly: 'How can we think *outside* the terms in which we *are*?' (Wynter quoted in Scott 2000: 206).

10 As is also the case in the initial discussion of machines in Deleuze and Guattari's *Anti-Oedipus*: 'Given a certain effect, what machine is capable of producing it? And given a certain machine, what can it be used for?' (Deleuze and Guattari 1984: 3). For Deleuze and Guattari a key figure here is then the *bricoleur* (involved as they are in 'tinkering about' and 'the art of making do with what's at hand' [translators note in Deleuze and Guattari 1984: 7]). Bricolage would, it seem to me, also be a way of thinking about the production of different devices.

11 See for example Marcel Mauss' *General Theory of Magic* (2001), itself a critique of J. G. Frazer's *The Golden Bough* (1983) (both authors position magic as a regressive form of thought).

12 To quote Andy Sharp (English Heretic): 'I don't think magic needs to know its name in order to work' (Burrows and Sharp 2009: 27).

13 David Burrows has written on this more abstract functioning of diagrammatic devices that allow a 'picturing' of different aspects of reality that are typically invisible (such as Black Holes) (see Burrows 2020).
14 I have in mind here recent uses of technology (and especially computer imaging) to present and animate different worlds and other space-times.
15 Technological development's reliance on colonial logics is explored in Louis Chude-Sokei's *The Sound of Culture* (Chude-Sokei 2016).
16 To quote Stengers:

Science, when taken in the singular and with a big S, may indeed be described as a general conquest bent on translating everything that exists into objective, rational knowledge. In the name of Science, a judgment has been passed on the heads of other peoples, and this judgment has also devastated our relations to ourselves—whether we are philosophers, theologians, or old ladies with cats. Scientific achievements, on the other hand, require thinking in terms of an adventure of sciences (in the plural and with a small s). (Stengers 2012: 2)

17 Burrows and I have previously used this diagram to think through Laruelle's Non-Philosophy project (Burrows and O'Sullivan 2019: 320).
18 We can also state this problem in more philosophical—or Kantian—terms. In the *Critique of Pure Reason* Kant maps out the components and parameters of a certain kind of device that is determinate of our experience (for example, with various a priori principles such as temporal sequencing—cause and effect—and so forth). We are always already inside this device or, rather, necessarily deploying it. For Kant there is limited use in speculating on an outside to this; all we can do is work out the conditions of any possible experience. Kant's project—as summarised by Michael Pendlebury in his book on Kant (Pendlebury 2022)—is to make what might be called this operating system opaque rather than transparent. So, once again, to see it *as* a device. The subject is not a substance in this sense and is more like a schema or diagram—or, again, a device—but one that thinks it's a substance. My own contribution here, in this essay and some of those that have come before, is to suggest that constructing a device within the device (a fiction within a fiction) might give us further purchase on seeing the latter—the self—*as* a device (and as a fiction).
19 It is worth pointing here to Amy Ireland's account of how blockchain technology might well prompt the emergence of other agents (seeing as it can guarantee a kind of consistency but not necessarily one attached to identity) and thus dovetails with the feminist critique of patriarchal 'representational schema': 'Web3 has the capacity to usher in a profound social paradigm shift because, among other things, it provides a totally novel notion of what counts as an agent—one no longer tethered to the male, the individual, or even the human' (Ireland 2022a: 59). There is also Ireland's account of 'patchwork' which, following a minoritarian and pre/non-representational schema, suggests other kinds of agency away from the human and especially male subject (Ireland 2022b):

Decoupled from a static, self-repeating human identity that continues intact throughout time, identity is freed as a shifting systemic structure that can be appended to certain complex assemblages at different times, running parallel but at different speeds and in different configurations, separate from the individuals we take to exist essentially and a priori, but which are indeed, part of a vertiginous array of systemic convergences. (Ireland 2022b: 71)

20 Although it is often science that is producing these other perspectives it does seem to me, once again, that fiction can be a crucial method here (especially when that fiction takes on and develops the findings of science). A good example of this—and one David Burrows and I discuss at length in *Fictioning* (Burrows and O'Sullivan 2019: 282-7)—is Peter Watts' Science Fiction novel *Blindsight* which involves a collection of different and neurodiverse characters and set-ups alongside other non-human entities and intelligences.
21 This collaborative project has the working title *Fictioning Community: The Non, the Ill and the Dead.*
22 Or a 'stopping of the world' as Carlos Castaneda might have it, which then allows the emergence of another world (see Castaneda 1974).

Part II
On Care and Repair

8

On Teaching and Writing as Care and Repair

This first essay of the second part of my book begins with some reflections on higher education in the UK today before moving on to some more personal reflections on teaching and on those themes and materials students have found have had most impact on their lives (and especially their mental health). It makes the case for care and repair as two key modalities or 'technologies of the self' (to partly borrow a term from Foucault). The former—care—in terms of an attitude and intention of empathy and concern; the latter—repair—in terms, once again, of a certain kind of self-authorship (or myth-work). This is connected to both magical and therapeutic practice and, more generally, to an expanded idea of 'life writing'.

The Larger Context

One thing that became apparent whilst teaching during the initial Covid years is that students are increasingly struggling with their mental health (as have been their teachers, but that's another story). As well as illness and any attendant fears about the virus itself this was, of course, partly to do with the various lockdowns—and with a feeling of isolation especially—but my sense is that many of these issues, especially around anxiety and depression, were already there before Covid and have simply been foregrounded by the pandemic. These mental health issues are complex and determined by all sorts of factors (only some of which I address here). Within higher education, for example, there is, the question of fees and student loans which means many students are already debtors before their adult lives have really begun (and with each subsequent Government review and policy change this situation seems to get worse). This can mean that there is an inordinate amount of pressure to succeed or, at least, that students will get some kind of quantifiable 'value' from their financial investment. I certainly don't blame the students for this, but it does bring about its own issues, for me and for them. The teacher/student relationship has, in some cases, become a service/customer one with all that implies.[1] For myself it means that there can be implicit demands from customers—or, at least, very particular expectations—which can militate against a certain kind of learning (expectations, for example, about acquiring 'transferable skills' or what the 'real-world' applications of their course might be).[2] For them there is, again, the ever-present tendency—which can be encouraged by the institution itself—to instrumentalise their learning. This is exacerbated by the various higher education metrics and league tables which increasingly focus on employability and job skills (so a particular kind of value and its measurement). Simply put, the spaces and places for a certain kind of learning, especially as regards critical thinking and creativity, seem increasingly scarce.

Then there are also issues arising from the larger national context which, again, Covid has exacerbated. Will there in fact be any job at the end of their degrees for example? And then further, thinking about the economic and political realities of the UK today, there are questions as to whether students will be able to afford rent, let alone buy a place to live (the latter seems increasingly like a pipe dream). The cost of living—or simply of maintaining a living of any kind—can seem impossibly high. Suffice it to say then that there are more than a few of these external socio-economic pressures on the young people I regularly come into contact with and, to say it again, this invariably has an impact on their mental health.

There are also other issues, it seems to me, at work here. Issues to do with the feeling of a lack of agency. As the lives of the young people I teach are increasingly determined by and dictated to by those abstractions—or hyperobjects as Timothy Morton calls them—that are beyond perception and, to a certain extent, conception too then a sense of individual autonomy has become increasingly eroded (Morton 2013). Things feel out of control. I'm thinking here of the way capitalism determines a restricted set of options (at least for most of us), but also of the impact it is having on the planet. In terms of the latter there really is a palpable sense of hopelessness and powerlessness as they watch—as we all watch—the ongoing ecological catastrophe unfold. In terms of the former, there seem to be fewer and fewer alternatives—or exits even—available to those who for whatever reason cannot or do not want to follow the more well-trodden and supposedly financially viable 'career' paths.

There is more to say here, for example about the failure of previous generations—my own included—to meet the larger ecological and environmental threats and dangers head on. And then also about the increasing polarisation and popularism in play within politics in the UK and abroad (and attending to the reasons for this). There is certainly continuing urgent work to be done exploring how change might be brought about on a national and then also a global scale which is really the only way some of these problems can be dealt with. However, this essay—as to a certain extent all of the essays in this book—is about going in the other direction and thinking around individual—and other kinds of collective—agency on a more molecular scale (to use a phrase from Félix Guattari). My focus is not, however, on how to 'act locally' exactly (in terms of co-ops or green politics or what have you)—although I am a firm believer in community and in local-universal circuits—but rather on how to meet the abstractions of capital. How to make sense of these larger forces, but also, despite them, to set up—and live—alternatives? Again, this is not to turn away from more global issues but it is to relate to them or track them in a different way.

Teaching Occulture: From Magic to Care

In the seminar room, teaching a final year undergraduate course on 'Occulture'—very broadly concerned with the intersections between magical and artistic practice—it was those sessions on claiming one's own determination or even writing one's own narrative that were most enthusiastically received.[3] Indeed, when the work turned from looking at objects out there (when this included various art practices and other cultural productions) to thinking more about ourselves and our own 'production of subjectivity'— so a turn to a kind of therapeutic logic (and, with that, taking a pragmatic/ constructive attitude to the materials under consideration)—then it felt like some real work was being done. This was also the case when students were able to articulate their own experiences and link these up to the materials (and practices) we were looking at. This is not to deny the importance of objective determinants and external causes. It was clear that many of the issues being experienced by the students were socially and economically determined (as I have very briefly laid out above). But it is to say that a sense of agency needed to be reclaimed on an individual—and a group—level or, again, that there needed to be a connection made between the themes we were exploring in the seminar and our own lives.[4] Some of this work was constellated around ideas of care and, paradoxically, also involved exploring other kinds of agency besides and beyond the self.

For example, we read Isabelle Stengers' short essay on magic, 'Reclaiming Animism', a key text on the Occulture course and one I have already referenced a few times in the essays in the first part of my book (Stengers 2012). Stengers writes about witchcraft as a practice of care for each other and for the planet. She also points out that there are other epistemologies and value systems out there besides the one that tends to dominate our life in the West and that it is crucial that we do not turn away from these for fear that they are regressions. This, for Stengers, would be to side us with those who burnt the witches. Magic—and the agency of what might be thought of as fictions (at least from a scientific perspective)—can have very real effects out in the world and especially for those individuals and communities who are looking for another way of being in that world. And then there were also texts from the witch/activist Starhawk that we looked at which again laid out a practice of modern witchcraft as a practice of care (see for example Starhawk 2003). It was especially Starhawk's linking of witchcraft to ecological concerns and with building community that was inspiring. All of this was done against the background of writers like Silvia Federici who in their historical work showed us that there had been other modes of existence—in particular more matriarchal and communal forms—and that there had been a brutal war waged against these (Federici 2014).[5] As such, our own more individuated (and competitive) mode of existence—with its attendant values and belief systems—could itself be seen as just one particular mode. It became, as it were, historically framed.

The war against the witches was a form of expropriation and primitive accumulation of women's bodies and reproductive functions (so a parallel to the enclosures acts). As far as this goes it was also the beginnings of the professionalisation of medicine and its attendant take-over by men. As such, magic, broadly understood, can be understood—to repeat the point above—as involving a different kind of care that is opposed to the capitalist sense of it (at least in some of its instantiations). And, as such, the figure of the witch (as we explored it in the seminar) need not simply be understood as an historical figure or, indeed, a superficial trope within our mediatised society, but can also be a figure that represents a set of values, practices and beliefs that might be taken up (as well, of course, as being an actually lived mode in the contemporary world in different ways, again as evidenced, for example, by Starhawk). Here the wisdom of non-Western (and/or pre-modern) epistemologies—and an understanding of the 'epistemicide' of Western imperialism—is especially crucial to attend to, as is the importance, following Raymond Williams, of demarcating those 'residual' cultures that might offer an alternative or an opposition to a dominant hegemony, from those that have already been incorporated into the latter (Williams 1980).

In the seminar we also turned to other cultural producers who, although not witches exactly, certainly explored other ways of being in the world and, with that, other ways of relating and other senses of value. Or 'a use of space and time contrary to the new capitalist work-discipline' to use Federici's words (Federici 2014: 177). The artist Carolee Schneemann for example and her 'gynocracy' and other mythopoetic practices and, especially, her relationship with her cats.[6] Or—a crucial figure for the course (and, again, one I have already mentioned in previous essays here)—Kathy Acker, and her writing practices, where at stake (or what we took from that work) was a drawing of one's own dream maps and a writing of one's own fictions.[7] Again, this claiming of an agency through reclaiming one's own narrative seemed especially important (which means this work dovetails, at least to some extent, with what has become known as 'life writing').[8]

To return to the question of control, there was also an emphasis—in the work of the seminar—on locating oneself in space and time or, at least, dislocating oneself from other, perhaps more dominant, senses of space and time. Indeed, Federici remarks that originally popular magic was a way for the poor to exercise some agency in a situation where they were subject to economic and natural forces outside their control. Magic, we might say, was a response to being overly determined by external factors. This desire for control seems important and in part explains the increasing turn to magic within our contemporary moment when, as I mentioned above, we are increasingly subject to forces beyond our control (or, in some cases, beyond our capacity to fully grasp).[9]

In relation to this we began the Occulture course by doing some work on J. G. Frazer's definition of 'sympathetic magic' from *The Golden Bough* and, with that, on different ideas of causality, for example action at a distance. In fact, part of this initial work was to disentangle possibly useful notions about and around magic from writers like Frazer who invariably positioned magical thinking as a regressive form or even an impoverished science. More generally we were interested in interrogating this anthropological take on magic that sees it from outside or from a modern Western perspective. But equally important here was the insight that magical practice does not always call itself magic and that, indeed, it is these kinds of practice that were often the most compelling not least insofar as they were more likely to escape cliché. Certainly, for those beginning seminars, magic became a name for other ways of knowing and other ways of being. Or, to give this a Deleuzian slant, other ways of affecting and being affected by the world.

As well as this work—which, as you can see from the names mentioned above, often turned to women's experience and their attendant writings[10]—there was also the reading of various texts on decolonisation that again emphasised care and community.[11] I have written more about this in 'Landscape, Trauma and Myth-Work', but to briefly repeat some of that in this context. We looked at Stefano Harney and Fred Moten's work on the undercommons with its call for 'Black Study' and the exploration of the haptic collectivity of the hold as a kind of care (Harney and Moten 2013). On a more abstract level, we looked at Denise Ferreira da Silva's exploration of a different system of value away from the 'universal' white Western—and philosophical—yardstick (her 'Equation of Value') (Ferreira da Silva 2017). Like Stengers' essay, Ferreira da Silva's essay and Harney and Moten's book were important texts for the seminar. If some of the texts around witchcraft returned to the scene of the witch hunts as a founding trauma of modernity (which although obscured is still very much haunting the present), then here the 'Middle Passage' was likewise identified as a further originary trauma. In fact, as Federici has persuasively argued, both these traumas are intimately connected.[12] We are living in the wake of slavery just as we can still smell the smoke of the burning witches (to use the phrase from Stengers).

Practices of Repair

Another way of thinking about these different kinds of care, especially when they involve writing and representation, is as the work of repair.

The latter work will take different forms depending on whether it is an individual or more collective endeavour, but it does seem to be the case that writing—when this also sometimes includes the mobilisation of other modes of representation alongside it—can allow this kind of repair to be activated and explored (as evidenced for example by the various texts I have referenced above). Writing, understood in its broadest sense, can be involved in producing a kind of cohesion for a subject or a group or a community in this way. This is not to say that writing is all that's needed, but simply that it can be an important part of this repair work.

To return to the teaching situation—and to turn to those forms of representation that might accompany writing—there was something especially important about the idea of drawing one's own maps or, more generally, making some kind of device (both practices I have mentioned in previous essays).[13] As another practitioner of magic has it (and, again, this is an idea that is a refrain in these essays) the magician must always make their own tools as part of their practice.[14] So there is, once again, a will to self-determination in play here. Some of the students that attended the seminar had a studio practice and so this emphasis on making chimed with the way they already worked across theory and practice, but even with those who were art historians it did seem that an emphasis on writing—and mapping out—something that implicated the self and thus might allow that self to explore other options (and other agencies) was especially useful.[15] A kind of expanded self-analysis was then partly at stake here.

Students produced fanzines, maps and diaries of pilgrimages, fieldwork reports, creative research files and journals, tarot cards, sigils and so forth all as accompaniments to the more straightforward essay format. In their diverse and idiosyncratic character such writing and drawing projects could not have been more different from the standardised image worlds of much social media (or for that matter from the standard academic essay format). Two key resources or further case studies here were VNS Matrix's fanzine *Hex* (2015) and Linda Stupart's spells in her book *Virus* (2016), both of these also raising the interesting question about the relationship of witches—and magic more generally—to their representation, not least in art.[16] As I suggested in the essay 'On Magic and Place' it does not seem to me that it necessarily follows that this representation—in this case, of magic by art—dilutes any force. In some cases, perhaps it can even increase it.

Also, important here—and as I have implied above as well—was that the seminar helped produce some community or even a collective agency at least of sorts (gesturing, perhaps, towards the fabled 'collective subject').[17] Although this was partly to do with pedagogical methods and, indeed, the willingness of participants to 'show up', it was also invariably connected to the themes and materials of the seminar.[18] Reading and talking about other modes of existence can blur over into experimenting with them. Working together can also mean working against atomisation and alienation (and as part of that against the algorithms that increasingly determine our individuated online lives). I will return to this area in a couple of later essays in this second part of my book and in relation to my own experiences outside of the pedagogical set-up, but certainly being part of a community can produce a decrease in anxiety which, generally speaking, seems to be tethered to a hyper-individuated mode of existence.

In relation to my own writing practice—and alongside my involvement in the collective performance fiction Plastique Fantastique (which might be seen, in this particular context, both as an experiment in the collective subject and, at least in part, as a magical practice)—I have also recently used writing as a device for both self-analysis and an attempt at self-transformation. During a year away from teaching—and before putting the Occulture seminar together—I had set myself the task of writing a novel. Writing this fiction allowed the summoning of figures and images that were both of me and not of me, and, with that, the writing process allowed a claiming of some of my own narrative and, indeed, opened up some space around my own sense (or fiction) of self. As I mentioned in my Introduction to this book, some of the essays collected here were prompted by that piece of writing which—looking back on it—was about my own care and repair. Although it was not a straightforward project—writing fiction, I discovered, is very different from writing theory/academic essays (almost as if it involves a different faculty)—it certainly produced a lot of material that I am still working through. Crucial here is the way that myth-work—in this case the writing of a fiction—'speaks back' as if it arrives from elsewhere and thus offers up information not otherwise available.

These kinds of practices—I'm thinking not only of my own fiction writing and essays (this collection included), but also the work of the students—are not a panacea to the problems I mentioned at the beginning of this essay. But they do seem to offer something important, perhaps as an accompaniment to any collective action/resistance (or collective work of repair). Again, they allow a claiming of a narrative or, more generally, a different production of subjectivity (to use Guattari's phrase again) (Guattari 1995b). In fact, to broaden this out slightly, in many ways magic—and especially magick (with a 'k')—seems to me to be a technology of the subject in this sense. Although, paradoxically it is a technology of the non-subject as well insofar as this work also involves giving attention to other agents and agencies besides the self (or besides the more typical fiction of the self we inhabit). Writing can allow a form of self-authorship to take place when this also means to change the idea of the self or even side-stepping the self so as to try other things out. This is gestured towards in the key magickal phrase 'Nothing Is True, Everything Is Permitted'.

Magic—as a practice of care and repair—can foreground a connection and relation with the non-human too insofar as it can move us away from overly human-centred/consumer logics. It can open us to wonder, for example, as the chaos magician Phil Hine has recently suggested (Hine 2022). Once again, magic is not only about self-determination—as I have laid out above—but also names a sidestepping of that self that has been determined. Or, put differently, care and repair can involve a kind of 'dropping down' of the human perspective into the world. This is also to simply affirm that there are different modes of existence out in the world that need to be valued, some of which can only be 'seen' by dethroning the human. These other ways of relating to the world will certainly be needed if we are ever to solve the larger issues of staying with the trouble/living in the ruins (as Donna Haraway, Anna Tsing and others have put it). It is also here that this apparently fringe/niche work on magic and occulture dovetails with some of the larger concerns I sketched out at the beginning of this essay. In particular, the *belief* in another kind of world and, with that, the cultivation of the imagination as a faculty seems important. The ability to imagine other ways of being and other kinds of relationship (with each other and the world) then, but, crucially, also to write or represent them in some manner too. And then also (and following this) to enact them in other ways out in the world. Imagination, and the work that follows from it, is itself a kind of care in this sense. It is also a form of repair when this is understood to involve the invention of figures and landscapes that one might 'take on' or inhabit as a way of 'going on' in the world. Figures and landscapes that might then speak back and offer up other knowledges and other perspectives.

Taking Control

The question of pedagogy today seems to me to be partly this. How to prepare students for a future that is increasingly uncertain? The old skills and knowledges these last years have at times seemed irrelevant or, at least, less appropriate. More important is this work of care and repair, of producing cohesion and, with that, some agency (as well, again, as linking up these questions of individual agency with larger infrastructural issues, so a kind of consciousness raising, broadly speaking). Once again, crucially this can involve the production of community—or a kind of scene—in and of the seminar. Teaching Occulture turns out to have been partly about this. To repeat the point I made above, it is as if there is something about reading others' attempts at taking control and building community that enables one's own thinking through of this field of operation. Teaching and learning then partly becomes about assembling an archive—a gathering of resources—with which to make or re-make oneself and one's community. And magic is also a catch-all name for those practices and value systems that are at odds with our present one (which, it seems to me, is increasingly bankrupt). Occulture dovetails with counter-culture in this sense.

I would not affirm practices of self-construction at the expense of other work. To loop back to a comment I made at the beginning of this essay, it has never seemed to me a question of choosing either the global or the local but, rather, of locating circuits between the two (or, as I have put it elsewhere, affirming the diagonal [O'Sullivan 2014a]). Work needs to go on at a variety of levels and, indeed, it is the circuits connecting these different levels which are crucial. As I have gestured to throughout the above, this emphasis on the self is also not an end in itself, or, put differently, is preparatory work for other perhaps stranger adventures. The exploration of other kinds of agency or other fictions of other selves. Writing especially seems to be about conjuring—summoning—these other fictions (sometimes more collective ones). But certainly, a platform of some kind is needed for these other experiments to begin. Or, put differently, it is only by making our own maps and writing our own narratives—and, as part of that, looking carefully at what's already there—that we can see where the exits are located and then what other kinds of devices might be required to set other things and even other futures in motion.

Coda

A scene by a river. There are trees and long grass that is blowing in a breeze. The sun is shining in a cloudless sky. A figure stands by the bank. They are mis-shapen or bent over somehow. Looking closer it's clear they have a blanket or cloak covering their head and shoulders. From a gap between the folds a withered forearm and claw-like hand reaches out holding a puppet of some kind. A further figure carved out of wood into a rough approximation of a hare—or, at least, there is a head, body and two outstretched hind legs. The hare is in the posture of boxing or dancing like those one can see in Spring. From beneath the bundle of cloth words come but they are mumbled and unclear. Only one phrase can be properly made out. '...I am the hare from the beginning of the world...' As the hare turns this way and that, the figure under the cloak sways gently from side to side and shuffles along, bare feet every now and again visible beneath the hem of the cloth. More mumbling, then another moment of clarity '...this message is not for you as you are now but for what you might become if you follow the uphill path...' With a quick sharp tug the hare is pulled back into that dark interior. The message has, it seems, been delivered. All is still for a moment. And then the figure with its companion now hidden stumbles off along the riverbank.

Notes

1 In relation to this see Sylvia Wynter's critique of the increasingly economic definition of the human which, in her words 'induces us all to behave as producers, traders or consumers' (Wynter in Scott 2000: 160).
2 As I mentioned above, I should make it clear here that I don't hold the students responsible for this. Why wouldn't you want to be clear on what you are getting for your money? Why wouldn't you want to see what the 'transferable skills' on your degree might be?

And, more generally, given the socio-economic climate, why wouldn't you want to secure your future at least to some extent? The issue is rather a general financialisaton of higher education that seems to be taking place which means teaching and learning become a kind of economic investment and, with that, there is the attendant production of an *indebted* subjectivity of and for students.

3 The point of departure of this course was this intersection but, as the title of the course suggests, we were also partly concerned with the tradition of 'occulture' (a term coined by Genesis P. Orridge) and in exploring a counter-cultural take on various magickal practices (especially those concerned with self-determination).

4 It is important to distinguish this claim to agency from what Mark Fisher, following David Smail, calls 'magical voluntarism'. This is defined by Fisher as 'the belief that it is in every individual's power to make themselves whatever they want to be' (Fisher 2018: 749). There are real limits to individual agency not least, as Fisher points out, class ones (and, with that—a key focus of Fisher—questions of 'social power'). It seems to me—as I hope is implicit in what follows—that there needs to be a kind of diagonal between the focus on external (objective) determinants and then claiming different forms of (subjective) agency. Or, to put this differently, there are two levels of struggle (and attendant pragmatics) and then various transits and circuits between these two.

5 In Silvia Federici's account of the witch hunts, the war against witches and popular magic more generally is understood as a war against a set of 'previously accepted practices and groups of individuals' (Federici 2014: 170). This included 'communal forms of life' (171) as well a 'broad variety of female practices' (174) (for Federici it was then predominantly a class war as well as anything else).

6 Burrows and I have addressed this particular inter-species relation at some length in *Fictioning* (Burrows and O'Sullivan 2019: 270-2).

7 Other figures—contemporary witches perhaps?—we looked at were Tai Shani and her work traversing feminism, fiction and performance (see, for example, Shani 2019); and Verity Birt and her eco-feminist mixed-media presentations and performances which, like those of Shani, also concern magic and, more broadly, a turn to other systems of belief (see the discussion of one of Birt's works in 'Archaeofictioning'). We also looked at the collaboration between artist Emily Hesse's and art theorist Andrea Phillips titled *The Witches Institution (W.I.)* (The Tetley, Leeds, 2022). This project and installation explored the contemporary figure of the witch in relation to the building of alternative institutions within existing institutions (as well as, more generally, the constitution of different archives).

8 See also Hélène Cixous' account of women's writing which, at times, reads like an invocation of Acker: 'I have been amazed more than once by a description a woman gave me of a world all her own which she had been secretly haunting since early childhood' (Cixous 1981: 246).

9 In terms of this desire for agency—and, indeed, in terms of 'writing one's own narrative'—we also looked in the seminar at QAnon. Here is not the place to go into this mythos and its attractions (I hope to do this in a future project), but what can be said is that apophenia—or the seeing of patterns and connections between (apparently) unrelated material—is a kind of magical thinking too. QAnon also involves the accusation of magical thinking to the 'elites' that are QAnon's avowed enemy (see Berkowitz 2020).

Work needs to be done in demarcating those narratives and fictions that are progressive and enabling from those which ultimately rest on reactionary views and exclusions (as with QAnon), but, crucially, and as Max Haiven has pointed out, the motivation—for meaning and agency (and for community)—is similar in each case (which is to say the attraction of and growth in QAnon, is the symptom of a more general sense of alienation, atomisation and lack of agency) (Haiven 2022).

10 Although this was not to say that the work was in anyway essentialist. Indeed, more than a few of the final projects looked specifically at the idea of the 'trans-witch' (especially in relation to performance) and, alongside writers like Federici, we also looked at the spells and performance/ritual protocols of non-binary poet/artist CAConrad (see, for example, CAConrad 2014).

11 And in relation to decolonisation, Amber Murray's essay on the Western imaginary of the witch (and a kind of 'spiritual othering' that can take place) also operated as an important corrective (2017). On the course we looked too at the phenomenon of 'WitchTok' and, indeed, further questions of race and representation that are invariably connected to these 'new' image worlds of social media.

12 To quote Federici:

The counterparts of the typical European witch, then, were not the Renaissance magicians, but the colonized native Americans and the enslaved Africans who, in the plantations of the 'New World,' shared a destiny similar to that of women in Europe, providing for capital the seemingly limitless supply of labor necessary for accumulation. (Federici 2014: 198)

13 In relation to this I should mention another course I was teaching at the same time as Occulture, this time to MA students, 'From Art Writing to Theory-Fiction'. Here many of the same issues—as regards practices of self-determination and/or the exploration of other modes of existences—were also at stake, although in that seminar they were looked at specifically in relation to different kinds (and genres) of writing, including autofiction and theory-fiction. This also included looking at those maps, diagrams, drawings and images that can accompany theory and fiction as, for example, with art writing. See my *On Theory-Fiction and Other Genres* (O'Sullivan, 2024b).

14 In relation to this idea and as case studies we also looked, for example, at Brion Gysin's dream machine plans and Austin Osman Spare's and Leonara Carrington's tarot sets.

15 The course was also structured around certain projects to be carried out outside the seminar room. The pandemic prevented some of these from happening (especially the more group-orientated ones), although there were more than a few journeys across different landscapes—with different forms of documentation—and, for example, experiments with producing tarot and other divination devices.

16 VNS Matrix gave out their fanzine at the *Transmetic: Ordonnance* performance event (curated by Lendl Barcelos and Tim Dixon) at Lewisham Art House, London, in 2015 (or, at least, that was where I got my copy). As well as being published in their book, Stupart's spells were also given away on sheets of paper at the *Still I Rise: Feminisms, Gender, Resistance* group exhibition, De La Warr Pavilion, Bexhill-on-Sea, in 2019. The mode of distribution seems as key as the form of these presentations in both these cases.

17 Elsewhere I have explored this question of the collective subject (and community more broadly) in relation to friendship (and through a reading of Spinoza's ethics) (see O'Sullivan 2004).
18 In relation to this we also had seminar sessions on collectives where we looked at Crass, Thee Temple ov Psychick Youth and then art collectives such as Array (see also the discussion of the former two collectives in Burrows and O'Sullivan 2019: 156–63).

9

On the Non-Human

This second essay of part two of my book leads directly on from the previous and involves a reflection on our relation to the non-human and specifically plants, animals and the natural world more generally. It makes the argument that we can be lacking an empathy or imaginative connection and that it is this—at least in part—that results in a 'resource extraction' mentality which then contributes to the issues of our Anthropocene. As with other essays in this second part, this one moves between a theoretical register and a more personal one (for example, involving memories and dreams of the landscape). It also attends to my own investments in certain writings and images about and around the landscape.

Other Value Systems

We share this planet with other entities but often our attitude to these (and the worlds they inhabit)—at least in the West and in modern times—is that they are a resource to be extracted. As far as this goes there seems to have been and generally still can be a lack of imaginative connection to or, more simply, empathy with our non-human co-inhabitants. Invariably we have seen these other beings as less than us and therefore as less valuable in some respects (although, of course, still valuable as a resource). In the previous essay—and, indeed, in various essays in the first part of my book—I have mentioned Denise Ferreira da Silva's work on foregrounding and critiquing a certain system of value in relation to whiteness and the ongoing colonial project (see Ferreira da Silva 2017), but we might note here that this same hierarchical system also denigrates both animals and plants (and the non-human world more generally) or, again, positions them as a resource to be exploited.[1] This value system is concretised by our capitalist mode of production (with its emphasis on competition and profit) and the attendant social relations and forms of consciousness. However, it is not the only value system and certainly not the only way of relating to the 'natural' world. We can see—even from the relatively limited perspective of modern Western subjects (to make a presumption here about my readership)—that pre-modern societies and cultures had a different attitude to the world and to the human's relationship to the non-human.

The same is the case for non-Western epistemologies. There are other systems of value and other ways other ways of relating to the non-human (besides extraction) which, for example, are animist in character or treat non-humans as persons (as, for example, in what Viveiros de Castro calls 'perspectivism' [Viveiros de Castro 2014]).[2] Looking away from our present moment and away from our present location—so towards other spaces and other times—reveals many different attitudes and value systems, some of which are themselves endangered. Put bluntly, the ongoing colonial project involves extraction but also the continuing erasure of alternative epistemological set-ups.

On one hand then it's certainly a question of doing the conceptual work—for those of us brought up in the West or in a predominantly Western framework—in order to try and understand these other value systems and knowledge frameworks (and there are increasingly various academic essays and books written on the latter). There can be a danger here that such work 'speaks for' these other knowledges and thus continues a kind of implicit erasure, but, generally, there has been an increasing awareness in the academy for the need to decolonise our more dominant knowledge systems—including the institution of the university itself—and attend to these other ways of knowing. However, it seems to me that to really relate to the latter—or, at least, for these other ways of knowing to have significant traction in our world as it is today (and, by that, I mean our capitalist world)—there need to be other forms of engagement, not least imaginative ones.[3] This means learning how to be compromised—to use an idea from that essay by Stengers that I have mentioned throughout these essays—by these other non-modern belief and value systems and, with that, working concretely and pragmatically on fostering other kinds of relationship with the natural world (or even, more radically, questioning the whole nature/culture division as set up in and by the West).[4]

It might also mean—as well as turning to the past and away from the West—inventing other value systems. So a turn to the future. Donna Haraway's work attends to this need for a radical future reorientation, for example in the way her writing explores various fictions—broadly understood—about other ways of being that might prompt us to live differently in the present. Hence, in particular, Haraway's interest in the Science Fiction writer Ursula Le Guin or, for example, her involvement in collective storytelling projects (see Haraway 2016 and Le Guin 1989). More generally, for Haraway it is the development of multispecies societies that offers hope here especially given global population increases (as affirmed in Haraway's slogan 'make kin not babies').[5] These kinds of hybrid and future-orientated communities can only come about through an expansion of the idea of 'family' and, more generally, from a dethroning of the human and especially the white, male, heteronormative subject. What is needed is a kind of 'dropping down'—as I have put it in the previous essay (and in 'A Thousand Devices')—from that autonomous and autocratic human perspective on to a plane of interconnectedness (or a plane of consistency to use a term from Gilles Deleuze and Félix Guattari).[6]

I want to stay with this idea of a necessary shift in perspective—or, again the 'dropping down'—but also shift this essay now to a more personal register. After all, if what I have said above is even partly correct, then in order to have traction in our world—if we really are to effectively move beyond theoretical supposition and slogans—then lines or circuits need to be made from this material to an actual lived life.[7] And the latter also needs to be carefully examined to see what resources might already be present (including imaginary ones) that, if need be, can be repurposed. Or, to repeat the crucial point above, our imagination needs to be engaged (and, perhaps, with that, there will need to be some self-sacrifice too).

In the Landscape

I have childhood memories of being out in the landscape and being fully immersed within it. Partly this is to do with pre-adolescence and simply having less going on (on one level anyway) to distract me, but, I think, it was also to do with an imaginative connection. I saw and thus inhabited the landscape in a certain way. This was the case with plants—especially trees and ferns and heather, which constituted the main flora of the North

Yorkshire moors where I grew up—but also with the geology of that landscape. In particular the peaks and valleys and other 'key-points', to use that phrase from Gilbert Simondon that I have turned to in previous essays.[8] Indeed, to stay with Simondon for a moment, my landscape was a network of these key-points where a kind of exchange between human and cosmos—the latter understood as a more radical outside—was possible (although I would not have put it quite like that back then). Was this then a throwback to a pre-technical mode of existence? Certainly, my experience—as that young person—might be understood as arising from what Simondon calls the magical mode of existence (which is characterised, in part, by this network of privileged key-points). And technicity—the mode that comes to supplant magic—might be understood as the progenitor of that extractive mentality I mentioned earlier. Simondon's key insight here is that these different modes are less dialectical or indeed simply progressive, but more involved in 'phase shifts'. So, with the existence or inhabitation of a magical mode for example there might be less a sense of regression—with all the problems that can imply—and more a sense that different modes can be co-present at any given time (so, this is not to call for a simple return to the past and nor is it a complete refusal of technicity which, after all, has brought about so many crucial developments in our world).

In 'Landscape, Trauma and Myth-Work' I attended more directly to the political nature of the landscape and especially the way that it is always already a scene of class war and other historical trauma. Indeed, we need to be careful in writing about landscape and the imagination that we do not affirm the more typical idea of landscape—and nature—as empty of human presence and as offering up an unproblematic escape. Although I would have been aware of private property and certainly frequented various disused industrial sites (such as old quarries), my own experience of the landscape when I was younger was certainly apolitical. But there are other registers on which we encounter the landscape besides what might be called—very broadly—the Symbolic. And, more crucially, how we encounter it—and then how we continue to relate to it—determines our attitude towards its value. For myself as that young person, the landscape was a place where different non-human entities and agents were active (when this included fictional ones too).

There is certainly here—in these experiences I am briefly gesturing towards—a different set of relations at work and a different value

Fig. 6.1 Mark Leckey, *O' Magic Power of Bleakness*, 2019, installation view, Tate Britain, London. (Photograph: Mark Blower. Courtesy the Artist and Cabinet Gallery, London)

Fig. 6.2 Sophie Sleigh-Johnson, *Cealdwiellla*, 2018, performance, Arcadia Missa Gallery, London. (Photograph: Tim Bowditch. Courtesy the Artist and Arcadia Missa Gallery, London)

Fig. 10.1 Neuschloss (with contribution from Anne-Marie Copestake), *Think smarter gateway error*, 2017, installation view, Room 113, Newcastle. (Photograph: Tom O'Sullivan. Courtesy the artists)

Fig. 10.2 Adjoa Armah, *The sea, it slopes like a mountain*, 2022, detail of installation, Auto Italia, London. (Photograph: Henry Mills. Courtesy the artist and Auto Italia, London)

Fig. 10.3 Verity Birt and Tom Sewell, *Crossings*, detail of installation, Energy Systems, Margate. (Photograph: Verity Birt. Courtesy the artists)

Fig. 14.1 Plastique Fantastique (David Burrows, Alex Marzeta and Vanessa Page), *Mars Year Zero*, mixed media installation, Southwark Park Galleries (Dilston Grove), London (Photograph: David Burrows. Courtesy the artists)

Fig. 14.2 Plastique Fantastique (David Burrows, Alex Marzeta, Simon O'Sullivan and Vanessa Page), *Plastique Fantastique Diagram of (Urb-Fux Glitter) Addiction*, 2015, performance, Wysing Art Centre, Cambridgeshire. (Photograph: Sylvain Deleu. Courtesy the artists)

system in play. It would be too crude to directly link up these mostly pre-adolescent understandings, experiences and perspectives with premodern and non-Western epistemologies and practices, especially as this might seem to imply a regression (in fact, to repeat the point above, I would say that these ways of relating are not 'pre' in any straightforward linear sense and indeed, to follow Stengers, that we should be very wary of what we label regressive).[9] But I would say that what we have here are other imaginaries at work within a more dominant imaginary if I can put it like that (or an imaginary before it has been fully co-opted by capitalist logics and values).[10] Returning to these other imaginaries and exploring them—or perhaps reactivating them in some manner?—seems crucial if we are to alter the trajectory we are on. From one perspective, our current crisis—at least as far as ecological issues go—is due to the way in which we have either 'forgotten', obscured or relegated these other attitudes and values (even when this work has sometimes been with good intentions).

Representation and Imagination

Art and literature—and aesthetics and poetics more generally—can, it seems to me, also involve and enable some of this work. As, for example, when representations of the landscape allow a different perspective on—and thus a different understanding of—our own landscape, both inner and outer. This is especially the case, for me, with landscape painting of different kinds, but also with other kinds of representations of landscape and, crucially, with performances in and around the latter. I go into some indicative and contemporary examples of these expanded performance practices in both 'On Magic and Place' and 'Archaeofictioning'. In terms of my own pre-history—before really engaging with performance (or, indeed, art theory)—artists like Paul Nash and Graham Sutherland (so a particular kind of English Modernism/Romantic Surrealism) were especially important, as was the tradition of 'Land Art' as for example with Richard Long (who was the subject of my own undergraduate dissertation).[11] Again, there can be a kind of 'myth' of nature (as emptied of human presence) in some of this work. Land Art especially can repeat the colonial trope of the explorer with the world as their blank canvas. But this work also presents a kind of optic on the landscape and, with that, affirms a certain valuing of landscape too (following Simondon, aesthetics here operating as a reminder of a magical mode of existence). Before my own interest in modern and contemporary art, tabletop role-playing games performed much the same function in my particular subjective set-up, again operating as a kind of device (amongst other things) through which to see the landscape in a certain way. In a previous essay I have mentioned the dangers of affirming a pre-modern idyll that can be in play in some of these role-playing games. That caveat aside, in my experience it can be as if a layer of fiction allows the actual landscape to be engaged with more fully or to be inhabited in a different way. Certainly those role-playing games activated an imaginative connection with the non-human. I go into this in a little more detail in my essay 'On Tabletop Role-Playing Games and Fictioning'.

And then there is also writing about the landscape, both factual (or 'ficto-factual') and made up. In terms of the former there is the genre of 'new' nature writing, perhaps best exemplified in our contemporary moment by authors like Robert Macfarlane (see for example 2012) and Roger Deakin (see for example 1999), both of these looking back to writers like Richard Mabey (see also Mabey's later *Nature Cure* [2005], a book specifically about landscape and repair). In reading authors like these we 'see' the landscape through their eyes, often accompanying them as they journey in and through a given place (and/or as they bring in other geographical and historical reflections, alongside the biographical). As with some of my comments above it is important that these kinds of works do not repeat the bourgeois trope of the landscape as empty and as escape (or neglect to attend to their own privilege), but at the same time it is important that works like these are able to emphasise the value of the natural world and of our different landscapes. Moving away from these ficto-factual accounts and turning directly to fiction (and to my own very recent reading interests) there are more recent works like Paul Kingsnorth's *The Wake* (2014) and Kazuo Ishiguro's *The Buried Giant* (2015). Both of these novels are evocative of landscapes of the past, but also present a different past to the one we might more typically presume existed. Kingsnorth's novel, following a book like *Riddley Walker*, plays with style and syntax as well in foregrounding its first-person narrative. Its imaginative power partly comes from the fact that the language is difficult but, once 'grasped', works to effectively transport the reader to another landscape. Ishiguro's novel involves a more disembodied and modern narrator, but the book is also imaginatively powerful in the various landscapes, set-ups and images it lays out. It plays with questions of genre too. Working with genre—or across genre—seems to be a key device in terms of presenting different perspectives.

In relation to pre-adolescence or that time when the imaginary is first assembling itself (and, once again, I am reflecting on my own past here as a kind of case study) there are also books by authors like Susan Cooper (*The Dark is Rising* [1973]), Alan Garner (*The Weirdstone of Brisingamen* [1960])—and, indeed, Ursula Le Guin (*The Wizard of Earthsea* [1968]). Each of these books is part of a series and all of them—and especially the first two—involve the imbrication of fantastical elements with a real landscape that the authors have a deep familiarity with. Or, we might say, the books are devices through which we see a given—and actually existing—landscape as magical in some senses and which, as such, changes our experience of those landscapes and thus, again, how we value them.[12]

A Different Mode of Attention

This imaginative connection can also be made by being out in the landscape and attending to it—or experiencing it—as fully as possible (as in some of the experiences of my own that I have gestured to above). It seems to me that it is often this simple move that offers all sorts of possibilities, not least for care and repair (although such access is increasingly restricted and, as I mentioned above, there is the question of who has the time and resources to follow this particular course of action).[13] This also relates to my own interest in walking—or pilgrimage—to certain special sites—or 'key-points'—in the landscape (something that Simondon remarks on as well in relation to the magical mode of being). As I have suggested in other essays here, walking or traversing the landscape in some manner seems to be a particularly effective method of activating the imagination. Once again this is not to empty out politics. The outside—by which I mean here the landscape—is always already marked in all sorts of ways, but that does not mean it cannot have this transformative effect. Indeed, in many ways a marked landscape is more powerful in these terms than one completely emptied of human presence (my own practices of pilgrimage involve journeying to these marked landscapes). I will return to this theme in 'Archaeofictioning'.

The imaginative connection I mention above also requires some work on this side of things. On what Félix Guattari calls the production of subjectivity (see Guattari 1995b), or, we might say, on that other device that we already are (hence the essays collected in the first part of my book). What other kinds of subjectivity (or other 'fictions of the self') are possible besides those that our capitalist mode of production and attendant social relations foreground? What other modes of being—with their beliefs, values, ways of thinking and acting—might be repurposed from the past for example (so, again, a turn to residual cultures), but also grasped from the future (utilising the findings of neuroscience for example, a theme of a couple of my earlier essays)? Is there a way of being in the world that is not solely determined by technicity and the subject/object split? A more magical mode (to follow Simondon once more) or a 'new' aesthetic mode that reminds us of that magical mode.[14] And, again, what devices—broadly understood—would enable or prompt this kind of work on the production of subjectivity?

Images and Other Fictional Entities

Once again Donna Haraway attends to some of these questions in her recent writings. For Haraway we need new figures—new avatars—that can engage our desires and can thus also operate as strange attractors to draw forth other futures. Indeed this—it seems to me—is what art can do, including those personal examples I mention above. In the chapter on 'Tentacular Thinking' in *Staying with the Trouble* (Haraway 2016: 30-57) Haraway gives us her own example of the gorgon-faced figure of Potnia Theron that might work in this way but, more generally she argues for a turning away from what she calls the Sky Gods—with their attendant Promethean stories—to the creatures and critters of the earth.[15] She also writes of cat's cradle games—and other knottings—as further figures (or devices) that conjure other ways of being in the world (or, which amounts to the same thing, foregrounds other worlds from within this one). Crucially Haraway attends to how different props are needed to enable different kinds of stories to be written and enacted (or simply to 'get a different story going').[16]

In a couple of the other essays gathered here I have mentioned the summoning of fictional entities and agencies and, indeed, more generally, the power of imaginatively connecting with figures and images (often through some kind of performance). Certainly, in a Buddhist context this kind of work can also provoke a different set of values to arise and, indeed, a different relationship to the non-human to take place (as in various practices around the figure Green Tara and a more ecological consciousness for example). Here it is partly how we engage with images—or that we engage with them actively in some senses—that seems crucial. We need to have a relationship with the entities that we have summoned or, as it were, have invited in. Hence also the importance of preparation and of taking these kinds of ritual engagements (and these fictional figures) seriously. Or, to put that differently, of sincerely entertaining an 'as if' so that transformation can occur.

Props and Devices

At stake throughout many of my own essays has also often been a kind of prop, but one that is at the same time a device. The latter has taken on different meanings, but in general has meant both the fiction of the self that we always already inhabit (something that allows the fiction of our world to 'get going') and that which might allow us to shift this fiction or at least make some space around it (and thus, perhaps, take on other fictions).[17] This latter device might then be something that foregrounds a different world from within this one when the right posture is taken in relation to it. Indeed, it seems to me that it is a question of perspective here and how this might be shifted through different devices. Again, it is in this sense that art and literature—or what I have also been simply calling fictions throughout these essays—can also work as these kinds of devices. To repeat the point above, they allow or enable a different optic to be set in place (and thus a different—and perhaps deeper—engagement to follow). Once again then it is a representation (a picture of the world to put it simply) within our own representation (the world we move through) that seems, at least partly, to be able to shift the register.

Representation is then partly here to do with seeing the world through another's eyes. It is the locating within this world of another perspective (and thus another world). Or, put differently, it is the locating of an outside (to our own subjectivities) through paradoxically looking further in and towards those fictions nested within our own fiction. In terms of this essay, this might mean to imaginatively occupy a different landscape within our existing landscape (as in those books we might have read when young). Or it might involve representing other worlds ourselves, that is, pursuing different kinds of world-building exercises, however rough or ready. Here the making of a world within this one—even if just done imaginatively (at first)—does something to our understanding and experience of the world we live within (if only reducing our belief in the later). As I've remarked in other essays there can be a kind of recursive re-bound effect in play with these practices of fictioning.

When thinking about our relation to the non-human then we might say that we need other kinds of devices—either encountering those already out there (perhaps forgotten or obscured) or making our own—that allow us to see our world differently or, again, see other worlds within this one. Devices that are less all-encompassing perhaps than the one we more typically—and perhaps necessarily (in some respects)—inhabit. Devices that are also perhaps more fragile, even more ephemeral. Indeed, part of the work here, it seems to me, is to care for these devices (alongside the non-human worlds they open up for us) and, indeed, repair those which in many cases have been neglected or needlessly broken.

Coda

On a Buddhist retreat and having been asked to locate a place in the landscape and stay there for a day, I find something begins to unfold or foreground itself. A connection with my surroundings and, alongside that, a sense of visitation of non-human agencies (the animals and plants but also 'larger' forces at work). The device here was the invitation and then the finding of the right place. This experience, which has stayed with me, was partly to do with the practice of meditation (that was part of that retreat) which shifts consciousness, bringing it more into the present moment. That and simply waiting until the mental chatter—and a certain kind of self-narration—had died down so that another kind of attention could come into play (and, with that, the imagination could become more fully engaged). This experience felt like a stopping of the world. It was a pause that allowed a seeing of myself as part of that non-human landscape I was situated in—and a seeing of that landscape as also part of me.

Notes

1. For a compelling account of this mentality—and for a selection of art practices that critically address it—see Gray and Sheikh 2018.
2. See the extended discussion of perspectivism in Burrows and O'Sullivan 2019: 186-90.
3. In our forthcoming work on *Fictioning Community* Burrows and I will attend further to the possibilities and limits of understanding other perspectives and how different devices might allow different kinds of relation (especially to divergent worlds) to be instantiated.
4. Stengers uses the phrase 'being compromised by magic' in her essay 'Reclaiming animism' (Stengers 2012). Viveiros de Castro maps out the Amerindian ontology which, in part, reverses our own nature/culture division, in *Cannibal Metaphysics* (Viveiros de Castro 2014).
5. Although this not to say that there are not dangers here or, at least, that we need to be careful in addressing these issues. Suggestions of 'population control' cannot but bring to mind other historical attempts and calls. We need always to ask who is it that will be most affected by such measures.
6. See especially the discussion of the relationship between becomings and the plane of consistency in the 'Memories of a Sorcerer III' section of the 'Becoming' plateau of *A Thousand Plateaus* (Deleuze and Guattari 1988: 248-52).
7. Hence, I take it, the increasing turn to autofiction and autotheory—and other kinds of ecofiction—as appropriate genres for thinking about the issues of the Anthropocene. In relation to the former see for example Anna Lowenhaupt Tsing's *The Mushroom at End of the World* (2015). In relation to the latter see for example Donna Haraway's 'The Camille Stories' that comes at the end of her *Staying with the Trouble* (Haraway 2016: 134-68). See also the discussion of these 'new' genres of writing in my *On Theory Fiction and Other Genres* (O'Sullivan 2024).
8. See note 10 of Chapter 4.
9. For Stengers the charge of regression means that we become complicit with those judgements that ultimately produced atrocities such as the burning of the witches (Stengers 2012).
10. For a more detailed take on other imaginaries—including those of the non-human (at least as fictioned by humans)—see Burrows and O'Sullivan 2019: 275-93.
11. A further key artist in this respect—one from the US rather than the UK—is Robert Smithson. I have written about Smithson elsewhere, including in my first book *Art Encounters Deleuze and Guattari* (2006), but, in this context, see also my account of a highly formative trip to the Spiral Jetty with a friend, Samudradaka, in O'Sullivan and Ståhl 2006.

12 I mentioned above that these books were part of my own adolescence, but it seems crucial to point out that this imaginary landscape was a shared one, especially with my twin brother, Tom (who, in fact, first referred to what he called a 'shared imaginary space' between the two of us).
13 And it is interesting that it is often looking back and remembering these experiences that is especially powerful (memory being a further form of representation).
14 In relation to this intention see also the theory-fiction based on 'found' documents edited by Phil Smith, *Living in the Magical Mode* (Smith 2022).
15 To quote Haraway:

> The terra-cotta figure of Potnia Theron, the Mistress of the Animals, depicts a winged goddess wearing a split skirt and touching a bird with each hand. She is a vivid reminder of the breadth, width, and temporal reach into pasts and futures of chthonic powers in Mediterranean and Near Eastern worlds and beyond. (Haraway 2016: 52)

16 Again, to quote Haraway:

> Ursula Le Guin taught me the carrier bag theory of storytelling and of naturalcultural history. Her theories, her stories, are capacious bags for collecting, carrying, and telling the stuff of living. 'A leaf a gourd a shell a net a bag a sling a sack a bottle a pot a box a container. A holder. A recipient.' So much of earth history has been told in the thrall of the fantasy of the first beautiful words and weapons, of the first beautiful weapons *as* words and vice versa. Tool, weapon, word: that is the word made flesh in the image of the sky god; that is the Anthropos. In a tragic story with only one real actor, one real world-maker, the hero, this is the Man-making tale of the hunter on a quest to kill and bring back the terrible bounty. This is the cutting, sharp, combative tale of action that defers the suffering of glutinous, earth-rotted passivity beyond bearing. (Haraway 2016: 39)

See also Ursula Le Guin's take on different storytelling props in 'The Carrier Bag of Fiction':

> So, when I came to write science-fiction novels, I came lugging this great heavy sack of stuff, my carrier bag full of wimps and klutzes, and tiny grains of things smaller than a mustard seed, and intricately woven nets which when laboriously unknotted are seen to contain one blue pebble, an imperturbably functioning chronometer telling the time on another world, and a mouse's skull; full of beginnings without ends, of initiations, of losses, of transformations and translations, and far more tricks than conflicts, far fewer triumphs than snares and delusions; full of space ships that get stuck, missions that fail, and people who don't understand. I said it was hard to make a gripping tale of how we wrested the wild oats from their husks, I didn't say it was impossible. Who ever said writing a novel was easy? (Le Guin 1989: 169)

17 Might this traversing across prop and device be put in more literary/linguistic terms, as forms of metonymy and metaphor? A prop would be part for whole (this seems especially clear with theatrical props but also archaeological remnants) and a device would allow a 'seeing like' or a logic of 'as if'.

10

Archaeofictioning

The practice of archaeofictioning can be understood as the making/writing of different pasts and thus also as the gesturing towards other possible futures. This essay explores this creative take on residues from the past, paying particular attention to how the latter might work as props for other narratives and, indeed, call forth other subjects. Important here is our relationship with our ancestors or a 'speaking with the dead.' Equally crucial is the idea that these other fictions need to be performed or enacted in some way so that they have traction in and for our contemporary moment.

The Survival of the Past

The past does not have the same reality as the present, at least for many of us in the modern West. That said, it did exist and there are remnants of it surviving into the present. Actual material remnants—which I will come to in a moment—and then the remnants in our heads, our personal and collective memories. In fact, Freud compares the psychic apparatus of the self to a city with different buildings but also ruins (Freud 2002). The past coexists with the present in this sense or at least, to say it again, evidence of it remains within our psyche.[1] This more or less defines the practice of psychoanalysis understood, in this context, as the giving of attention to those aspects of the past that continue to determine the present. A particularly pointed example of this is trauma which maintains a strong presence or, in fact, often an absence—an absent presence even—in our memories. Trauma dramatically announces the continuing impact of the past on the present, even when this is in some senses obscured.

To turn from that inner landscape and to look outwards—to the different landscapes we all live in and through—there are residues of this past that survive here too (including of various traumas). Some of this evidence of the past is on the surface and more or less plain to see (if one is looking to see such things at least), but other elements of the past are buried beneath the ground. Archaeology is the practice of excavating these residues and then also reconstructing the past—or even different pasts—from any material remains. It is worth remarking here straightaway that there might be still other pasts that have left less in the way of material remains or that have had their material remains destroyed or further obscured in some manner. Perhaps even pasts that have been 'written' over with other—more recent—pasts (as with those transitional monuments that 're-purpose' already existing artifacts or those buildings that have been built on the site of previous buildings or other inhabited sites).[2] Our landscapes are also marked by these obliterations and other kinds of obscuration. A certain kind of repair work might then also be important here, especially when it moves between individual and more collective trauma (or follows the local-universal circuit I have mentioned in a previous essay). Or, following this, when it is able to summon forth another kind of community.

Archaeology versus Art

In one sense art practice involves an opposing tendency to archaeology. Certainly, it is not necessarily concerned with the past. Indeed, often it is pitched towards the future, as evidenced by the various manifestos that especially accompany avant-garde practices (and as the name avant-garde suggests). More generally art practice might be said to be future orientated or 'call forth' its people—a people adequate and appropriate to it—as Gilles Deleuze would have it.[3] But there are similarities between these two disciplines or practices. Both are involved in a kind of composition or in the 'making' of something in the here and now that also gestures to an elsewhere. The making of a different world perhaps (or at least the imagining of the latter)? Elsewhere David Burrows and I have written at length about those practices that embody fictions in this way (see Burrows and O'Sullivan 2019). We called this materialisation of other fictions within our present reality a practice of fictioning. But might there be a sense too that archaeology, despite being turned toward the past, is also involved in its own kind of fictioning practice in and for the present? And even, following this, that it can have its own kind of future orientation?

Archaeologists might understandably baulk at this suggestion. After all, archaeology is a science that is intent on accurately reconstructing an actual past reality, at least as far as this is possible. It does not make things up. In many ways its status as a science (or the way in which it follows the scientific method) means that it can work precisely to question previously accepted stories. But on the other hand, archaeology certainly needs to produce a narrative—of what happened in the past—using those 'props' it digs up (alongside other material evidence and already existing records). There is then here a similar desire for meaning that we find within other forms of storytelling (again, including art). A desire to make sense of things—in this case the different finds and other residues—that are often, on the face of it, meaningless. A desire to map out a context and, with that, locate ourselves in relation to the latter. Or, put differently, there is desire to reconstruct some kind of whole from fragments. To produce a consistency and a coherence.

Other Narratives

But might there be yet another kind of archaeology hidden within this one? One that is less interested in the truth of the past (if there were such a thing), but concerned rather with constructing other fictions from found material (or even, again, fictioning the found materials)? It is said that all history is written from the present and, in the same way, all archaeology is also necessarily conducted in the present too. So an accompanying question here might be what kinds of conditions in the present—and, more specifically, what kinds of subjects and communities—might produce or write these other kinds of accounts?[4] And then, in turn, what 'new' subjects (or, more generally, persons, human and non-human) might be called forth from these other histories or, indeed, fictions? Here the writing of a different narrative and a calling forth of a community adequate and appropriate to it seem to be the same or at least a similar operation.

One of the useful things about the past is that it is more or less inexhaustible. There is always the possibility of telling a different story (and thus of summoning another people, to turn once more to Deleuze's phrase). The same goes with archaeology. There is always more to be found. And residues and remains can always be re-interpreted. Indeed, archaeology is also partly about this practice of re-interpretation. In fact, might it be that we are always already 'interpreting' finds using a more or less unconscious framework? A dominant narrative that is in place and that is then reinforced by the evidence produced by any excavation. It wouldn't be the first time that scientific practice had operated in this way, as a kind of rationalisation of a prior investment (as in 'we see only what we want to see'). We live in and through a tissue of these narratives and other discursive set-ups (or what Lacan would call the Symbolic). It is these stories that give our lives meaning and context. But, of course, these narratives also invariably involve exclusions and, once again, obscurations. To repeat the key point here, other accounts—other fictions—can be written. The past is always there to be reclaimed in some senses.

Archaeofictioning

Might this reclaiming involve what Adnan Madani has called 'archaeofiction'? Madani suggests that this could involve a practice of speaking with the dead.[5] Certainly, archaeology involves a communion with our ancestors just as those older cultures communed with their ancestors too. Donna Haraway in her speculative fiction that comes at the end of *Staying with the Trouble* also writes about future symbiotic creatures and communities that are attentive to the past and to the 'Speakers of the Dead' as a way of moving forwards into a different future (see Haraway 2016: 166-8). Indeed, as we progress further into the Anthropocene this is an increasingly important practice, one that is both ethical and aesthetic. A witnessing before the dead and then, perhaps, the enacting of rituals (broadly understood) that take us out of our own time and connect us with other times and their inhabitants.[6] Rituals that summon other modes of existence from within the present one.

Certainly, looking to the past—and conjuring the dead—places us in a sequence. We become connected both to those who came before us and, with that, also to those that come after. We have a responsibility—however much of a cliché that might sound—to this future and to those other future people (when this includes other creatures and non-human communities). On the one hand this is simply to identify a larger temporal context for a given self. This can help break with alienation and an increasingly prevalent atomisation (and, as such, this attitude has something in common with certain Buddhist meditations that bring to our awareness our connection with all beings existing through space and time). Once again, the imagination (or, in a Lacanian frame, the Imaginary) is important here and especially, in this context, our ability to imaginatively connect across time.

As implied above, this also has an important ecological aspect insofar as it prompts us to understand that the earth is a shared home and that our actions today will have consequences tomorrow. In fact, we are already experiencing these future consequences (the Real is asserting itself despite the stories we might be telling each other). The future, it increasingly seems, is hurtling towards us. To repeat the point above, there is a need to realise—to actually grasp on a deep level—that we necessarily share our world with others in other places but in other times too.

To take up and develop Madani's term then, but also to make it into a verb, archaeofictioning would not be exactly like 'experimental archaeology', where different practices from the past are reconstructed and re-enacted in order to 'solve' problems. How an antler can be used to dig a mine, how a wooden sled can be used to move massive stones, and so forth. But it might have something in common with these insofar as it might also involve an enactment of some kind, either an interaction with any residues or a kind of performing of different fictions with and around them in some manner. Again, using these finds—or perhaps representations of them—as a prop so as to enact something different. Perhaps to summon a different past and thus a different future? Or even, more radically perhaps, inventing new props that somehow resonate with older objects and finds. New kinds of 'future-past objects' for new kinds of 'future-past rituals' perhaps?

Case Studies

An example of what I have in mind here is Anne-Marie Copestake's ceramic object based on the Folkton Drums, themselves enigmatic objects—made from chalk—that were found in a child's grave in North Yorkshire. It's difficult to work out what the Folkton Drums are exactly or what their original purpose was. They are an example of a rare neolithic find with figurative elements—the suggestion of a face or, at least, eyes and nose—that appear alongside more abstract markings. They appear to be representations of urns or vessels but are also entities (or representations of the latter). Certainly they seem to summon a world. For myself they operate as a kind of temporal anamorphosis or, indeed, as time-travel devices (and increasingly I have found myself returning to visit them where they are on display in the British Museum).[7] Copestake's object, that is not an exact copy but a kind of re-versioning of one of the drums—and as such a kind of summoning of them—was shown as part of an exhibition by the artist collective Neuschloss with the title *Think smarter gateway error* (see Fig. 10.1 in the colour plate section). Neuschloss' own work involved a further image of one of the drums and then other technical devices (in this case speakers) in order, we might say, to activate the drums (both the original ones and the representations) in and for our contemporary moment. The soundtrack—the clatter of footsteps and closing doors, the ambient hum of an electrical cabinet and then the brief appearance of a visitor (a security guard?)—accentuates the sense of some kind of institutional setting, but works as an interference or cut into the actual setting of the exhibition as well. The accompanying text by Neuschloss also makes reference to institutional mental health policies, in this case concerning the university (where some of those involved in the group work).[8]

The installation was then an intervention into the institution or, we might say, it involved a utilisation of the past so as to call something different forth. It seems to me that this exhibition can then be understood as involving a turn to the past as a kind of resource, but that it was also about adopting a certain perspective and posture in the present, broadly understood, so as to allow these different objects to do their work (to activate the anamorphosis I mentioned above). And this work, at least partly, seemed also to be about foregrounding a certain idea of care, although one that, like the drums themselves, it is less easy to pinpoint exactly or give an exact discursive account of. Perhaps it is a care of the imagination?

Moving away from the British landscape, a second example of what might be called archaeofictioning is Adjoa Armah's exhibition at Auto Italia gallery in London in 2022. This exhibition was titled *The sea, it slopes like a mountain* and involved the presentation of a number of handmade objects alongside a sound work (spoken word along with recordings of the sea and of birds) and texts.[9] Armah's research practice for these different works included walking between slave forts on the Ghanaian coast with invited guests and then, crucially, the making of the objects—that are like props—which are coated with the collected sand of the different beaches. The work is complex, involving different elements and multiple references, but I want here to briefly focus on the objects. These are based on various Ghanaian musical instruments and other devices—for example a staff or pole with a finial (see Fig. 10.2 in the colour plate section)—used to clear or secure a space (for example for healing) or to allow mediation and communication across worlds (including from the living to the dead). Encrusted with the sand, these object-props seem to be from a deep past or, at least, they reference older artifacts (as well as those in European museums). But they also gesture towards a different future (they are not archaeological finds that gesture only to the past).[10] Certainly, there is a sense that they might be used to call something forth from the landscape. There is also here a sense of the re-telling of a particular story, and, with that, a re-enactment or a re-staging of history. Again, it is especially the way the objects imply a future performance as well as being inspired by one—in terms of the walks Armah conducted—that is compelling. Armah herself refers to these objects as sketches or prototypes, as 'not the thing, but the thing that makes the thing happen' (Armah 2022). This sense of dramatisation is further emphasised in the way the objects are positioned on a stage in the gallery space.

At stake in Armah's practice is then a different idea of time from that of typical linear sequencing—a summoning of different pasts and futures through staging and storytelling. There are connections here with a group like Black Quantum Futurism and their own project of 'event mapping' (see Phillips 2018). Indeed, Armah's practice reminds us that there is a certain idea of time (and thus of the past) that itself needs decolonising. Calendars and clock time—and with that ideas of historical sequencing—are invariably tied up with a Western mind set and, indeed, with a colonial project. In order to disrupt this kind of temporal set-up and then also suggest other possibilities and relations with the past (not least for those groups and communities who experience this form of time as an ongoing colonisation) then props and other devices will be needed. And, alongside these, new rituals of repair will need to be enacted too.

To return to the British landscape, there are also those contemporary art practices that involve attention being given to different marked sites and, especially, those that involve a performative element that seeks to activate these sites in some manner. I looked at some examples of this kind of work in 'On Magic and Place'. My third case study is a more explicit case of this kind of archaeofictioning (if it can be called such) and one that is, crucially, also an eco-feminist reclaiming of the past: Verity Birt's research and multimedia presentation *Crossings* (see Fig. 10.3 in the colour plate section).[11] Alongside a number of strange assemblages—more props perhaps?—made by the artist Tom Sewell, Birt showed a film that partly focussed on the landscape and included standing stones and neolithic cup and ring markings in the North of England. The film was made during the initial Covid years and seems to concern an intention to set up a space of healing (the virus is mentioned in the voice over). In particular, digital imaging and sequencing allow the exploration of a different poetics of the landscape. There is, for example, the switching between different scales (or the micro and macro) and the layering of text and voice over image (much of which foregrounds the imbrication of the human with the landscape). And then there is also the way the technology allows the insertion of one space within another or a kind of nesting of different worlds. There is as well the use of animation, most strikingly with a neolithic beaker that is superimposed and set spinning in or over the filmed landscape. Animation is a further way of superimposing or layering different places and times.

Important here, alongside the human residues and marked landscape, is also the other flora and fauna of this landscape which Birt interacts with. It seems to me that at stake in Birt's practice—and in this collaborative exhibition with Sewell—is an idea of care for these other non-human entities and agents in both the past and the present.[12] And, once again, it is the journeying through and across a given landscape to these different sites that is important, almost as preparation for any kind of ritual (for example of healing) that might then take place. Indeed, walking seems to be an especially productive way of interacting with the past as it is manifested in our landscape and thus also of gesturing towards other possible futures.[13] Walking in this sense (and as is the case with Armah's practice too) can itself be a performance and work as a kind of summoning.

Mythotechnesis

At some point in the not-too-distant future this idea of archaeofictioning might also take on a different and, as it were, more real and urgent aspect. Technological developments—and especially developments in AI—suggest that the reconstruction of the past might become increasingly accurate or, at least, believable. At the time of writing 'deep fake' algorithms are being used to bring old photographs to life. The past is increasingly being animated in new, technologically mediated ways. It seems inevitable that the past will continue to be resurrected in this way and be presented as reconstructed fictions especially when AI dovetails with virtual reality (VR) technology (for a kind of theory-fiction about this—in relation to the military-entertainment complex—see Audint 2017).

What might the implications for an understanding of archaeofictioning be here? Certainly, the latter might be a name for this new pursuit or discipline of resurrection and reconstruction. But, following my comments above, might it also name a more diverse and expanded field of practices; the making of other objects and the devising of other rituals that summon the past—and, once again, crucially, different pasts—in different ways and for different reasons? Technology might well play a part in this. The increased processing speeds of computers and the ubiquitous availability of imaging and editing software means that 'new' relationships to our pasts and new kinds of hybrid worlds are already being produced (as in the way—as I mentioned in relation to Birt's work—one space or time can be 'inserted' within another).[14] In our book on *Fictioning*, Burrows and I suggested the name 'mythotechnesis' for some of this work that involves a collaboration with this technology. These kinds of collaborations might well involve the production of different communities of the dead or of different landscapes of the past for example (with the utilising of different props to actualise—or simply perform—these other space-times). The question here, of course, is who is making and coding the technology? What commands are there at source? Who is producing these other pasts and for whom? Mythotechnesis is never a neutral business.

Being with the Past

To return to some of my initial comments above it does seem that these practices of more experimental archaeofictioning can be a way to claim (or re-claim) the past and might, in this sense, also be thought of as repair work. Certainly, to practise archaeofictioning (as I have developed the term) is to occupy a past that is different to what can, for some, be a moribund present (and thus, once again, to gesture towards a different future). But terms such as 'claim' and 'occupy' perhaps already name a mode that is too tethered to the self as it exists in the present (and, indeed, to a Western mode of subjectivity). Might archaeofictioning instead involve a kind of 'being with' the past—and especially different pasts—and, as such, also being with other entities from those pasts? Again, this complex and open relationship to other pasts seems crucial in terms of our own future and survival as a species.

Coda

Let us imagine a scenario. There is a clearing in a wood and a fire. Around it are gathered different people and creatures, some recognisable, some less so. They have been brought together—a communion of sorts—to enact something. Perhaps it is a ritual? Or simply a 'being together' with other species. And in this circle, it turns out that those objects and signs did not mean what we thought they did when we first unearthed them but had a much stranger and more urgent purpose. And these peoples of the past are not like us at all—their reality is very different—but certainly they are, in part at least, something that we might become (after all there are different temporal circuits and loops at stake here). In this place, in this circle in this landscape, with these props gathered here—alongside others that we have made and brought ourselves—a performance is taking place that allows causality to become reversed. These beings of the past are offering up an image of a different future. Of what we might become by taking on a certain posture and perspective, one that involves seeing this diverse gathering here as our own community.

Notes

1. For Henri Bergson the past also 'subsists' (see Bergson 2004). We don't perceive this past, fixated as we are on the present and our more utilitarian interests, but it can present itself, most spectacularly with involuntary memory when a kind of gap in the sensory-motor apparatus (our habitual and reactive mode of being) allows it to be 'seen'. It seems to me that ritual (a particular kind of performative act in a particular location) might also allow this kind of travel, as might some other kinds of device (I will return to this at the end of this essay but see also the discussion and diagram in 'Time Circuits and Temporal Loops' and the discussion—and further diagram—in Burrows and O'Sullivan 2019: 90-1).
2. An indicative example of a transitional monument is the Ruthwell Cross located in the borders of Scotland (once Northumberland) that has both pagan and Christian signs and markings (see the discussion in Orton 1998). In terms of buildings on previous sites one need only think of the practice of building churches on pre-Christian sacred sites.
3. See, for example, Deleuze 1989 and the extended discussion of this future orientation in Burrows and O'Sullivan 2019: 16-21.
4. In relation to this there is also the idea (and Science Fiction trope) of a future archaeology looking back at our present 'as if' it is the past. See also Kodwo Eshun's essay 'Further Considerations of Afrofuturism' which begins with a future—and in this case alien—archaeologist visiting our planet. Here a Science Fiction perspective works as a device to show us something more typically obscured within our own time (Eshun 2003). See also Fredric Jameson's figuration of the genre of Science Fiction as itself an archaeology of the future (Jameson 2005) and Burrows' and my own thinking through of 'Science Fictioning' or the enactment/materialisation of Science Fictions within art practice (Burrows and O'Sullivan 2019: 295-313).
5. Madani discussed this notion in a seminar for 'Advanced Practices' at Goldsmiths in March 2021 at which I gave a presentation on fictioning.
6. A call for new ceremonies perhaps that can work across divides and gather communities together and as called for by Sylvia Wynter (see Wynter 2015).
7. We can also turn from art practice and look more explicitly to writing here and to those works of fiction that involve an element of the past as a kind of anamorphic time-travelling device. For example, and as I mentioned in 'On Magic and Place', there is Alan Garner's novel *Red Shift* where a found prehistoric stone axe allows this travel and accessing of other times (Garner 1973).
8. To quote from the handout to the installation:

    Think smarter gateway error focuses on this coincidence of two creative responses to institutional contexts, both of which draw on the particular presence of the 'Folkton Drums'. The work utilises the connection and communication implicit in this coincidence as a way to intensify the reversal of the 'staff well-being centre'. (Neuschloss 2017)

9. For further information on the exhibition and images see https://autoitaliasoutheast.org/projects/the-sea-it-slopes-like-a-mountain/ (accessed 4 April 2023).
10. To quote from the Auto Italia website, these objects are 'selected for their function as sonic, linguistic, spiritual, historical, bodily and social technologies':

    By staging objects in this way—holding on to modes of encounter and making meaning in the world beyond the comprehension of the colonial imagination—Armah creates an ambiguous historical moment and point of reflection, in which various moments, belief systems and places form a syncretic chorus. (Auto Italia 2022)

11 For further information on the exhibition and images see www.veritybirt.co.uk/Crossings (accessed 4 April 2023).
12 Or a 'world populated by relics, beings and the scars of past events' as the exhibition handout puts it (Lock 2020).
13 For a compelling example of this 'walking as method' of activation of different pasts in the landscape see the *Weird Walks* series of fanzines.
14 See my essay on 'Art Practice as Fictioning' for a thinking through of technologically mediated practices that involve this kind of layering and imbrication of different spaces and times (O'Sullivan 2014b).

11

Dreaming as Method

Dreaming can be a method of escape from an existing set-up and a way to imagine other modes of existence from within this one. This essay explores this double aspect in relation to various 'case studies' of dream work—including Kathy Acker's dream maps and Susan Hiller's collective Dream Mapping *project—leading also to AI and its production of other image worlds. The essay begins, however, with a brief account of the dream work of Carl Jung and especially the idea that a dream is to be treated as a landscape to be circumambulated. This relates too to some of my own therapeutic experiences that have involved navigating imaginary landscapes—with their different figures—and which I introduce later in my essay. I end with a report back on an important dream I have had that also relates to the landscape theme of many of these essays.*

Landscapes and Dream Perspectives

Dreams arrive from some other place and also present another place to us. Another way of putting this is that dreams are fictions, but ones that are more directly connected to our lives than some of the other fictions we might encounter. They are after all authored by us in some respects (although in other respects they are definitely not authored by us). Dreams are also a fiction we inhabit more fully than, for example, a novel or even other more immersive set-ups (although see the following essay on tabletop role-playing games). Most of the time when we dream we are not aware that we are in a fiction at all. Hence the sense of full immersion which might tell us something about that other 'fiction of the self' that we are also fully immersed in but more or less necessarily oblivious to.

For Carl Jung a dream was to be approached as if it were a strange and idiosyncratic landscape that needed to be 'circumambulated.'[1] Jung also suggests in other writings that an appropriate method for dream interpretation is that the dream be turned in the hand as if it's a complex and multifaceted object.[2] It is in both of these senses that the dream is to be approached on its own terms rather than interpreted using a ready-made schema.[3] Despite what I have said above about the dream's connection to the dreamer, for Jung it was also important that a dream is not necessarily 'owned' or, at least, that it was to be understood above and beyond the consciousness that had dreamt it (although not necessarily the individual). Any interpretation of the dream was to be made from within the dream perspective. Again, the dream had its own integrity and logics that were different and not reducible to the events and so forth of waking life. That said, for Jung there was a meaning to dreams. What happened in that other place—or what it was there to tell the dreamer—was to do with rebalancing the psychic state of an individual. As with Freud, there was then a diagnostic character to Jung's dream work, although Jung's writings on dreams draw on an older—pre-scientific or magical—paradigm of dream analysis.

As well as being untethered from the dreamer's consciousness (and conscious intentions), for Jung the dream was also beyond typical space and time, at least as lived in and by the conscious self. Insofar as the dream offers this other experience it also demonstrates that our usual experience of space and time is a local property of the (awake) subject. In a situation in which our sense of space and time is increasingly becoming commodified—for example in terms of time there is now a monetarisation of packages of time (the gig economy) and, more generally, there is an increasingly omnipresent 'attention economy' in play—then these other senses of space and time (and especially different dream times) seem increasingly important. This is also to foreground other kinds of attention or even the importance of a certain kind of inattention. Following Henri Bergson on this point, a pause in our more typical habits of attention and what Bergson calls the sensory-motor apparatus—which is what, in part, dreams announce (not least as they arise from the sleeping body)—can allow other times and other landscapes to foreground themselves (Bergson 2004).

The dream might also allow some perspective back on the dreamer. This certainly seems to be the case with lucid dreaming that enables this other perspective on the self to be taken on. As I have suggested in previous essays there is always already a nesting at work in our experience in and of the world.[4] We are a self-model situated in a world-model even before the dream fiction occurs. It's not easy to step outside the model that one is necessarily within. But dreaming—and especially lucid dreaming—suggests that one can turn in the other direction (which is to say—somewhat counter-intuitively—that this outside perspective can be produced through a turning inwards). The dream can be a device—and a method—for seeing the fiction of the self as a fiction in this sense.

Dream Maps and Dream Diaries

Dreaming is also related to writing fiction more generally which, after all, is also the making of a world within a world (or, to follow the image I put forward above, the drawing out of a landscape within another landscape). As I mentioned in my essay 'On Teaching and Writing as Care and Repair', some of my own writing has involved this working out of a landscape of the self (and, as such, the relating of an interior world with an exterior one) and then also, crucially, the following of various figures and avatars that emerge from within that landscape so as to see what they might do and say. There is a connection here with the idea of mapping out dreams, as for example with Kathy Acker's dream maps which accompany some of her writings and which I have also referred to throughout these essays (see Acker 1984). Certainly, a map—or, again, a landscape—seems the right way to 'picture' these non-typical space-times. Drawing one's own maps seems especially important given our increasing dislocation and dissociation in space and time—the feeling of being lost or not in control—and, indeed, the increasing difficulty of imaging our individual relationships to the larger abstractions that can seem to determine our lives (again, see my essay 'On Teaching and Writing as Care and Repair').[5] Dream maps can be part of this project of locating ourselves in a particular time and place.

Acker's maps are idiosyncratic and non-linear and see her using different registers and resources to record and present her dreams (for example, at times, turning to pre-modern and non-Western imagery).[6] They do not tell a straightforward story or, if they do, it is one that can be entered into at different points, or that offer up different trajectories to follow. They are often to do with journeys in this sense. Crucially, although involving a radically distributed authorship in one sense (or certainly a fragmented self), they are also *her* maps. They involve what might be called a kind of self-mythologising and, with that, a remaking of the world (as Acker remarks at the end of the image-text sequence 'The Journey', from *Blood and Guts in Highschool*: 'So we create this world in our own image' [Acker 1984: 164]). More generally, Acker's books also show the connections between dreaming and writing fiction.

As well as dream maps and other ways of imaging dreams (especially drawings) there are also dream diaries that are often used as a resource for writing or, more generally, for making art (in relation to a key figure for these different essays see for example William Burroughs' *A Book of Dreams* [1995b]). Here the fact that these dream worlds and images arrive unbidden as if from somewhere else makes them especially important for making something that is both of the world (that accompanies a given self) and not of that world too. And then there is also the fact that the dream diary is a record or representation of what is already a representation that is itself within a representation. Do these succeeding representations always detract from the dream or can they in some cases focus certain aspects, not least for those beyond the dreamer? Written accounts of dreams and dreaming can also allow a larger community—of readers—imaginative access to what was a private experience and, as such, they change the valence of the dream. I will return to this idea of dreams and community below.

Summoning Figures and Other Fictions

In previous essays in this second part of my book I have written about the importance of different images and figures in terms of engaging our desires and, specifically, the need for 'new' kinds of figures and images that are appropriate and adequate to 'living in the ruins'. On the one hand these images and figures can be found in the actual past or a projected future but, it seems to me, they can also arrive through dreams. Indeed, to repeat the point I made above, dreaming (like writing) allows the summoning of something that is both of you and not of you (and thus speaks back to you). Although I suggested above that Acker, for example, is involved in claiming her own sense of self, her dream maps and writings are also about disabling or sidestepping this sense of self too.

In relation to this 'speaking back' there are also those dreams that seem especially important or that appear to be more meaningful than others. My own experience is that many dreams can be relatively easily understood in terms of waking life (for example those about and around anxiety) but then there are also dreams that seem to come from further away and that are at the same time somehow more meaningful. These dreams are often accompanied by an atmosphere and a particular kind of vividness that can be absent in those other more 'everyday' dreams. It is also my experience that these more special dreams do seem to come from another time. They are often cryptic, involving composite images and landscapes. They are prophetic somehow or, at least, gesture towards a future.[7] Invariably they are remembered and, as such, call out to be reflected on or, returning to Jung, circumambulated. And I think Jung is right that they seem to be about correcting a given trajectory or, certainly, suggesting other paths for a subject. I offer a brief report of one such dream in a coda to this essay.

Is this to introduce a hidden agency behind the self? A deeper assignment at work? Some of Jung's writings would seem to suggest this (as does—in another vein—the idea of collective archetypes). But we do not need to wholly subscribe to the idea of a more authentic self that is 'revealed' in dreams in order to assert their importance and to find them meaningful. Rather, dreams, once again, are the production of fictions within the fiction of the self. Fictions that we might take on or follow (at least to some extent). Another way of putting this is that dreams are not simply to be dismissed as illusions and residues from waking life but they are also not evidence of a deeper or 'truer' reality. Like other fictions then, dreams might be seen as offering other possibilities or indicating other modes of being. So different agencies and assignments perhaps, but not a final 'real' one. In this sense—to return to the point I made above—they allow for a kind of exit from an existing set-up.

Another personal example of this blurring of the real and imaginary (and, indeed, the locating of exits)—albeit at a bit of a tangent from dreaming—is some work I have recently done around my anxiety and, specifically, an enquiry into what lies beneath that. This work involved tracking sensations and feelings as they arise in and on the body and then staying with those and seeing what else—especially certain images or narratives—arises and what information they might offer up (for example in relation to what I say above about changing track).[8] This work has put me in touch with some very early memories but also with some other images and narratives that are stranger and less tethered to 'reality'. These important images often involve a landscape with different features and marks but also different characters and avatars. Some of these are from my own fiction writing that I have mentioned above and in a couple of previous essays. In fact, it is as if these figures (or avatars) from that invented narrative had been actualised somehow in a landscape (just as the writing of that novel involved its own summoning of figures and landscapes). Equally important is how this imaginary landscape has become superimposed on the real one I live in and move through (which has also resulted in my growing interest in pilgrimage).[9] I realise some of this is cryptic. I think perhaps necessarily so as I'm not sure myself what this means exactly or what kind of answer it is to my own struggles with anxiety. But clearly this work involves conjuring certain images that attract me or engage me in certain ways.

This other landscape seems to be a resource then, although the path towards it is not always clear. At times it does not feel enough to pitch against the loops of anxiety; but at others it feels as if it can contain that anxiety somehow. Or as if the latter is itself a feature—a shadow perhaps—in and on that landscape. I have figured this dream work as a conducting of my own personal and therapeutic myth-work that is increasingly dovetailing with my academic and artistic interests. I share these personal experiences here in the hope that they might resonate and that at least some of the above is useful for your own work of care and repair.

Dream Machines and Other Devices

In the above I have suggested that dreams can be a resource for writing and other creative projects (as well as being more directly therapeutic). This is especially the case as they can allow or prompt a certain amount of self-narration (as is also partly the case with the therapeutic experience I have briefly outlined above). But, as I've implied as well, dreams offer a glimpse of other possible modes of existence, even future possibilities. Elsewhere David Burrows and I have written about the importance of dreaming for various writers (for example Carlos Castaneda) and especially the way a dream can involve a shuttling of perspectives or the taking on of another viewpoint (Burrows and O'Sullivan 2019: 53-5). In that writing—on what we call fictioning—this dreaming was also connected to drugs that open up other realities from within this one. Certainly psychedelic drugs involve a kind of waking dream, and, again, one that can offer up all sorts of information. These different devices involve a shift in perspective on the self for example. They can also involve a transportation to other landscapes and, indeed, other times and, as such, offer up a broader context for understanding a given subjective set-up.

Another example of a kind of dream fictioning device is Brion Gysin's *Dreammachine*. This relatively simple technical device—all that's needed is a turntable, light bulb and cut-out pattern—works to shift perspective and open up other worlds from within this one. Crucial in all this—in activating the device—is to set an intention (even if that intention is to undercut conscious intention).[10] In our book on *Fictioning*, Burrows and I coined the term 'mythotechnesis' to refer to those practices that operate at the intersection of—or involve a collaboration between—technology and the human more generally. Gysin's *Dreammachine* would be an example here, but it seems to me that mythotechnesis might also be a term that can be applied to various AI experiments in image production, from the algorithmically produced Google DeepDream images and animations to more recent AI systems that produce 'new' images from language prompts (as in DALL-E). At the time of writing ever more advanced AI systems are on the horizon that will be able to generate moving images from prompts. AI announces a revolution in animation in this sense. More generally virtual reality—itself understood as a fiction within a fiction—might also work to show us something about the fiction we always already inhabit. And when these VR systems dovetail with AI-generated animations then we will increasingly find ourselves in complex landscapes of layered fictions. As I mentioned in the previous essay, crucial here is the question as to what kinds of community are involved in this generation of different landscapes and thus also what kinds of community are called forth by them.

And then there are also the recent AI writing programmes such as ChatGPT. Certainly, these can produce narratives that are not exactly intended, but that nevertheless might offer up further resources for other kinds of set-up. Again, for Burrows and myself it is the possible collaboration with these machinic devices (rather than the focus on any threat to humans from them) that is important. With ChatGPT, for example, it is already 'as if' something is speaking back to us even though this thing is not a being; nor does it have agency, strictly speaking. These experiments in word and image generation can, however, be productive. Another way of saying this is that these other image worlds and landscapes although not exactly intended might be followed *as if* intended (so there is something similar here to how we might 'read' dreams).

Collective Dreaming and Other Communities

There is also the practice of—and various experiments with—more communal or collective dreaming. An example here is the *Dream Mapping* project of the contemporary artist Susan Hiller where collective maps—or kind of dream diagrams—were produced following a conscious intention of a group to dream together. Important in this particular project is that the collective dreaming was conducted outside and in a very particular place, a field in England.[11] The idea of a community of dreamers that exist both in a 'real' landscape and in a dreamed one seems important here, as does the idea that the composite map that was produced—from superimposing the individual dream maps of the participants—is itself nested within a further 'real' map. Elsewhere Burrows and I have suggested that it is this— the different kinds of relationship between an apparently real set-up and a fictional one—that is an important characteristic of different fictioning practices and how different components and props can work across these two registers or ontological levels (see Burrows and O'Sullivan 2022).[12] We used Monica Wittig's fiction *Les Guérillères* and the various communities and practices around it (and within it) as a case study of this complex nesting function with its various plays between real and fictional communities (Burrows and O'Sullivan 2022: 45-7). There is the especially intriguing question here of the relationship of a fictional community to real objects (that summon that community), just as with other real collectives and communities there is the question of the role of fiction—and particular texts (for example manifestos)—in calling them forth. This has been important to Plastique Fantastique, the performance fiction (and community) I am part of and where the real and the fictional have always blurred or interacted in these kinds of productive ways.

More generally, however, there is the fact that different communities—and different cultures—work with collective dreaming and/or affirm sharing dreams as an important practice. Indeed, it seems to me that it is also the case that a 'new' community might need to draw its own maps—including dream ones—alongside whatever other devices it might use in order to cohere itself as a community. In fact, I think there is a more general set of relations to be drawn out here between a device, a map/landscape and a community. As if any two of these are needed to produce the third term (Burrows and I will be returning to this question of the relationship between maps, devices and communities in a sequel to *Fictioning*, tentatively titled *Fictioning Community: The Non, the Ill and the Dead in Contemporary Art and Philosophy*).

At the end of my 'Memories of a Buddhist' essay I briefly go into my own experience with a kind of collective dreaming or dream work, in which anonymised dreams were looked at by a group (so visiting—and circumambulating—a kind of composite landscape) and, indeed, helped cohere that group and provide further directions or prompts for its work. In that case it became interesting in the group to track the shared features and tropes of different dreams, but also to look at how these dreams had a relevance and traction outside the dream (and the particular set-up of the group), that is, in the wider lives of the participants.[13] Or, put differently, how the dream moved from fiction to reality (and how different aspects of our group work then re-entered our dreams). That work also involved looking at dreams alongside other fictions (including more performative ones) and, indeed, more mythic narratives.

I have recently worked too on a parallel writing project with a friend, Ola Ståhl, which involved sharing imaginary landscapes and dream times and, especially, seeing what composite landmarks and figures emerge from between the two of us (and then, crucially, what they might say back to both of us). Put bluntly, we were looking for some information. Certainly the material we produced—that included different fictions alongside the discussions and explorations—feels valuable, albeit not in any straightforward way. It was as if we were sharing dream maps and landscapes, but also looking for the common images and pathways within the latter. Indeed, this work—like some of the other experiences I mention above—involved the generating of a kind of fictional community of figures and avatars. A community that Ola and I were both part of in some sense (so we too were figures in those landscapes). Dreams can offer up shared meaning in this way. This is something that seems increasingly crucial in a contemporary set-up that foregrounds individualism and which often replaces more personal meaning with consumerism (and competition). Meaning here partly means connection and a perspective that sees—and actualises—different kinds of relation and with that foregrounds other kinds of value. Or, put differently, this kind of 'dreaming as method' can itself be understood as a form of care and, as such, also be a component in a practice of repair.

Another example of dreaming as method, again, in a collective sense is Justin Barton's philosophical writings on fiction (or what might be better called theory-fictions). In particular, Barton attends to the resonances between dreaming and fiction and then also to the connections between these two and what he calls the 'group subject' that might offer a possible 'escape-path' from the 'ongoing disaster of capitalism' (Barton 2021). For Barton, dreams are an indication of another mode of perception in the same way as literature operates, for Barton, as a lens on to non-ordinary worlds.[14] Dreaming, for Barton, is also intrinsically connected to both the planetary and what he calls lucidity, both understood as fundamentally different kinds of consciousness to our more usual (and restricted) one that is determined by capitalist logics. Dreaming has an importance beyond any individual dreamer in this sense, naming as it does a method for accessing these radically different modes of perception (and of being).[15] Following Barton, might it also be that dreams can be understood as 'incursions' from the outside? They are certainly—to repeat the point above—a kind of subjective technology that nevertheless allows an access to something radically non-subjective.

Dreaming of the Future

In order to have further traction in our world the other landscapes and possibilities that have been at stake in this essay need actualising in waking life. I mean this not just in the sense of allowing the dream information to alter a personal trajectory (for example) but also in terms of other—wider—possibilities. Using the dream material—and perhaps associated fictions—to make something different (a different map and a different device perhaps?). Dreaming of other futures for example which might then work to help pull that other future forth (or to summon a community). A sense of porosity, between different realities seems important here as is simply investing less in what we are told is reality.[16] It has often been said that the inability to think beyond capitalism is a failure of the imagination. But it's difficult to think/imagine beyond the conditions that you are in and, which in many senses, set the parameters for any imagination (what is consciously imagined, if I can put it like that, can be an image of something already present). Dreaming seems to offer something important here. A method for getting out of—or working around—this epistemological and even ontological predicament.

Coda

I remember dreaming of a moorland landscape with broad hills and deep valleys. A dark landscape that would occasionally be lit up by the sun emerging from behind fast moving clouds. And then seeing there on the horizon in huge letters the word: LAND. It was as if this word was a backdrop and the landscape was a stage set or space for a performance. I remember how this dream stayed with me (I think I probably dreamt it when I was 15 years old or so) and how memories of it have recurred over the years. I think it was prophetic in terms of my moving away from the city but even, thinking about the dream as I read over some of these essays, in terms of this book too that somehow seems to be connected to that dream (or even called forth by it). It's still unclear to me what that dream means (circumambulation certainly seems more appropriate than interpretation), but it has operated as a trigger in different areas of my life. It has had real-world effects, although sometimes this has only become clear to me in hindsight. Although I would not make any claims that it offers up any clear information for any utopian project, it has certainly shown me—and continues to show me—the power of images and fictions (as well as of landscape) in terms of any transformative project.

Notes

1 To quote Jung: 'While "free association" lures one away from the material in a kind of zigzag line,...the method I evolved is more like a circumambulation whose centre is the dream picture' (Jung 1978: 14).

2 Again, to quote Jung (who is demarcating his method from Freud):

The change in my attitude toward dreams involved a change of method; the new technique was one that could take account of all the various wider aspects of a dream. A story told by the conscious mind has a beginning, a development, and an end, but the same is not true of a dream. Its dimensions in time and space are quite different; to understand it you must examine it from every aspect—just as you may take an unknown object in your hands and turn it over and over until you are familiar with every detail of its shape. (Jung 1978: 12)

3 Hélène Cixous makes a similar point—contra Freud—towards the end of her own meditation on dreaming and writing (and what she calls 'The School of Dreams'): 'Like plants, dreams have enemies, plant lice that devour them. The dream's enemy is interpretation... We must know how to treat the dream as a dream, to leave it free, and to distrust all the exterior and interior demons that destroy dreams' (Cixous 1993: 107).

4 See the Brassier quote in Chapter 1, note 12.

5 See also Walter Benjamin's account of an important dream:

Suddenly, and with compelling force, I was struck by the idea of drawing a diagram of my life, and knew at the same moment exactly how it was to be done. With a very simple question I interrogated my past life, and the answers were inscribed, as if of their own accord, on a sheet of paper that I had with me. A year or two later, when I lost this sheet, I was inconsolable. I have never since been able to restore it as it arose before me then, resembling a series of family trees. Now, however, reconstructing its outline in thought without directly reproducing it, I would instead speak of a labyrinth. (Benjamin 1979: 318–9)

See also the diagrams and maps gathered in Clarke and Kivland 2017 that use Benjamin's account as a device or prompt for a gathering of other experiments and lost diagrams.

6 And in this sense—especially in the look back to Aztec and Mayan imagery—the dream maps look to Burroughs too (see, for example, the interview with Burroughs 'Journey though Time-Space' that also deals with the bringing of the past and future into conjunction and, indeed, the way the cut-up can work as a tool of divination [Burroughs 2008: 38–48 and 28]).

7 In relation to this, dreams have sometimes been a resource for the performances of Plastique Fantastique. For example, a dream of something called the 'Ghawkin' then worked to partly call forth a performance that was itself concerned with summoning whatever figure this word named. See the *Plastique Fantastique Ribbon Dance Ritual to call forth the Pre-Industrial Modern* that was part of *The Event* (curated by Andy Hunt) in Birmingham in April 2007 (images here: www.plastiquefantastique.org/performance02.html [accessed 18 Jan 2024]).

8 I want to take this opportunity to offer my thanks to Mandarava who facilitated this somatic exploration with care, attention and generosity.

9 This is especially the case with different parts of the South Downs where I now live but also and especially journeys to sites like Avebury and Stonehenge (so specific marked places in the landscape).
10 See also Susan Hiller's curated group exhibition *Dream Machines* that, in this context, might be said to be an exercise in gathering together examples of these dream devices (Hiller 2000).
11 In a relatively recent commentary on her work of the 1970s Hiller suggests that the important thing about the dream-mapping project was how it involved the portrayal of a place rather than a location and, indeed, how this means such maps refer back to medieval maps like the Mappa Mundi. For Hiller it is also especially important that these maps are drawings, involving various demarcations, both real and imaginary (see Hiller 2010). The resonances with Acker's Dream Maps are clear insofar as the latter are also drawings of places in this sense (might we even say they are Acker's own *mappa mundi*).
12 See too the New Mystics project where AI collaboration (with contemporary artists) is also foregrounded in what might be called a collective dreaming project. (www.newmystics.xyz/about/ [accessed 18 January 2024]).
13 This project carries on our investigations begun in O'Sullivan and Ståhl 2006.
14 Here is Barton setting out the intention behind *Outsights*, his impressive collection of essays on different literary works:

> The aim is to break open a view of the outside of the ongoing disaster, and to do this by concentrating on eleven works—all of them are texts—which in different ways do not fit well within the forms of knowledge and expression that are elements within the constitution of ordinary reality. To one extent or another these texts are all instances of what can be called 'the anomalous'. (Barton 2021, n.p.)

15 See also The Occulture's collectively written book *Ludic Dreaming* that positions 'dreams as an ethicoaesthetic practice', a form of re-enchantment that might be set against some of the more dominant logics and modes of our 'information saturated culture' (The Occulture 2017: 14).
16 I am reminded here of what Mark Fisher says of 'capitalist realism', that it 'is like a pervasive *atmosphere*, conditioning not only the production of culture but also the regulation of work and education, and acting as a kind of invisible barrier constraining thought and action' (Fisher 2009: 16).

12

On Tabletop Role-Playing Games and Fictioning

This essay leads on from the previous in terms of its attention to other imaginary landscapes. It also extends some of my previous work on fictioning in making the case that tabletop role-playing games can be understood as world-building technologies. In particular the essay focuses on the emotional engagement and imaginative immersion of the gaming experience but also, crucially, the collaborative and collective aspects (including the way they allow for different experiments with other forms of agency). The prompt to start this investigation was my own memories of tabletop role-playing games—itself activated by my recent introduction of these games to my own children—and how this helped set up an imaginary space that is still important to me.

Through the Gate

What is at stake with tabletop role-playing games? That is, besides the entertainment they offer or besides their status as games? Although I no longer play them as immersively as I once did (the phase of truly being in those worlds for me was relatively short, perhaps four years from age 12 or so to 16), they have had a determining effect on my imagination and, I think, on the various life choices I have made. In many ways the art and theory worlds I have lived in and moved through seem in retrospect a logical progression from those other worlds, albeit these latter worlds are more 'worldly' and more politically urgent as it were (but, if I'm honest, usually less vivid). That said, I have recently taken on the role of a 'Game Master' for my own two sons and have now watched them enter into what always seemed to me another space-time. Put simply, they too have become caught up in exploring these other parallel worlds. Indeed, I remember clearly when, as it were, the penny dropped. When the two of them realised that this was not simply a game, but something else altogether. Something much stranger, but also more magical.[1] It was as if they had gone through a gate and, with that, had entered more fully into the characters (and the landscapes) they were playing. Since then, the elder of them has been hooked and the refrain that I once spoke is now on their lips: *Dungeons and Dragons* (which is the game we were playing) is not simply a game. It's a way of life. Quite an over-the-top statement, but for a time it really was as if this were the case for me, as it is for them now. There is much more I could say here about their adventures. About how easy it is for them and their friends to enter these worlds, switch perspectives and so forth (and then also deeply experience various emotions within the game). About the importance of preparation—of setting a context—so as to allow this other kind of inhabitation to effectively take place (although I am often surprised too at how few 'props' are needed for the shift in perspective to be made).[2] And then also about how these tabletop games relate to other games—that are also more than games—that they play 'outside'[3] (what is now called LARPing—live action role playing—although, for them, there are not necessarily any costumes or other props, besides that which is found lying around). Some of those observations and reflections might appear in some other writing—some more fiction perhaps—that is, in a more appropriate form to what seems to be happening in those worlds and with those children (and, looking back, in my own childhood) especially when on the cusp of adolescence (which, it seems to me, is when our imaginaries are predominantly formed).

In fact, my own experiences with role-playing games were also split between live play—out on the moors in the North of England in my case (something I have mentioned in a previous essay)—and then playing various tabletop role-playing games themselves which, in many ways—when I first encountered them—somehow extended that live play and, again, made it more vivid (despite them coming after and being one step removed from the play outdoors). I remember like it was yesterday the first actual tabletop role-playing experience which was *Dungeons and Dragons* (this was the first and most important game, though others followed).[4] The slight puzzlement about what we were doing and how we should be doing it (the game was initiated by an older boy) and then the moment it all fell into place. Again, the penny dropped. I was hooked.

Or we were. For this history I am briefly laying out is not just about me but about my twin brother too. We both entered that world—as we did many others—together.[5] There is also much more to say about this, but it is not just my own story and so I leave it to one side—except to draw something important from this determining factor. There were always two of us (at least) and so there was always already a community and a discourse happening around these experiences and this world creation.[6] The experience of role play was precisely shared.

World Building

I want now to move a little deeper in, to shift, at least to some extent, from the realm of memories (and my own biography) to something more theoretical. Or, as I said at the beginning of this essay, to think about the importance of these games beyond the games themselves. So, first of all, I mentioned 'world creation' above and, clearly, with role-playing games there is a kind of world making that goes on beyond fiction per se. In these games one is actually living 'in' the fiction as it were (or, at least, shuttling between the fiction and the reality outside of this). As a character in the game one is making decisions that determine outcomes. In fact, even here things are more complex as there are two positions to occupy. One is the Game Master who has initially built or, really, written the world (even if they are using a pre-prepared scenario, they need to add detail, narrate the encounters, bring the world to life [and I should also say here that my experience was that these worlds were always more successful when written by the Game Master]). And then there are the players who then enter into that world and, with that, continue the world building or give it another dimension.

In passing it is interesting—for me at least—that universally it was my twin brother who would function as Game Master whereas I would be the player (or one of them). I think this determines a certain take on the imagination. A focus on construction and a generosity in building a world for another (and then the satisfaction of seeing that world being interacted with). A perspective of and on the games as a whole as it were. And then the other position, more oblivious to the scaffolding and the 'behind the scenes' work and so forth. More a sense—and perspective—of just being thrown in (so, perhaps, more spontaneous). In fact, both are—of course— needed, and, in fact, the two make the game, which is to say without the

Game Master there is no world, or if there is, it is one that is chaotic, perhaps too spontaneous. And without the players the Game Master has simply penned a fiction. These worlds need building *and* animating. They need to be invented and then believed in—interacted with 'as if' real—in order that everything can take off and, with that, become something that is greater than its parts.

So, there is already something interesting in play here. Something to bring to the table (!) in relation to current debates around world building (within art and theory worlds). Or, put differently, there is here a situation in which worlds are created and then lived out, at least to a certain extent, by others. Again, the worlds at stake are co-produced in this sense. This certainly resonates with—but, I think, also adds something to—for example, Donna Haraway's interest in 'string figure' games and, indeed, other communities of world building (Haraway 2016). Although Haraway does look to art practices and collaborative workshops too, it seems to me that these are often a pale imitation of these other experiences of gaming (I'm aware that some of this is to do with my own history and of what went in, as it were, at a certain age). It's certainly the case, as I've already mentioned, that art can extend certain images and logics apparent in these role-playing worlds,[7] but, I think, it can also detract from, or dampen down, what are often the most interesting and intense aspects. The sense of immersion, or simply of play, for example. Perhaps as well the lack of judgement that's typically involved (something that I think is also important in my experience of collaboration and other collective set-ups).

Imagination and Anamorphosis

I have written elsewhere, with David Burrows, about how art scenes are often a pale imitation of other music and club scenes (another of the worlds I inhabited after role-playing games) (Burrows and O'Sullivan 2019: 164-66). And, for example, that the intense and exciting experiences art can offer are not as intense or exciting—for me—as those I have had in the spaces and places of club culture and, especially, free parties (although it is perhaps also the case that art practice can extend certain characteristics of these experiences or develop them in interesting ways [this seems to be especially the case with collectives and performance]). A similar point might be made in relation to role-playing games which are also more all-encompassing (although, again, age—pre-adolescence—has a role to play here). As far as this goes, role-playing games bring something different to theory/art debates around world building. Or, more simply, they bring a different kind of world making to the fore, one that is then occupied, or imaginatively lived out if I can put it like that. It's also in this sense that they can foreground the idea of the 'fiction of the self'—a theme of some of these essays (especially in the first part of my book)—insofar as they enable the taking on of other fictions, which then—as I've mentioned before—enables a certain kind of perspective back on the self.[8]

One thing that is especially apparent here is that this is the building of a world within a world. Tabletop role-playing games involve the instantiation or enactment of a different world within this one. There is a kind of anamorphic logic at work in how the game can suddenly foreground another reality from within this one and how a more 'dominant' reality then backgrounds itself (this is part of the 'penny drops' moment I have referred to a couple of times earlier).[9] Hence also the importance of context and how one is introduced to these games (and thus how ones take them on). In fact, perhaps this tells us something about what a world actually is. It is not as if role play involves the building of an actual world (although LARPing can involve 'real' costumes and props). But then, on the other hand, what is an actual world? It might well be that a certain material reality is required, but there is also an imaginative component to a world. Certain images, and, of course, a belief in that world that goes with this. Or, put slightly differently, any given world needs a subject that goes along with it and, as it were, fully inhabits it. There is, crucially, an emotional aspect to this as well. For a world to be made it needs to be felt too.

Magic and Fictioning

We might usefully turn here to those accounts of reality that attend to its 'constructed' nature. For William Burroughs, for example, reality was a kind of script that could be cut in to (see Burroughs 2005). Burroughs demonstrated that as well as the Imaginary (and the emotions in and of the body) reality is also produced through language (or through the Symbolic, to stay with a psychoanalytic register). We can track this logic of editing further forwards to Burroughs' experiments with audio cut-ups and then to artists like Genesis P-Orridge and Thee Temple ov Psychick Youth where the cut-up is applied to TV (so audio-visual material) and, indeed, becomes a mode of life (see P-Orridge 1992). We can also turn in the other direction and look further back to where the cut-up method dovetails with magickal practice per se (as, for example with the various practices of Austin Osman Spare [Spare 2007]). Again, it's not exactly that a material reality is altered—although there might be aspects of that reality that are changed—and more that a Symbolic and Imaginary (and emotional) change can take place. Or, to repeat a point I made above, a different fiction is taken on or inhabited.

And then there are also those other accounts of world building we find with philosophers like Alain Badiou (see Badiou 2009 and my discussion in O'Sullivan 2012: 126-38 and 148-63) or any of the more recent writings on world making, especially those which follow a more abstract and conceptual—or diagrammatic—logic. There seems to be a particular attention to this within certain theory worlds at the moment, which is to say, a moment when our present world—in the West—seems increasingly bankrupt.[10] Certainly, there is an emphasis here on how a different world might be made from within this world.

It is here that some of the logics and experiences of role-playing games might be brought more specifically to bear. They might flesh out some of the architecture of these abstract world-building enterprises. Indeed, any world that is built within this world needs to be inhabited or lived somehow as well. It is not as if an abstract idea of a world can all of a sudden be instantiated materially. It also needs to be imaginatively (and emotionally) engaged with. As Burrows and I have suggested in *Fictioning* the production of new and different social imaginaries seems a crucial part of any utopian/liberating project or world-building exercise in this sense. It is certainly within the realms of art—broadly conceived—that we see explorations of and experiments with these other imaginaries (our own work focussed on Science Fiction and the more non-human imaginaries in play there [see Burrow and O'Sullivan 2019: 275-93]). But with role-playing games there is an even closer occupation of a different imaginative space, and, again, an accompanying emotional aspect. This can happen, of course, with reading fiction, but with role-playing games two other factors are also in play. First, one is more fully 'in' the fiction. As I described it to my two boys, one becomes a character in the book (so, again, one takes on another fiction). And second, this experience is shared. Again, one might say that a reading experience is also shared between presumed author/narrator and reader. Nevertheless, there is something more co-constituting within role play. Something more than simply the reader 'constructing' the text. At stake is not only a more vivid—and present—world within this one, but an agency as well that is, as it were, co-produced within that world (and even a sense of freedom that can come with this).

Other Perspectives and Other Worlds

Alongside this immersion there is also the way these games emphasise the importance of perspective and the shuttling between different perspectives. They demonstrate that there are always worlds within worlds that depend on these different perspectives. In fact, following some neuroscientific accounts (and the many references I have already made to this material) it seems as if it's more accurate to say that we are always inhabiting a model or even that we are a model within a model (see Metzinger 2009 and the discussion in previous essays). It is in this sense that role-playing games also demonstrate a particular logic about nested fictions that is always already at work. We are always already involved in role play. Or we are always already playing a fiction within a fiction.

This emphasis on different perspectives is even more the case with recent role-playing games and, especially, those written by communities and/or as part of an art practice. I'm thinking for example of David Blandy's *The World After* (2019) that allows for all sorts of non-human avatars and, more generally, foregrounds multispecies role play (so allows a closer relation to non-human imaginaries). Role-playing games can allow for more radical experiments in shifting perspectives in this sense. The experimenting with other, perhaps stranger, fictions of other selves and perhaps non-selves too (which thus allows for, or implies, a more radical world building). I am now less involved in the world of tabletop role-playing games but from some of my students who are more involved I can see that this attitude towards gaming (especially with more recent games)—that it allows for all sorts of experiments around perspective and, indeed, different experiences of collaboration and collectivity—means these games can play an important part in any personal or political project of transformation.

Of course, there is also the more complex—and urgent—business of making actual worlds. Real struggles to change material reality. It is these, really, that need to be brought into encounter with any abstract reasoning about world construction (and here, crucially, it is the question of the real agency of different subjects that needs attention). But it seems to me that tabletop role-playing games might also provide some insight here, not so much into the material production (or the abstract working out) but, once again, in foregrounding the importance of the imaginary in the inhabiting of another world and the importance of emotions in engaging with it. So, once again, a kind of in-between—or diagonal—between the material and the abstract. Role-playing games also demonstrate the ability we have, at least to some extent, to take on other fictions more generally. It is in this sense of allowing us to explore and experiment with different forms of agency (including those beyond or besides the human) that these games might also be understood to be involved in certain kinds of care and, indeed, repair.[11]

Coda

Recently my experience of tabletop role-playing games—or at least my memory of playing them and introducing my children to them—has taken on a new importance insofar as I can now make the connections between those experiences and the other imaginary places and spaces that are at stake in some of these other essays. But the importance also crosses over to how I inhabit different landscapes or am able to see them as containing certain virtualities. I can imagine myself—or avatars of myself—in and on these different landscapes and as having a different kind of agency there. Another way of putting the idea of world building that this essay has been concerned with is as the actualising of these other virtualities within the world. I think fictioning is also a good term for this project which, for myself, is necessarily connected with landscape and performance and, indeed, with other practices of care and repair.

Notes

1 I think this 'penny drops' moment is akin to what Peter Wolfendale and Timothy Franklin suggest is the 'depth' aspect of what they call the tabletop role-playing game aesthetic. In their essay Wolfendale and Franklin make a convincing case that although this aesthetic might have similarities with others—as found in painting, theatre and literature—it is the way in which it is uniquely collaborative and dynamic that singles it out, or, in their words: 'We experience this depth when we see the consequences of our choices spiral out of our control, producing interesting and unforeseen results, suggesting new and exciting ways in which the world can be filled in' (Wolfendale and Franklin 2012: 219).

2 Might it also be that these games worked especially well in the pre-internet age (insofar as there was less competition for attention, for example, from digital and social media)? Certainly, in the 1980s for example there was a vibrant 'underground' culture of game design and playing (alongside mail order self-published zines and such like). On the other hand, it seems to be the case as well that the internet has opened up the possibilities, not only in multi-user online gaming, but also in the proliferation and availability of all kinds of self-published and fringe tabletop role-playing games. As in other areas—I'm thinking especially of art writing and artist's books—ubiquitous digitalisation has also brought about a renewed industry of small presses and self-publication (this relates to what has been called the 'long tail theory' of the internet and the increasing availability of 'niche' products).

3 There are also the computer games they play—screens being a ubiquitous element to all aspects of their lives—and in which another kind of world building and role-playing (to a certain extent anyway) is at stake. A recent contemporary example here that begins to dovetail with *Dungeons and Dragons* is *Elden Ring*. In relation to the intersections and interferences between screen-based games and contemporary art practice see Jamie Sutcliffe's curated show *Trouble in Outer Heaven: Portable Ops Plus*, at Southwark Park Galleries in 2021 and his accompanying essay 'Vocal Cord Parasite' (Sutcliffe 2021c). I will need to leave it to others to track through the thematics and implications of these kinds of games—in relation to play, fiction and reality—but it certainly seems to me that virtual reality, and even more so augmented reality, radically reorients the idea of fictioning (understood here as the instantiation of fictions within the real) and that we will increasingly see what is now called the 'gamification' of reality that arises from the implementation of these 'new' technologies (and their logics) across different aspects of life.

4 One of the other games in particular is worth mentioning here, *Traveller*, which was the Science Fiction equivalent of *Dungeons and Dragons* and, as such, involved more explicit world building (in terms, for example, of the flora and fauna, level of technological development, and so forth of a given planet).

5 And, as such, what I write here is indebted to those shared experiences and our ongoing conversations (as well as Tom's ongoing experiences of these games).

6 In relation to this—and, indeed, the footnote above—I should also say that the following comments are further indebted to a wider 'community of interest'. Although this is true for many of the essays collected here—the idea of a single author as origin of ideas is certainly a fiction (as different essays have attempted to point out and explore)—I want to acknowledge the various conversations and discussions I have had around tabletop

role-playing games and world-building, especially as the games themselves foreground this kind of collaborative and distributed knowledge production. See also the note below.

7 There are cases where the intersections between role-playing games and art practice are successful or, more particularly, cases when art practice involves a perspective on—and mobilisation of—some of the logics and themes of role-playing games. See for example Lesley Guy's writings on role-playing games and collective art practices and her work as part of the collective *Totaller* (Guy 2024). See also the games (and miniatures) of *Blue Mountain Arcturus* (Allan Hughes and Mark Rohtmaa-Jackson) and the essay by them, 'Citadel of Chaos' (Hughes and Rohtmaa-Jackson 2022). This essay is a reflection on their work in an exhibition that was curated by them (*Polymorph Other*, Queen's Hall Arts Centre, Hexham, 2019) and which was itself a take on Joanne Tatham and Tom O'Sullivan's collaborative art practice. Hughes and Rohtmaa-Jackson's essay develops an especially interesting idea of the 'wargaming table' as a magical set-up and what they call an 'inconsistent technology of representation' (Hughes and Rohtmaa-Jackson 2022). A further role-playing game on display at that group exhibition was Timothy Linward and Peter Wolfendale's *Dice Cult* (2018), a very strange—and mythopoetic—role-playing game rule book which, in this context, brings a further resonance between role-playing games and philosophical investigation (see also my comments above—in note 1—on Wolfendale's philosophical reflections on tabletop role-playing games (and their particular aesthetic), written with Timothy Franklin [Wolfendale and Franklin 2012]).

8 For an interesting case study of this role play—and imaginative occupation of another reality—see the ongoing 'Mythogeography' project of Phil Smith and his collaborators. At stake here is 'walking as method', but also an idea of treating the world as a game space (hence the set of 'rules' and protocols in, for example, *A Plymouth Pantheon* by Crab and Bee [Smith and Billinghurst 2019]). See also the games of the art collective *Inventory* (playing football on the Strand in London for example) that—like Smith's project—look back to the 'ludic experiments' of the Situationists ('The situationist game is distinguished from the classic notion of games by its radical negation of the element of competition and of separation from everyday life' [Debord 1957]).

9 Might this also be understood as a kind of magical function of tabletop role-playing games? In relation to this see the various writings and curatorial projects of Jamie Sutcliffe which, as well as anything else, also show the resonances between gaming and art and magic (Sutcliffe is part of Strange Attractor publishing and has himself edited a collection of texts on *Magic* [Sutcliffe 2021a]). Another interesting connection here is that Phil Hine, leading exponent of chaos magick in the UK (see the brief mention of Hine in 'On Teaching and Writing as Care and Repair') was also an avid *Dungeons and Dragons* player in his youth and, indeed, contributed an article to *White Dwarf*—the key *Dungeons and Dragons* magazine—in the 1980s on sigil magick.

10 See for example Patricia Reed's itemisation of what constitutes a world ('Worlds are composed of contents, the identification of those contents, and by the configuration of content-relations within—semantically, operationally and axiologically') and what it means to inhabit a world ('worlds are made concrete through manners of doing and saying that affirm a coherence between its contents and the identities of its contents, as well as content-relations therein') (Reed 2021: 1). Reed calls for us to learn 'inadaptation' towards the mono (but small) world we currently inhabit and then, also, 'to think referential frameworks for an unconcretized otherworld (an affirmative labour, for which

inductive modes of knowing are inadequate because there are no memories available from a world that has yet to be inhabited)' (Reed 2021: 5). This is part of Reed's larger project—carried out across recent writings—to affirm 'the difference between the making of a common world vs. the making of worlds in common' (Reed 2021: 3).

11 And then there is also the way in which role-playing games are increasingly used as a kind of therapeutic method or device, allowing individuals to imagine themselves differently and, again, experiment with different forms of agency (thanks to Alexis McGlone for conversations around this point).

13

Memories of a Buddhist

This essay involves a personal reflection on Buddhist practice as a technology both of the self and of the non-self. As far as the former goes, I argue that Buddhist practice offers many important techniques and methods that are amenable to the West (especially with various kinds of meditation practice). In terms of the latter, the essay makes the case that some of these practices also gesture towards other modes of being outside the alienated subject. At stake here is the looking to other cultural practices not to co-opt but to see what might be useful in terms of our own mental health crisis and sense of atomised existence. My essay ends with a long coda that reflects on my experiences with group work in and around myth.

Buddhist Practice

I have had two different experiences of sustained Buddhist practice that have had a significant impact on my life. The first is with Triratna (which was known as the Friends of the Western Buddhist Order when I was first and more involved).[1] The second is the *vipassana* tradition of meditation as taught by S. N. Goenka.[2] In fact, I have also had experience of *vipassana*—or 'insight'—meditation within Triratna, specifically with the *anapanasatti* practice which I will come to below. As far as Triratna goes, I have been involved as well with various therapeutic/'myth-work' practices (and retreats) that are partly in that tradition or certainly took place within a Western Buddhist context. I look briefly at those—which have often also involved group work—in the last section of this essay, 'On Groups and Myth-Work'. In what follows I want to think more generally about the impact this involvement with Buddhism has had on me and thus also the impact of these kinds of practice on a subject in the modern West in the twenty-first century. I'm keen not to generalise—and am aware that my perspective is specifically of a white male subject—but I want to try and attend as well to this impact beyond my immediate life situation and, as such, make an argument for the importance of these practices, not least for what seems like a mental health crisis in the modern world (or the modern Western world at least).[3]

Triratna

As far as Triratna goes there are a number of characteristics (if that's the right word) that, I think, are worth highlighting:

1. *Community*. Not only are there important friendships that I have formed through my involvement with Triratna (see point 5, below), but, more generally, it has offered up a community that has been accessible, welcoming and, in many ways, deeply nourishing (on what might be called a soul level, when this names something—a kind of register of feeling—situated between the intellect and the body). Traditionally this community is understood as the *sangha* or the community of those 'going for refuge' to the three jewels of Buddhism (the other two being the *Buddha* and the *dharma*, both of which I'll come to). It is this going for refuge that defines a Buddhist (when this is pursued at ever-deeper levels of commitment). There are many different aspects to this community, but to pick out three relevant ones in this context. First, there is a sense of a common focus and, with that, a common intention which to a certain extent binds the community. Second, there is a culture of sharing and, with that, a sense of openness and generosity. And third, there is an emphasis on honesty and, to a certain extent, non-judgement. All of this—the sense of community broadly understood—can also, more simply, be seen to be connected to Buddhist ethics and the emphasis on 'right speech', 'right action' and so forth. The broader purpose of this ethics is to produce favourable conditions for practices such as meditation.
2. *Meditation*. The meditation practices I have learnt with Triratna have helped with my mental health.[4] They have, in the past, brought about at least some peace of mind and a general feeling of positivity. This is in fact the intention of the foundational practices taught by Triratna: mindfulness of breathing (attending to the breath) and *metta bhavana*

(cultivating positivity). Both of these involve developing increasing awareness and, with that, attending to that which we perhaps more typically do not attend to (distracted as we can be by countless other factors). Meditation offers other rewards too. Important, in my case, is that it allows for the generation of a perspective on the whole of a life. Or, to put that differently, it allows or enables the placing of life within a larger context. Seeing it all laid out, as if it were a landscape (to return to a trope I've used throughout these essays). This is especially the case with a third practice that is central to Triratna: 'just sitting' which involves simply observing—without reaction or judgement—what arises in experience. Meditation brings about a certain amount of self-knowledge in this respect, although, crucially, it also points towards—and allows a kind of 'experience' of—non-self. I'll return to this. It means too that practices like this link up with what I have said in other essays collected here about methods or devices that allow for a shift in perspective.

3. *Ritual*. Although ritual practices can be difficult to engage with for a Western subject (in my experience at least), when they 'work' something very powerful happens. I have written about my early experience of Triratna puja (a kind of devotional practice) elsewhere (O'Sullivan 2001) but more recently I have had experience of puja and ritual which operated more specifically as a kind of device that shifted things (for me). Important here was the participants in that ritual 'acting out' various scenarios (for want of a better word) within a framework. Or another way of saying this is that they were involved in exploring their own personal myth within, again, a larger (mythic) context and then also, crucially, being witnessed doing this by the other participants (again, see the final section of this essay, 'On Groups and Myth-Work'). This also involved various props so as to foreground or add detail to these other narratives. In fact, I'm not certain this latter example of ritual was entirely Buddhist (it had as much in common with certain Western therapeutic techniques such as encounter groups), but it was Buddhism that had brought these participants (and teachers/leaders) together and set up the frame as it were (in this case a particular retreat). There is more to say about ritual and how it engages one in a different manner to other practices—that it is about not just the head, but the emotions and the imagination also—and how, it would seem to me, an engagement like this needs to happen so as to be able to bring about transformation. As

well as operating as a device in this way ritual also offers up a framework for understanding how more artistic devices (for example performance) might work. Certainly the Buddhist rituals I have been involved in, as well as involving various objects and props—and other people—and being performed in front of different shrines with different figures and images, have also involved the summoning of fictional entities.[5] Although, in this case, insofar as the effect of these entities is real then fictional does not seem quite the right word.

4. *Retreats*. This is really part of point 1 above, but it does deserve its own category as it certainly has its own distinct flavour and impact. In Triratna retreats are set up in a very particular way. On the one hand they are comfortable. Warm rooms, good food, lots of fresh air (they are often in the countryside, though not necessarily so). One is looked after (and, as such, is able to recuperate). There is also a relatively structured programme to follow which, as such, 'holds' one (early morning meditation sits and then various other activities and sits throughout the day, often ending in puja). But on the other hand, retreats can also involve more uncomfortable experiences. Indeed, the set-up—and the programme—is like a platform that can reach out into some other more difficult stuff. After all a retreat is a retreat from the world so that one can engage with the self without distraction. On one level then, a retreat simply sets up favourable conditions so that other things might arise or so that one can safely journey in to some other, perhaps darker, places. A retreat is a space and time set apart from the everyday in this sense. A liminal space even. There is no doubt that it's a privileged space. Not everyone has the time and money to go on retreat. But it is not a holiday. Or an escape. Indeed, taking a long hard look at oneself is often what we are encouraged not to do, distracted as we can be by social media, consumerism and the like. I should say too that it's my experience that time can also be experienced differently on retreat. Or, at least, a certain idea of capitalist time—and productivity—can be sidestepped which means, once again, other perspectives (and a more creative mode of responding to the world) can come to the fore.

5. *Friendship*. This is also really a part of point 1 but there is something different about individual friendships that are developed and deepened

as opposed to the more general community of practitioners—the sangha—that is part of Buddhist practice. Or, at least, with friendship that sense of community takes on a different inflection. Partly, as with all friendship, it is simply the business of being honest, deploying more of yourself and then also trust.[6] Often it means being seen in one's totality (as far as that is possible)—the best and worst—and being accepted for what one is. So, again, non-judgement is important here. Or, perhaps that should be, there is an acceptance of the particular fiction of the self that is there on display as it were (even an understanding that this fiction is something generic). There is also something important about shared experience here and, again, a certain amount of shared intention (as well as shared practices of disclosure). Friendship can break with alienation and atomisation in this sense. It can mean there are at least two of you. This means that it also relates to collaboration although it is not necessarily the same (in my case, for example, collaboration is not exactly friendship—or not only that—and, in fact, can involve the production of a further fiction [I will return to this in my final essay in this book]).

6. *The Buddha*. It's interesting that this comes so low on my list. Certainly, the Buddha as a figure who gained enlightenment (or, in this context, has seen through the fiction of the self) is—as I mentioned above—one of the three jewels. There are complex matters to unravel here to do with (spiritual) hierarchies and also perhaps with what a figure like the Buddha means from a Western perspective (if indeed it means anything).[7] But certainly, what can be said is that Buddhist practice involves a visualisation of ideals—or, at least, a moving towards certain inspirations (or, more generally, certain images). It is this that also operates as a motor *for* practice (so faith or *sraddha*). These figures—the Buddhas and Bodhisattvas—are like strange attractors in this sense.[8] They engage and animate our desires in different ways. Again, it is interesting to think about the kinds of figures in the West that also do this. Triratna has done some of this work, for example 'uncovering' pagan/non-Christian figures and images. Elsewhere I have also referred to other attempts at working this through—especially in terms of mobilising the imagination—not least in terms of exploring non-human relations. The Buddha too can be thought of

in other—more abstract—ways. As a kind of embodiment of a reality (behind any fictions), although this does not, it seems to me, mean that this reality is an actual place as such, more a reservoir of possibilities (a virtual realm as it were). Can there be a Buddhism without the Buddha? Certainly, in some traditions, if you meet the Buddha (on the road) it is suggested you kill them. This would seem to imply that a figure like this, as well as being an attractor, can also operate as an impasse.

7. *The Dharma.* Equally interesting is that this—the teachings of the Buddha—also comes in lower down my list (a reminder here that the *dharma* is the third of the three jewels). On the one hand the *dharma* is the tradition and teachings that have been passed down and which originated with the Buddha. These can have traction on a life even if it's in the modern West. The central idea of impermanence or 'conditioned co-production' seems self-evident insofar as this then produces a certain amount of suffering—or *dukkha*—in a being who desires permanence.[9] But it is the work of Buddhism to understand this reality on ever-deeper levels (and specifically in a non-conceptual manner). And then, of course, the *dharma* is the path out of this predicament (as the teachings say, there is suffering, but there is a way out of suffering: this is the Buddha's key insight—and that this path can be taught). But it might also be suggested that *dharma* is anything that helps that insight or, even, helps one practise. *Dharma* is any set of instructions—or any device perhaps?—that shows up the truth of impermanence and, perhaps, suggests as well how to live appropriately in relation to that (might, for example, Spinoza's *Ethics* be understood as a dharmic text in this sense insofar as it also maps out an ethics and path towards an experience *sub specie aeternitatis* ['under the aspect of eternity']?).

Vipassana

At this point in my reflections on my involvement in Buddhism, I want to pivot away from my experience with Triratna (and their methods and practices) to *vipassana* as taught by S. N. Goenka. Although superficially similar—it is a meditation practice after all (and, in fact, Triratna does teach *vipassana* meditation too)—there is something radically different about this practice (it seems to me)—as well as some other aspects which *vipassana* foregrounds:

8. *Self-knowledge*. To begin with, the practice of *vipassana*, almost as a side effect, throws up memories and images of the past (so it relates too to what I mentioned above in relation to the 'just sitting' practice). It also allows a linking of these together. An understanding, for example, that different fears are all isotopes of the same fear (ultimately, of death).[10] Put simply, *vipassana* allows a grasp of ever-deeper causality and our implication within that. On a bodily level this also involves real work and real struggle (more than other meditation practices I have been involved in). *Vipassana* is a practice of staying with one's experience, of simply watching what it is that's going on (in this sense, it is again a kind of 'just sitting' practice) and thus experiencing impermanence in and on the body. Indeed, this is the 'method' of *vipassana*: to simply be present—and aware—as things arise, then pass away. In fact, more specifically, the method is to gradually increase the focus of awareness (of and on the breath and body) whilst also reflecting on this impermanence (so, conceptual thinking does have a role here as a kind of prompt). There are then very simple instructions to *vipassana*—the device is not complex—but the results are very profound indeed. If all this sounds quite calm—even in a way objective (*vipassana* as a kind of first-person scientific investigation)—my own experience is that it invariably involves sitting with (sometimes excruciating) pain (partly because it involves 10 days of hours of sitting meditation). Indeed, there is a sense that this pain *is* the self (as well as being part of the method too).

9. *Non-self*. What can follow, with some sits, is a kind of letting go and an experience of non-self. Or, to put this differently, an experience (often of intense joy) but without a self experiencing it. There can also be, for example, a different sense of both time and space in play (in a more radical—or deeper—sense than I mentioned above in relation to retreats). Hour-long sits can seem—on reflection—to have lasted seconds. There can be a sense of vast spaciousness too (and, with that, often a loss of location). On a more mundane level—the implications of this practice away from the sits as it were—there is a loosening of the sense of self or even, to return to some of my comments above, the 'seeing' of this self in a larger

context. Or, perhaps that should be the holding of the sense of self more lightly, seeing it as only part of the picture as it were. *Vipassana* offers this broader perspective. I mentioned the Triratna practice of *anapanasatti* above—a similar practice of developing increasingly focussed attention on impermanence (through attention to the breath)—and this also had a similar effect for me, albeit less prolonged. A loosening of the self—and, with that, the production of a kind of a blissful state that had been, as it were, self-created. There is something about this kind of self-knowledge—that a certain amount of satisfaction can be found within (rather than without) that is important too. But there is also something even more important about the flexibility this allows because a little bit of a gap has been opened up between stimulus and response (to return to a Bergsonian idea I have mentioned in other essays).[11] Inside the meditation practice, and then outside of it too, one is able to more creatively respond to what comes one's way, rather than simply reacting in a more habitual manner. Insofar as the self is a bundle of habitual reactions, then this means the self is also transformed to some extent.

Ultimately then Buddhism—as it has become instantiated in the West (at least, in my limited experience of the two traditions I have been discussing)—offers a series of practices, based on certain teachings, which, are beneficial to mental health on all sorts of levels. They can produce a healthier, happier individual (although they are certainly not a kind of 'cure all'). But these practices also gesture towards something else, to a fundamentally different mode of being in the world.[12] This is almost a utopian project (in the terms that François Laruelle understood 'effective utopia' perhaps [Laruelle 2004: 26]). Or, to put this differently, Buddhist practice can offer a view from elsewhere (or even a view from nowhere).[13] *Vipassana* especially can offer a sense of what the enlightened viewpoint actually is. A being in the world, but without a self. Between the two practices or traditions I have laid out here there is something important in play about getting some perspective on the fiction of the self, and, with that, producing some space around it (and especially its reactive mechanisms). It is this that also gives one the impression that sincere Buddhist practitioners are often 'more themselves'—more fully singular—as if an understanding of the self as a fiction allows a more careful cultivation or, indeed, narrating of that fiction. It is here that Buddhism has resonances with other techniques and technologies such as the Western traditions of the 'care of the self', although in this case the latter must also be figured as a kind of care of the non-self too.[14]

Detached from the name Buddhism or—to gesture back to a point I made earlier—from the Buddha, it does seem to me that these practices of introspection, especially when deployed in relation to other methods and practices (such as community and ritual practice) seem to enable a kind of repair to take place, understood here as the making cohesive of a self (that follows from having a clearer perspective on what a self is). But it also, to repeat the key point here, extends the idea of what a self is or can be. It stretches it out somehow—again, as if it is a landscape—in fact, ultimately it blurs some of the boundaries between inner and outer—offering up more material for what I have been calling myth-work (or, again, the work of repair). It is also here that one of the key paradoxes of these essays once again foregrounds itself insofar as these practices are about the self but also the non-self too. Or, put in a slightly different way, they are about the making of a self and the seeing of that making as the making a fiction.

Groups and Myth-Work

The group can operate as a device that allows other things to come into focus. Group work—or simply the exploration of what comes up in a group where trust has been built up—is a powerful way of exploring certain dramas and narratives, fantasies even (in the Freudian/Lacanian sense).[15] When this work is accompanied by myth-work, or the exploration of different myths and fictions (and especially playing them out somehow and/ or seeing how they have contemporary relevance) then these explorations about the different stories we tell ourselves can have even more of an impact on a life.[16]

As far as the group itself goes all it needs is a gathering of individuals committed to the process (not least of regular meetings) and, at least to begin with, someone (or perhaps two) that can hold the process and keep the device from tipping over. But what is the process? On the one hand it is simply to be with others and notice our reactions to what is said or done in the space the group has opened up. This will also involve being willing to speak our own truth when this simply means attending as closely as possible to our own narratives and any associated affects should they arise. As far as this goes honesty is key. The device doesn't work—or only works poorly—without the latter. And, again, trust. Trust that one will not be rejected whatever one says or otherwise reveals. This lack of judgement is the very atmosphere in which these important stories can be played out and individuals can go to those places that they might hitherto have avoided.

What can transpire in this atmosphere is that one is able to access and, perhaps in some cases, act out certain scenarios that are more typically obscured (although no less determining of one's way of being in the world for all that; in fact, their hidden natures can often mean they have more of a determining role). The group operates as a particular set-up that allows this insofar as it provides a cast of characters for whatever drama is being asked to be played out. It is often said that one always finds oneself in the same group, with the same cast of characters—for example, the one person one is attracted to/falling for and the one whom one wishes wasn't there (if only they were not part of the group, then things would be more workable). The reality is that we bring these characters—alongside the associated dramas—with us. We project onto the group our hopes, fears and other psychic realities. So a kind of landscape with figures as it were. When seen in this way, the group reflects back to us these same aspects (so the others there operate as a kind of mirror).

At least to begin with. Working in a group can also mean these projections eventually give way and we see individuals for what they are (or, at least, we see more of what's there). That is, if we can continue to suspend our judgement. There is something very powerful about witnessing someone else play out their narrative, and, with that, actually experience whatever affects—or, indeed, trauma—brought them to the group. So, the device partly involves watching a performance then, but one that is no less real for being performed. Again, this is a theme of some of these essays—that representation can increase the power of any initial event. This means that these different narratives are framed in a particular way. It also means that one gets more involved in these narratives or performs one's own narrative.[17] On the one hand this is to simply recognise something common at work in and with the various participants in a group—that there is after all something universal in human suffering for example.

On the other hand, there is also a kind of transmission of affect at work in these kinds of set-up (which is in fact, I think, related to our common natures). It only takes one of the participants to begin this kind of work and then the rest can follow the path downwards (which is really, ultimately, where the group—if it's functioning as a group—is always heading).

But in order to step up and into the round (to mix metaphors a little) and say your bit does take courage. Here the courage is to do with taking a risk and, ultimately, allowing yourself to be vulnerable and to be seen being vulnerable. Again, being willing—and prompted—to show what one would rather keep hidden. It's an easy thing to say, but invariably very difficult to follow through in practice. The method—such as it is—is then this bringing out of that which is in the shadows—and often in shame— and putting it on display. There is a resonance with writing here insofar as the latter can also involve this making apparent of the obscured (if not the making public of the often very private). For myself I have often figured this as turning towards a darker landscape hidden within this one and also, at other times, as visiting a kind of 'basement' (some of the recent fiction I have written explores this further). I realise these comments (and these spaces and places) are somewhat clichéd, but it certainly seems to be the case that both take on a reality when I have been in groups and involved in serious group work. And it has also been clear to me (often in retrospect) that it is going to these places that allows some real repair work to be done. Once again, the device only works if judgement is suspended (or at least any judgement is 'owned'; in this way watching one's reactions to whatever is being said or played out by others is part of the process too). To not be judged, to be accepted—to still be loved perhaps?—when one has revealed what one is most ashamed of is transformative (seeing as it is rejection, in some form or other, that has often brought many of the participants to the group).

How does myth fit into this? On the one hand it can work as a kind of preparation. A setting up of an external scene or context (or again, a particular landscape of sorts). The group is a device in the theatrical sense as well as anything else.[18] Myth can also provide some details that might be seized on to get things moving. Myths express something universal, or, if not universal, certainly they communicate something that tends to have resonance with more than just one individual (they are certainly culturally specific but can be trans-personal too in this sense). They also seem to operate across time (or, perhaps that should be they are situated in their own 'dream time').[19] A myth can help with the process of turning towards what we fear or are ashamed of and with bringing to light that which we would rather keep hidden. Myth is itself a kind of device in this sense.

Myth can as well provide some meaning and context to whatever narrative is being played out. It can be a way of making sense—of stitching together—the events of a life. Introducing an external myth into a group set-up can also work to suggest—or prompt—other more personal myths which can then be explored against this backdrop. Here we return to the idea of an individual's particular myth-work or, again in Lacanian terms, their structuring fantasy. For Lacan the barred (or alienated) subject (which is what we always already are) has a particular relationship to their object of desire. Or, we might say, has a particular structuring story that is told around and about this object (I map this out a little more in 'Fiction as Desiring Work'). Lacanian analysis is partly about changing this relation or again, 'traversing the fantasy'. In a way group work also allows this reconfiguration—even, perhaps to a certain extent, a rewriting of the fantasy—especially when that group is already looking at other myths.

I mentioned above about the importance of having someone who can 'hold' the group. They are not exactly like an analyst who, amongst other things, plays the part of taking on the analysand's projections (and also, at times, undercutting or wrong-footing them). In many ways it is the group itself—that device again—that works as the analyst in that sense. So, a kind of gathering of fictions if I can put it like that. The group leader is more a guide of sorts, although this is not to say they won't do some sidestepping. Certainly, they are part of the group, which means they will be involved in working through their own process. Key, however, is that they are also able to get some distance or maintain another kind of perspective. To be in the group, but not entirely of the group. They need to be able to step in and right the device when required and, more crucially, to know when this is required and when, rather, just to let things play out. In a way it is simply experience that seems to make a good group leader—they have been in groups and understand how the device works—but it also takes an individual who has been down to that other landscape and, to a certain extent, has become familiar with its landmarks and way stations. Which is to say it takes an individual who is aware of their own structuring narrative or their own myth (as well as other, perhaps older myths). Another way of saying this is that such an individual is able to move between worlds, when these worlds are simply what is typically apparent and what invariably is hidden. What is above and what is below. And this means that such an individual will not always appear in control. Certainly, they will not be offering any 'ready-made' solutions or paths to fulfilment. They are very far removed from a guru in this sense, closer to the analyst in many ways. Crucially, it also takes an individual who wants to help others. Compassion, ultimately, is the essential pre-requisite. Someone willing to stand with you—and not to judge or turn away—as you conduct your own myth-work.

Coda

Reflecting on what I have written above—and on my experiences with this kind of group work—it occurs to me that it has always involved working with representations, or, more precisely, fictions within fictions. This is the case with the dream work that was carried out in some of these groups, but also with the puppets and other props that were gathered together and put on display or used in different ways (see endnotes 18 and 19). And then, perhaps more generally, there is the idea that the group itself is a representation. The group exists in a space set apart from 'reality' but also nested within it. Here once again it is the group as a kind of theatrical device that seems at stake. A device that when activated can allow something previously obscure to become foregrounded.

Notes

1 More or less all my understanding of Buddhism—certainly on a conceptual level—comes from Sangharakshita's teachings (an especially important work for me was *The Survey of Buddhism* [Sangharakshita 1993]), but, more generally, from various teachers in the Triratna tradition (including Rijumitra who first introduced me to the above book through a year-long reading group in Leeds in the mid-1990s).
2 For a writtten account of Goenka's teachings and practice see Hart 1987.
3 As such this essay operates as a supplement of sorts to the first academic article I published that also reflected—in part—on how Buddhism had influenced (and might continue to influence) my life and scholarly/artistic trajectory (see O'Sullivan 2000).

4 I am aware of the limits—and possible dangers—of positioning mindfulness as panacea to all problems and issues (as in the way these practices are introduced in all sorts of institutional settings and contexts). Certainly, the causes of mental health issues are many and varied. To a certain extent I go along with someone like Mark Fisher for whom depression, for example, is socially produced and thus must also be tackled on that level (see also my comments in 'On Teaching and Writing as Care and Repair' about what Fisher identifies as the dangers of 'magical voluntarism'). But I think too that a full spectrum approach is needed in dealing with mental health issues and that meditation, alongside the other Buddhist methods and technologies I lay out here, can be a highly effective part of this approach.

5 In particular there is something important about the shrine, a particular kind of set-up—or another device perhaps?—that can then prompt a certain kind of experience (especially as it represents one's desires and aspirations).

6 See also my article on 'Friendship as Community' that was about a parallel experience of friendship (in relation to the places and spaces of club culture) and how that also produces community (O'Sullivan 2004).

7 I have addressed some of these issues—from a more philosophical perspective—in a previous article on Buddhism in relation to the finite-infinite relation and the philosophy of both Gilles Deleuze and Alain Badiou (see O'Sullivan 2014c).

8 Buddhism has both an ascetic aesthetic and one of abundance or proliferation in this sense. The latter is especially the case with the cosmic fictions and landscapes of various Mahayana sutras and, especially, within Pure Land Buddhism. In the context of the essays in this book these pedagogical and instructive stories involve a multiplicity of avatars and fictions (on Pure Land Buddhism see Ratnaguna and Sraddhapa 2016).

9 In relation to the implications of conditioned co-production for Western subjectivity see also Nagapriya's *Exploring Karma and Rebirth* (Nagapriya 2004) (I want to take this opportunity to thank Nagapriya for discussing various aspects of Western Buddhism with me over the years).

10 More generally Buddhism offers a context to think about death and, indeed, involves practices that might, at least in some senses, prepare one for it. See for example *The Tibetan Book of Living and Dying* (Sogyal Rinpoche 1992).

11 For a fuller account of the importance of this 'gap'—following Henri Bergson—in relation to an alternative production of subjectivity see also O'Sullivan 2013.

12 In terms of this—and, more generally, a Western take on Buddhist tradition and practice—see also Rodney Smith's *Awakening* (Smith 2014). This book, as well as turning to Western science and psychology in its exploration of another mode of being, also has the merit of offering up practical experiments and techniques (and, in this sense, has connections with other Western takes on non-self, for example the movement [and process] 'Liberation Unleashed' [see www.liberationunleashed.com/ [accessed 18 January 2024]). I want to take this opportunity to thank Samudradaka for this reference but, more generally for his ongoing friendship and for numerous conversations about Buddhist practice over the years.

13 There are connections here with the nemocentric subject as evidenced by the title of Ray Brassier's essay ('The View from Nowhere') that explores this idea of a kind of non-subject or of experience without a self (Brassier 2011).

14 See, for example, the various practices mapped out in Hadot 1995 and Foucault 2005.

15 Although this is not to fully explain what happens in a group as the process is more mysterious in many ways and takes place on many different levels (or, said differently, being 'in' the process is a very different matter to reflecting on it).

16 What follows relates to my experience with this kind of 'myth-work' in the 'River of Soul' group led by Atula and David Findlay, with Mandarava and Nagasiddhi as facilitators/organisers (see www.riverofsoul.co.uk/, accessed 18 January 2024). Towards the end of the essay, I write a little more about what makes a good group leader, and it is these two individuals (in fact, really all four of the above) that have served as my model. More generally I would like to take the opportunity here to thank them and the other participants of the two groups I was part of in 2017 and 2018.

17 Re-enactment can certainly bring about the same effects/affects as the original event, but it is also interesting how a (second order) representation can sometimes increase a given effect/affect (rather than diluting or decreasing it) (see also the next essay 'Notes on Performance Fiction').

18 The group I was involved in also involved puppets—made by Mandarava—that were used to play out these myths (so a set-up within a set-up) and then as well, at times, the making of other objects (further props?) and, in my case, masks. Again, watching a fiction—especially one that is clearly staged, but that involves 'real' objects too—seems to allow a reflection on our own fiction. In the group I was involved in we also brought in other objects (and figures)—from our life—and put them on display. Gathered together in this way—or, once again, framed in a certain manner—they took on other significances and operated as props for our own and, indeed, other's narratives.

19 Again, the group I was involved in also used dream-work more explicitly—and from a broadly Jungian perspective—in a kind of group exploration of anonymised dreams and especially their associated landscapes. This was a method specifically developed by Atula (see also the brief discussion in 'Dreaming as Method').

14

Notes on Performance Fiction

My final essay—composed of notes towards some definitions—explores different aspects of performance, including audience, performers, props and scripts, different spaces and places and then also the general 'scene' of a performance. It draws on my own experiences within the 'performance fiction' Plastique Fantastique especially in thinking through the way performance can work to dislodge the fiction of the self and, indeed, suggest other modes of fiction, including collective ones (so this essay also works as a return to some of the discussion in the first part of my book). It is in this sense that performance fiction can be understood as a kind of magical device.

Performance Fiction

There are different ways of understanding what performance is (in relation to contemporary art) and then also what might be at stake in a practice that involves performance alongside fiction, especially when this tends towards ritual and, to a certain extent, channelling too. Reflecting the themes of many of these essays (and especially those in the first half of my book), in what follows I am especially interested in how this kind of performance can—as well as anything else—work to dislodge the fiction of the self and, indeed, suggest other modes of fiction, including collective ones. Performance fiction might be understood as a kind of myth-work in this sense but also as repair work too.[1] What follows includes very broad definitions and some implications/inferences drawn from my own experience (by and large) within this genre (if it can be called as such) and specifically as a member of the collaborative performance fiction Plastique Fantastique (with some indicative or illustrative performances from that group listed in the notes [with links to documentation]).[2] As such, although these notes are my own take (and certainly not to be taken as definitive statements about Plastique Fantastique), they are deeply indebted to the group—David Burrows, Alex Marzeta and Vanessa Page (amongst others)—and, especially, to conversations with David.

1. *Performance happens in front of an audience and as such is both live and public.* This was complicated during the Covid pandemic—for Plastique Fantastique—insofar as venues were closed and, as such, we did virtual performances over Zoom.[3] Nevertheless, even in this situation there was an audience that consisted of the other members of the group and then, eventually, the Zoom performances were also broadcast (so they were always intended for an audience in this sense). It might be that a performance can be pre-recorded, but even then, it is certainly intended for viewing. What this means is that there is a certain amount of performing *for* that audience (even if the performance is for a more imagined spectator). The audience makes up part of the performance in this sense, or, at least, functions as part of the scene of the performance. It is partly this that differentiates performance from ritual—the latter often tending to the more private (or, at least, not necessarily intended for an audience)—although performance might certainly involve elements of ritual. It might be that the audience is also directly involved in a given performance in some manner, but, more generally, it certainly needs to be interpellated. It is this that differentiates performance art from, say, theatre, although this is another porous border, with some theatre moving towards performance and vice versa. When a performance happens in front of an audience who are involved or arrested in some way, then in my experience the device—the different components of the performance—clicks into gear and things begin to happen.[4] All of this does not mean that a performance is always hospitable or inviting. Indeed, it might be deliberately blunt. Or the performers might even turn their back on an audience or, more generally, perform as if an audience is not there. Nevertheless, the audience is there—even when blanked—and, as such, is part of the set-up of a performance. In fact, might this apparent refusal to engage on one level mean that another kind of engagement is at work on another level? A refusal to communicate can also be an opening to other forms of communication (non-verbal, affective and so forth). Or, put differently,

a given performance can sometimes be for another kind of audience within the audience that's there (or work to call forth this other audience).

2. *Performance involves a performer or performers.* On the one hand this is obvious. Invariably there is a figure or set of figures doing the performing (perhaps with additional audio-visual material, or, simply, different sounds and images). But it is sometimes the case too that the performers are not quite themselves. They are there but also not there. Or they are there but also something else insofar as they have entered into that performance space.[5] The idea of channelling—of sidestepping an existing set-up so as to allow something else to come through (something that is both of the self and not of the self at the same time)—seems crucial here or, at least, has been important to the performances I have been part of. This relates to the important idea that art can 'speak back' to its progenitors as if from an elsewhere (as I have mentioned in other essays collected here, it tells you what it is or where it wants to go). In fact, sometimes this channelling is acted out rather than real. Or, more accurately it is located in a grey zone between being real and being pretend. I'll return to this below. Performance can operate as a laboratory for exploring the fiction of the self in this sense and, especially, for seeing this fiction as a fiction (insofar as it offers a perspective back on the self from elsewhere). It can also allow the 'trying on' of other fictions—the taking on of different characters and avatars, for example—or, indeed, the exploration and testing out of more collective fictions. This is especially the case with those collaborative performance practices—such as the one I am involved in—that foreground this group fictioning aspect. Again, this is not a becoming exactly (in the Deleuzian sense) although, following Deleuze, there might be a kind of capture of affects. Performance is then not exactly the 'real' becoming of these other fictions, but it is not exactly pretending to become them either.[6] It's situated between these two, on an edge between so-called reality and fiction—so a slippery to place to occupy—hence also the way a performer can be both in the performance and looking on as it were (the 'looking back at the self' perspective I mentioned above).

3. *Performance involves gestures, words and props.* In fact, it might not involve all of these. It might, at its most simple, involve just the spoken word or even just gesture. But, again, in terms of the performances

that I have been involved in it tends to operate in and through a variety of registers (including the discursive) and with a variety of different material components.[7] This also includes various machines or other technical devices that extend or, at least, alter the human set-up (most simply, a microphone). Sometimes these machines might be used against their originally intended purpose or are mixed in with other more analogue instruments as props. To again use a term that David Burrows and I coined in *Fictioning*, such performances can be a form of 'mythotechnesis' when this names the intersection of fiction and technology and, especially, a performative experimentation with the latter. More generally, performance can involve a collaboration with these machines and other objects. A collaboration with various non-human agents. In my case performance has also invariably involved written scripts or protocols. The latter work as a kind of scaffolding that holds things together or stops them coming apart at any rate: something that is there—a kind of prompt—but that might be departed from too (and invariably is). After all, a performance is also about summoning something unexpected, something that cannot be fully worked out from this side of things. Sometimes this written text can work on its own—as its own work—as well as this kind of prompt; as a record of what went on, but also, perhaps, as a script that might be repeated elsewhere. When a performance is especially concerned with building or summoning a world then it might also involve some further props (a world needs at least some details like this). It is not as if these need to be accurate or realistic exactly. Indeed, they might be amateur, more 'thrown together' or just involve an 'outline' as it were. In fact, this foregrounding of the representational status of these props—so not the use of real things but representations of things—seems important (I'll return to this below as well). Or, to say the same differently, with performance it is more often the case that representations are put into play.

4. *Performance involves a scene.* If the performers and props (broadly understood) are the material components, then the scene—that I have already mentioned in relation to the audience—is the larger context. On the one hand this scene is simply the history of performance that means it works as a meaningful genre or is something that signifies. But it might also mean the context of contemporary art more broadly

when this includes as well the spaces and places of such art (not just galleries, but those spaces and places that have been designated—even temporarily—as a space for performance). As well as anything else (and alongside any issues and impasses) contemporary art opens up a space where things can happen that are unlikely to happen elsewhere. Following on from my comments above, a scene—or different scenes— will also involve different groups of people in different locations. Different countries and, within them, different towns and cities, for example, have different art scenes, with different expectations therein and, following this, often with different sets of audience responses. This becomes very apparent if you do a similar performance in different locations.[8] As David Burrows has pointed out these scenes might also be understood as the generator of art more generally (see Burrows 2010). This is to foreground what is already in play in this essay: that art, here performance, is always more than simply the intention and product of a single author. It is always already collectively produced in some senses. To stay with Burrows—and to repeat a point I made above—a scene might also be understood in a larger and more inclusive sense as involving different non-human actors.[9] So, props again but also, perhaps, other fictions (that operate as effective agents in a milieu, to return to that idea laid out in my first essay). We are beginning to move away from a certain register of reality and conscious intention here and, with that, to widen performance's realm of possible agents and operations. A performance involves the working together of these different material agents, but then it can also involve a summoning of other more immaterial agents too. Is this a real summoning or a fictioned one? When push comes to shove, is there a difference (or, again, as I suggested in my first essay, if a fiction has real effects, then is it, to that extent, real)?

5. *Performance is both presentation and representation.* On the one hand the history of performance—or a history anyway—is one of breaking the frame and, with that, presenting life as art.[10] Performance is part of an avant-garde tradition of introducing non-artistic media and material into the realm of art (in this case it is especially the body that is introduced). A couple of key antecedents of performance in this sense are Dada (and especially the Cabaret Voltaire) and the Situationists

(especially with the creation of situations), although both of these also—and crucially—pitched their practices against existing definitions and practices of art. In terms of the latter—the Situationists—there is an attempt at reclaiming life away from its representation (or away from what Guy Debord called 'The Spectacle'). In terms of the former—Dada—there is an intention to break with an all pervasive 'reality effect' (and with a certain regime of sense that is both cause and effect of that). More generally, both Dada and the Situationists were concerned with uncovering or foregrounding another way of being from within this one, and, crucially, enacting this other mode. Performance can also be understood as the acting out of something different within the everyday or that is then set against that more typical reality as a background. Here the nesting of one set-up within another does something to our more typical perspective. Performance can allow a point of view back on the pre-existing world in this sense, which is then also seen *as* another kind of set-up. This is a curious and compelling aspect of performance—even a kind of 'side effect'—that produces this 'outside knowledge' through a counter-intuitive method of performing another reality.

6. *Performance is a fiction that transforms.* In many ways all of the above points are covered by this idea that performance is a fiction, but certainly there are practices—again, what Burrows and I have called 'performance fictions'—that foreground this fictioning aspect.[11] These practices are specifically concerned with a kind of narrative function (even a storytelling function) and especially one that is embodied in some manner. This might be explicit or it might be implied by the various performers, props and so forth. Key here is that the performance might not only be telling a story but also, again, embodying—or instantiating—it in some manner. In fact, a performance fiction might involve both of these perspectives at once. So speaking about another place but also, in some senses, from that other place too (this is the 'as if' reporting back that I mentioned above). Performance can be a kind of materialisation of a fiction in this sense. In order for the fiction to work at least some of the above protocols and set-ups need to be in place. The audience needs to 'buy in', at least to some extent. The performers need to be not only who they are but also these other figures who will have

arrived. The props need to have been assembled. The right scene needs to be set up and present too. And, alongside this—and partly enabled by it—there is also the strange nesting of representation that can then be put to work. In terms of that last point—and to broaden things out slightly—it seems to me that we are always already 'in' a performance in some senses. But to return to perhaps the key point in what I have laid out here, performing within that performance seems to show us something about the performance we always already are (as if it allows an outside perspective on this). This effect of performance—and specifically performance fiction—seems to operate whatever any other function of narrative might be in play (so, again, is a kind of secondary effect that uses the storytelling function to do its work).

All of the above components make up what might be thought of as a kind of device. It's not exactly that this device has a pre-set purpose, more as if it is being set up with no knowledge—or no exact knowledge—of what might then occur. The set-up is produced blindly in some senses, which is what makes performance sometimes tricky but always generative. But when it does work, when it all clicks into gear—or, as I say above, when the device starts working—and one can hear the right sort of whirring, then one is taken up and away as sometimes is the audience too (or, to say the same but from a different perspective, something else is made present or, at least, foregrounded). All the preparations before a performance (and, indeed, all the definitions and reflections written above) are simply a platform so as to allow this other stranger functioning to do its work. Performance is a magical device in this sense, one that might be set against or even re-purpose other more technical devices or, indeed, mobilise other more aesthetic devices. It is a simple kind of device in many ways, but complex too insofar as it operates on a number of different registers, signifying and asignifying (or affective). Performance fiction more specifically can also be both a device and a representation of a device. Indeed, to repeat the point above, sometimes all of this magical functioning is simply a staged fiction with the performance operating 'as if' it really was summoning other entities. But then this is the more secret functioning of performance fiction that blurs this edge between real and 'make believe' (after all, from a wider perspective both of these are just set-ups which are invested in to one degree or another). And that also goes for the fiction of the self too which, in this context, is simply one further component of the scene or device, itself a particular performance fiction that, at times, needs to be set aside (or stepped away from) so that those other fictions can then get up and begin do their work.[12]

Coda

I remember a performance in an old chapel. We were all on a stage in amongst various props, objects and other devices. All of us had microphones and instruments of one kind or another. Behind us there was a projected film of animations and images with other scenes and stories being played out. The sounds started quietly enough. A gentle drone with some percussion and the occasional word spoken aloud. Gradually though the sounds got louder with more layers added and instruments joining in. Louder still and soon it was deafening. Someone on stage was shouting out a call and response to the other figures there. A series of names perhaps? There was a lull and someone else suddenly shouted out 'where's the dragon?' Then again, louder this time, 'WHERE'S THE DRAGON?'

From the back of the dark hall, something appears. A mass of gold with some kind of long pole coming from one end. On the end of the pole is a painted wooden cut-out of a dragon's head. The body is moving in time to the music, then weaving in and out of the gathered crowd. The dragon progresses towards the stage, its head bobbing up and down in time to the sounds that have now built up again to a frenzy. There are other members of Plastique Fantastique down there in the crowd dancing like insects. There's singing from the front and more images on the screen. The call and response starts up again. More names are shouted out. It's all on an edge. All just about to collapse. But then it doesn't. And because it's not collapsing, it sails that edge, tacks into that wind. It's as if this dragon has been called forth by something that moves through all of them gathered there. Something that all the rehearsals had been preparing for. All that work had simply been a platform, put together piece by piece, that has now allowed this other thing to foreground itself. And all the while the other avatars of Plastique Fantastique are focussed on the various instruments and other devices up on that stage, pushing them further and further, allowing them to work back on all this; to tell them—and the others gathered there—where they need to go. And from out here—looking back at this set-up—it looks as if the whole arrangement had been planned somehow. As if this scene that is now here had called back to all of them from some future time so that they might gather and enact it. And, as always, this is the puzzle of it all. From this side of things there is the struggle and the practice. The taking of a chance and of trying this and then that out. And then, when finally it's done, it's as if it had already been done or was always going to be like this. In fact, could be no other way. There is a whole crowd of figures on that stage now. Some other deeper assignment is at work that has used this performance and this gathering as components in its own summoning. And there it is now, apparent to those who are on the look out for such things. A second dragon that doubles the wooden one still dancing in the crowd there. It stretches its huge wings, turn its head to survey the scene then takes off and begins its climb into the sky.

Notes

1 This is then to return to and develop some aspects of the concept and practice of performance fictions as laid out in *Fictioning*, defined in that book as 'producing "a zone of activity that once entered produces a shift in how relations are understood and formed" (Burrows), and that describes a presentation and performance that "speaks back to its producer—or simply goes beyond any straightforward intention" (O'Sullivan)' (Burrows and O'Sullivan 2019: 5–6).
2 For an initial attempt at mapping out the different operating protocols and, indeed, various components and materials of this collaborative practice (again, from my side of things), see O'Sullivan 2010. For a more recent attempt that also extracts some protocols and parameters (in relation to myth-work) see O'Sullivan 2016a. And finally for another take on Plastique Fantastique and, indeed, collective art practice as the production of a 'holding pattern' for points of collapse (and also as a practice of 'Non-schizoanalysis') see Burrows and O'Sullivan 2014. For an archive of Plastique Fantastique performances and other installations, objects and texts see www.plastiquefantastique.org/index.html (accessed 18 January 2024). My comments in this essay relate to Plastique Fantastique performances up until 2021.
3 See Plastique Fantastique's *Zoom Ritual to Tell Stories*, part of *This is a Not-Me* (curated by Mark Jackson), IMT Gallery, London, 2020 (available at: https://imagemusictext.com/exhibition-this-is-a-not-me/, accessed 18 January 2024).
4 This 'taking off' has been my experience with a number of Plastique Fantastique performances, but especially the *Summoning the Bitcoin Fairy* at Southwark Park Galleries (Dilston Grove) in September 2016 and *The Seed Archive Breakout and the Burning of Elon Musk*

(Mars Year Zero) at the same venue in September 2019 (see www.plastiquefantastique. org/performance31.html and www.plastiquefantastique.org/performance44.html, both accessed 18 January 2024). I think in both cases the architectural set-up played a key part. I give a brief fictioned account of the second of these performances in a coda to this essay (see also Fig. 14.1 in the colour plate section for an image of the installation by Plastique Fantastique).

5 See for example *Myth-Science Fiction: Evolution of Time-Stretcher*, performed at various venues in 2014, and which explicitly involved the 'taking on' of other avatars (see: www. plastiquefantastique.org/performance25.html, accessed 18 January 2024). Another example that involved a kind of channelling (and included Harriet Skully as part of Plastique Fantastique) was *Diagram of (Urb-Fux Glitter) Addiction*, also performed at various venues in 2015 (see: www.plastiquefantastique.org/performance26.html and www.plastiquefantastique.org/performance27.html, both accessed 18 January 2024) (see also Fig. 14.2 in the colour plate section).

6 On this point see the presentations and discussions—on the relationship of Magick and art (and especially performance)—in Burrows and Sharp 2009.

7 For an account of the gathering and assembling of various objects and props—in relation to the performance *Plastique Fantastique 24-hour Puja for the People-yet-to-Come*, at Space Station 65, London, in 2006—see Lynch and O'Sullivan 2007.

8 There is in addition the question of performances that are outside in the landscape. In these cases, performance also works to transform that set-up or, at least, our perspective on it (as was the case with the *Plastique Fantastique Ribbon Dance Ritual to call forth the Pre-Industrial Modern* that took place in an urban landscape, Birmingham city centre, in April 2007 (see: www.plastiquefantastique.org/performance02.html, accessed 18 January 2024) and *Plastique Fantastique Triple Castration Ritual: Welcome Tat-Not* that was part of *The Visitation* installation and took place in the rural setting of Tatton Park as part of the 2010 Biennale there (see: www.plastiquefantastique.org/performance11. html, also accessed 18 January 2024). In each of these cases the performance also changed the sense of what these places—or landscapes—are *for*.

9 For more detail on art scenes in this sense—understood from a Deleuzian perspective—see Burrows 2010.

10 See for example the practice of Carolee Schneemann (and the discussion in Burrows and O'Sullivan 2019: 270-2).

11 For a theoretically informed account of a performance fiction in this sense—*The Chymical Wedding*, a parade and ritual performed at Tate Britain in January 2008—see Burrows and O'Sullivan 2010. This article additionally tackles a crucial issue—for Plastique Fantastique—that also concerns the fiction of the self: shame. Shame is a kind of subjective/non-subjective technology that tells you something about where you are and, indeed, the limits of a certain sense of self.

12 The setting aside or disabling of the fiction of the self—in order to summon other fictions—was in play in the performance *Cloud Gives Birth to New Animal: Plastique Fantastique Welcome Neuropatheme*. There were two versions of this multimedia performance, the first at Performance Space, London, in October 2012 as part of *Performance Matters* (organised by Gavin Butt and Lois Keidan), and the second at the ICA, London, in January 2013, as part of *Long Live the New Flesh*, curated by Open File (Tim Dixon and Jack Brindley).

Afterword

In place of a conclusion, I want to offer up four further brief reflections—or inflections—on some of the key themes of my book and especially the process of writing about them.

Magic and Anamorphosis

Looking back at the 14 essays—all of them initially drafted over a period of two years—it seems to me that they constitute a set-up or context for something else to take place (as I have intimated in a few of the essays themselves). Another kind of work perhaps? Or a performance of some kind? Certainly, there is a limit to writing scholarly (or even partially scholarly) essays about magic and myth-work. Something else needs to be enacted for the kinds of transformations at stake to take place. But on the other hand—and as I hope I have made clear in at least some of the essays—writing can also, at times, be its own myth-work or, indeed, constitute a magical technology of sorts. Although writing is necessarily intended it can involve an unintended summoning too. This is especially the case with techniques like the cut-up—as well as with fiction more generally—but it seems to me that any and all writing can involve a sidestepping of the self. Writing 'speaks back' in this sense. Or it can seem as if it came from another place, which in some senses it has (this is why it has such a connection to psychoanalysis and schizoanalysis).

Indeed, besides the arguments put forward, these essays have ushered a number of different figures and props on to a kind of stage, which has then allowed other things to come into focus (at least for myself).

The writing process seems to involve these anamorphic moments when a different set-up becomes foregrounded within the one that is more familiar (which is another way of putting the 'speaking back' I mentioned above). As I've suggested in some of the essays, this can also be the case with reading which, at times, can produce these anamorphic shifts (especially with works of fiction and works that involve fiction). Writing can frame the fiction of the self—a key concern of these essays—in this sense too. It can give a kind of perspective back on that fiction which then allows a little space to be opened up. This also means—at least in some cases—that other fictions can be taken up or entered into more fully.

Myth-Work and Its Devices

This shift and the way fiction enables it has also been at stake in some of those artworks I have looked at as case studies of myth-work (many of which involve writing and all of which involve performance in some sense). Often this myth-work has involved some kind of temporal shift too or an actualisation/activation of a different space-time. Throughout the essays I have often gathered these ideas around the figure of the device. Indeed, another take on what these essays have been about—and as I also mentioned in my Introduction—is as the locating and tracking of these different devices that allow different perspectives (and times) to be further enacted or performed in some manner.

For myself and in my own myth-work, this has meant an opening up of all the cupboards to see what's in there and then laying it all out as on a tabletop or as a landscape (to return to a further key theme of these essays). Hence the inevitable repetitions with some of my other writings (and the referencing of the latter throughout). What components might be repurposed for other ends? And then what, perhaps, needs discarding? In fact, some of the more directly therapeutic writing that was part of this self-enquiry did not make it into this book, but certainly, reading these essays through, it's clear they all come from this personal investment. Making a device in this way—as well as anything else—allows you to 'see' the device that you are (to give the fiction of the self this other inflection) and, with that, perhaps also see other devices that might be out there (and crucially to see these other devices *as* devices).

Autowriting versus Collaboration

Despite some of my comments above—and my attempt to do something a little bit different with this book—to a certain extent what's been laid out in these essays is also familiar territory. Or, at least, there has been a certain amount of control at stake. It's not easy to shrug off the genre one is more used to (or located within). On reflection it seems to me that in order for writing to really 'speak back' as if from some other place then something else needs introducing into any restricted set-up. Or, perhaps, something else needs to be lured in so as to disrupt that set-up? There needs to be an opening at any rate. A gap in any chalk circle that is drawn. Collaboration can allow this interrogation of a given archive and an 'opening up' of a given self. A collaboration also opens the door to other stranger collaborations with other agencies and, indeed, helps us understand the collaborations we are always already partaking of.

This is a key paradox of my essays (that follows from concerns I have always had). They are both about the fiction of the self and an attempt to track other agencies always already at work 'beneath' or besides this self (when this includes fictional agencies too). Collaboration, although it can be difficult, works as a kind of counter-tendency to autowriting in this respect. The latter is an important genre or practice in many ways (not least in exploring the fiction of the self), but it seems to me that a device built by a collaboration might offer up further insights into those other agencies that are always at work. That kind of device might also be a little more open to redeployment elsewhere, untethered as it is from a single author, however fragmented or distributed the latter might be.[1]

Writing as Care and Repair

Writing these essays has also increasingly been a survival strategy of sorts. In particular, and again looking back, it was the ongoing relationship with the work that kept me going during some difficult times (and especially the process of returning each day to the drafts and reading them over to see what I had been about). It is in this sense that writing has been my own repair work (as implied in some of my essays), conducted alongside those other enquiries into care and repair more generally (so, to say it again, locating circuits between my own subjectivity and other resources and agencies, as well as circuits between the present I am in and other pasts and futures). The knotting together of a self then—from out of these various lines and loops—that at times seemed as if it might come apart (especially during those initial Covid years). But alongside this, writing has also been a way of loosening up some other already tightly tied knots (in my case—as I've mentioned a few times—a self that is an especially anxious set-up) so as to be able to explore other fictions and other landscapes. Once again, and somewhat paradoxically, the care and repair of the self can involve attention to that which is outside the fiction of the self too.

As I've mentioned in some of the essays, at the outset it wasn't clear what this writing project was going to be about—there weren't any blueprints or plans—more a case of identifying some of the key signifiers and 'quilting points' that had asked to be written out. What objects, practices and especially texts had foregrounded themselves as important (in my own writing and artistic practices and teaching, but also life more generally)? Why were these important? How were they working? Then, crucially, what implications might be drawn from them? I hope my attempts to answer the latter question especially mean that what I offer up here is more than just a looping around of a given fiction and that some of it might be useful—or perhaps work as a trigger?—for your own myth-work and practices of care and repair.

This is a book about magic and myth-work then, but one that is also itself a case in point: a book about care and repair that is also my attempt at these two practices. Perhaps this is to say nothing more than that a book can be a very particular kind of device and that a book about devices can itself be a particular kind of device too.

Note

1 I think this might be the case with *Fictioning*, the book I co-authored with David Burrows and which these essays operate as a supplement to (although, of course, I am not the best judge of that) (Burrows and O'Sullivan 2019).

Bibliography

Acker, Kathy (1984), *Blood and Guts in High School, Plus Two*, London: Picador.

Acker, Kathy and M. Wark (2015), *I'm Very into You: Correspondence 1995–1996*, New York: Semiotext(e).

Alado-McDowell, K. (2020), *Pharmako-AI*, Newcastle-on-Tyne: Ignota.

Amaro, Ramon (2019), 'As If', *e-flux*, available at: www.e-flux.com/architecture/becoming-digital/248073/as-if/ (accessed 18 January 2024).

Armah, Adjoa (2022), 'In Conversation: Adjoa Armah, Abe Odedina and Hannah Catherine Jones', *Auto Italia*, available at: https://autoitaliasoutheast.org/events/in-conversation-adjoa-armah-abe-odedina-and-hannah-catherine-jones/ (accessed 16 October 2023).

Artaud, Antonin (1995), 'Ci-Git/Here Lies', *Watchfiends and Rack Screams: Works from the Final Period*, ed. and trans. C. Eshleman and B. Bador, Boston: Exact Change, pp. 191–239.

Asprem, Egil (2018), 'The Magical Theory of Politics: Meme Magic, the Cult of Kek, and How to Topple an Egregore', available at: https://contern.files.wordpress.com/2018/05/asprem-magical-theory-of-politics-nova-religio-pre-print-may-13-2018.pdf (accessed 5 September 2021).

Audint (2017), 'A Century of Zombie Sound', *Futures and Fictions*, ed. H. Gunkell, A. Hameed and S. O'Sullivan, London: Repeater, pp. 347–78.

Auto Italia (2022), 'Auto Italia, Projects, The sea, it slopes like a mountain'. Auto Italia, London, 28 April 2022 – 24 July 2022: Adjoa Armah', exhibition page, available at: https://autoitaliasoutheast.org/projects/the-sea-it-slopes-like-a-mountain/ (accessed 4 April 2023).

Badiou, Alain (2009), *Logics of Worlds: Being and Event 2*, trans. A. Toscano, London: Continuum.

Badiou, Alain and É. Roudinesco (2014), *Jacques Lacan Past and Present: A Dialogue*, trans. J. E. Smith, Columbia University Press.

Barthes, Roland (1973), *Mythologies*, trans. A. Lavers, London: Paladin.

—— (1989), 'The Reality Effect', *The Rustle of Language*, trans. R. Howard, Berkeley: University of California Press, pp. 3–10.

—— (2011), *The Preparation of the Novel: Lecture Courses and Seminars at the College de France (1978–1979 and 1979–1980)*, trans. K. Briggs, New York: Columbia University Press.

Barton, Justin (2015), *Hidden Valleys: Haunted by the Future*, Winchester: Zero Books.

—— (2021), *Outsights: Disappearances of Literature*, available at: https://infinite-distance-b83ea.web.app/justin-barton-and-mark-fisher (accessed 1 April 2022).

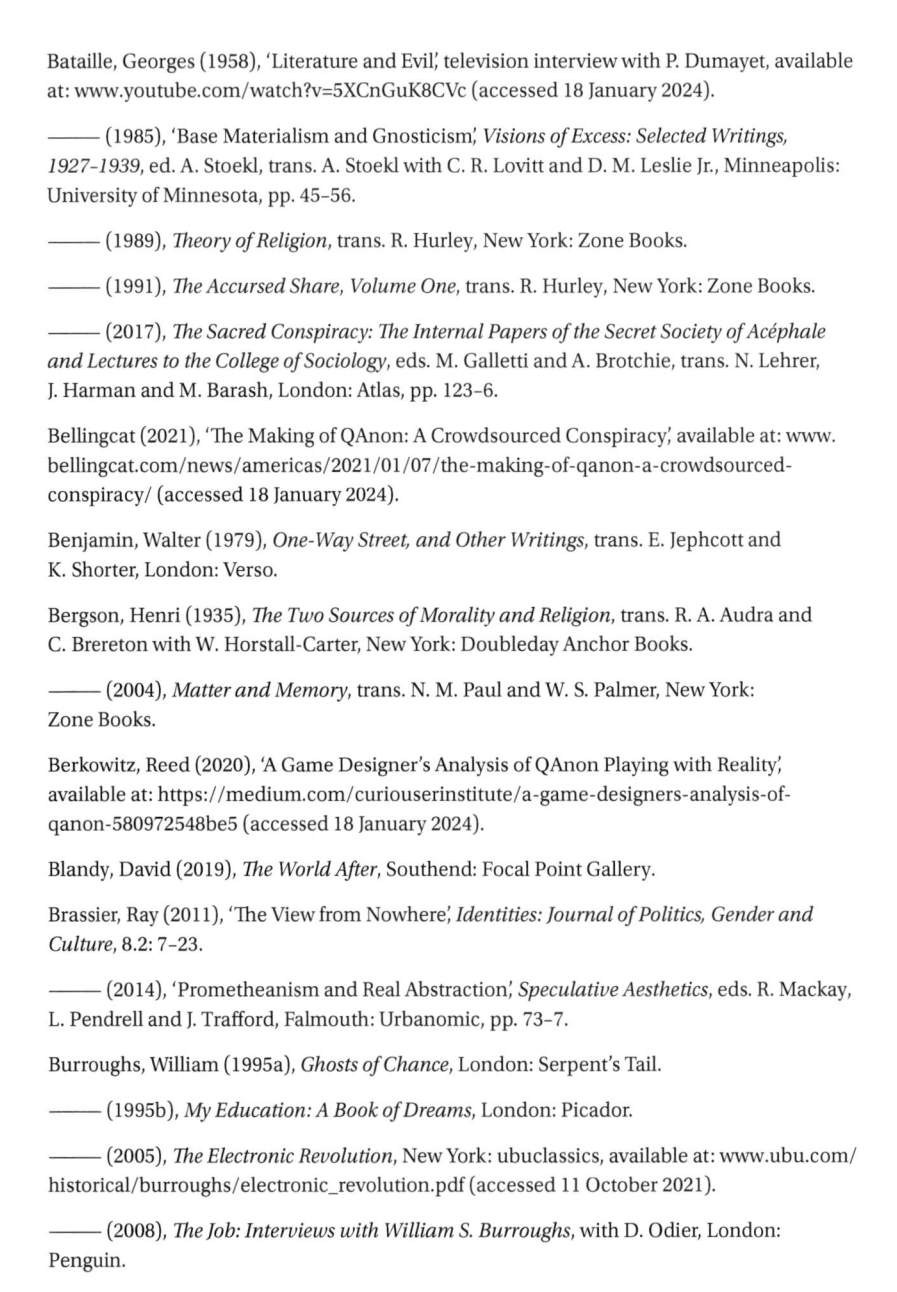

Bataille, Georges (1958), 'Literature and Evil', television interview with P. Dumayet, available at: www.youtube.com/watch?v=5XCnGuK8CVc (accessed 18 January 2024).

—— (1985), 'Base Materialism and Gnosticism', *Visions of Excess: Selected Writings, 1927-1939*, ed. A. Stoekl, trans. A. Stoekl with C. R. Lovitt and D. M. Leslie Jr., Minneapolis: University of Minnesota, pp. 45-56.

—— (1989), *Theory of Religion*, trans. R. Hurley, New York: Zone Books.

—— (1991), *The Accursed Share, Volume One*, trans. R. Hurley, New York: Zone Books.

—— (2017), *The Sacred Conspiracy: The Internal Papers of the Secret Society of Acéphale and Lectures to the College of Sociology*, eds. M. Galletti and A. Brotchie, trans. N. Lehrer, J. Harman and M. Barash, London: Atlas, pp. 123-6.

Bellingcat (2021), 'The Making of QAnon: A Crowdsourced Conspiracy', available at: www.bellingcat.com/news/americas/2021/01/07/the-making-of-qanon-a-crowdsourced-conspiracy/ (accessed 18 January 2024).

Benjamin, Walter (1979), *One-Way Street, and Other Writings*, trans. E. Jephcott and K. Shorter, London: Verso.

Bergson, Henri (1935), *The Two Sources of Morality and Religion*, trans. R. A. Audra and C. Brereton with W. Horstall-Carter, New York: Doubleday Anchor Books.

—— (2004), *Matter and Memory*, trans. N. M. Paul and W. S. Palmer, New York: Zone Books.

Berkowitz, Reed (2020), 'A Game Designer's Analysis of QAnon Playing with Reality', available at: https://medium.com/curiouserinstitute/a-game-designers-analysis-of-qanon-580972548be5 (accessed 18 January 2024).

Blandy, David (2019), *The World After*, Southend: Focal Point Gallery.

Brassier, Ray (2011), 'The View from Nowhere', *Identities: Journal of Politics, Gender and Culture*, 8.2: 7-23.

—— (2014), 'Prometheanism and Real Abstraction', *Speculative Aesthetics*, eds. R. Mackay, L. Pendrell and J. Trafford, Falmouth: Urbanomic, pp. 73-7.

Burroughs, William (1995a), *Ghosts of Chance*, London: Serpent's Tail.

—— (1995b), *My Education: A Book of Dreams*, London: Picador.

—— (2005), *The Electronic Revolution*, New York: ubuclassics, available at: www.ubu.com/historical/burroughs/electronic_revolution.pdf (accessed 11 October 2021).

—— (2008), *The Job: Interviews with William S. Burroughs*, with D. Odier, London: Penguin.

Burrows, David (2010), 'An Art Scene as Big as the Ritz: The Logic of Scenes', *Deleuze and Contemporary Art*, ed. S. Zepke and S. O'Sullivan, Edinburgh: Edinburgh University Press, pp. 157-75.

―――― (2020), 'Science Fictioning Singularities: The Diagrammatic Imaginaries of Physics', *Data Loam: Sometimes Hard, Usually Soft. The Future of Knowledge Systems*, ed. J. Golding, Berlin: De Gruyter, pp. 38–64.

―――― (2024), *Fictioning Devices: The Cosmopolitical Functions of Contemporary Art*, London: Bloomsbury.

Burrows, David and S. O'Sullivan (2010), 'The Chymical Wedding: Performance Art as Masochistic Practice (an Account, the Contracts and Further Reflections)', *Angelaki*, 15.1: 139–48.

―――― (2014), 'The Sinthome/Z-Point Relation or Art as Non-Schizoanalysis', *Schizoanalysis and Art*, ed. I. Buchanan and L. Simpson, London: Bloomsbury, pp. 253–78.

―――― (2019), *Fictioning: The Myth-Functions of Contemporary Art and Philosophy*, Edinburgh: Edinburgh University Press.

―――― (2022), 'Science Fiction Devices', *New Perspectives on Academic Writing*, London: Bloomsbury, pp. 39–52.

Burrows, David and A. Sharp, with J. Cussans (2009), *Magick*, London: Stanley Picker.

CAConrad (2014), *Ecodeviance: (Soma)tics for the Future Wilderness*, Seattle and New York: Have books.

Castaneda, Carlos (1974), *Tales of Power*, London: Simon and Schuster.

Ccru (Cybernetic culture research unit) (n.d.), 'Hyperstition', available at: https://web.archive.org/web/20030204195934/http://ccru.net/syzygy.htm (accessed 5 September 2021).

―――― (2017), 'Lemurian Time War', *Ccru Writings 1997–2003*, Falmouth: Urbanomic/Time Spiral Press, pp. 33–52.

Chare, Nicholas (2011), 'Writing Perceptions: The Matter of Words and the Rollright Stones', *Art History*, 34.2: 244–67.

Chiang, Ted (2019), *Exhalation*, London: Picador.

Chude-Sokei, Louis Onuorah (2016), *The Sound of Culture: Diaspora and Black Technopoetics*, Middletown, CT: Wesleyan University Press.

Cixous, Hélène (1981), 'The Laugh of the Medusa', trans. K. Cohen and P. Cohen, *Signs*, 1.4: 875–93 (reprinted in *New French Feminisms: An Anthology*, eds. E. Marks and I. de Courtivron, Hemel Hempstead: Harvester Wheatsheaf, pp. 245–64).

―――― (1993), *Three Steps on the Ladder of Writing*, trans. S. Cornell and S. Sellers, New York: Columbia University Press.

Clarke, Helen and S. Kivland (2017), *The Lost Diagrams of Walter Benjamin*, London: MA Bibliothèque.

Cooper, Susan (1973), *The Dark Is Rising*, London: Macmillan.

Cussans, John (2010), 'The Para-Psychic Properties of Marmalade', *Performance Fictions*, ed. D. Burrows, Birmingham: Article Press, pp. 15–46.

Deakin, Roger (1999), *Waterlog: A Swimmer's Journey through Britain*, London: Chatto and Windus.

Debord, Guy (1957), 'Report on the Construction of Situations and on the International Situationist Tendency's Conditions of Organization and Action', trans. K. Knabb, available at: www.bopsecrets.org (accessed 18 January 2024).

Deleuze, Gilles (1989), *Cinema 2: The Time-Image*, trans H. Tomlinson and R. Galeta, London: Athlone Press.

—— (1994), *Difference and Repetition*, trans. P. Patton, New York: Columbia University Press.

Deleuze, Gilles and F. Guattari (1984), *Anti-Oedipus: Capitalism and Schizophrenia*, ed. J-A. Miller, trans. R. Hurley, M. Seem and H. R. Lane, London: Athlone Press.

—— (1988), *A Thousand Plateaus*, trans. B. Massumi, London: Athlone Press.

Deller, Jeremy (2013), *English Magic*, London: British Council.

Edison Harding, Douglas (1961), *On Having No Head*, London: Shollond Trust.

Eshun, Kodwo (1998), *More Brilliant Than the Sun: Adventures in Sonic Fiction*, London: Quartet.

—— (2003), 'Further Considerations of Afrofuturism', *CR: The New Centennial Review*, 3.2: 287–302.

Federici, Silvia (2014), *Caliban and the Witch: Women, the Body and Primitive Accumulation*, New York: Autonomia.

Ferreira da Silva, Denise (2017), '1 (life) ÷ 0 (blackness) = ∞ − ∞ or ∞ / ∞: On Matter Beyond the Equation of Value', *e-flux*, 79, available at: www.e-flux.com/journal/79/94686/1-life-0-blackness-or-on-matter-beyond-the-equation-of-value/.

Fink, Bruce (1995), *The Lacanian Subject: Between Language and Jouissance*, Princeton: Princeton University Press.

Fisher, Mark (2009), *Capitalist Realism: Is There No Alternative?*, London: Zero.

—— (2014), *Ghosts of My Life: Writings on Depression, Hauntology and Lost Futures*, London: Zero Books.

—— (2016), *The Weird and the Eerie*, London: Repeater.

—— (2018), *K-Punk: The Uncollected and Unpublished Writings of Mark Fisher (2004–2016)*, ed. D. Ambrose, London: Repeater.

Foucault, Michel (1984), 'What Is an Author?', trans. J. V. Harari, *The Foucault Reader*, ed. P. Rabinow, New York: Pantheon Books, pp. 101–20.

―― (2000), *Ethics: Subjectivity and Truth (Essential Works of Foucault, 1954-84, Volume One)*, trans. R. Hurley, ed. P. Rabinow, Harmondsworth: Penguin.

―― (2005), *The Hermeneutics of the Subject: Lectures at the College de France 1981-82*, ed. F. Gros, trans. G. Burchell, London: Palgrave.

Frazer, J. G. (1983 [1922]), *The Golden Bough: A Study in Magic and Religion*, Basingstoke: Macmillan.

Freud, Sigmund (2002), *Civilization and Its Discontents*, trans. D. McLintock, London: Penguin Classics.

Garner, Alan (1960), *The Weirdstone of Brisingamen*, London: Harper Collins.

―― (1973), *Red Shift*, Glasgow: William Collins Sons and Co Ltd.

―― (2022), *Treacle Walker*, London: Fourth Estate.

Gauthier, Xavière (1981 [1976]), 'Why Witches?', trans. E. M. Elsinger, *New French Feminisms: An Anthology*, eds. E. Marks and I. de Courtivron, Hemel Hempstead: Harvester Wheatsheaf, pp. 199-203.

Genosko, Gary (2022), 'Schizoanalysis and Magic', *Deleuze and Guattari Studies*, 16.4: 529-44.

Gilroy, Paul (1995), *The Black Atlantic: Modernity and Double-Consciousness*, Cambridge, MA: Harvard University Press.

Glissant, Édouard (2010), *Poetics of Relation*, trans. B. Wing, Ann Arbor: University of Michigan Press.

Gray, Ros and S. Sheik (2018), 'The Wretched Earth: Botanical Conflicts and Artistic Interventions', *Third Text*, 32.2-3: 163-75.

Gruppo di Nun (2022), *Revolutionary Demonology*, Falmouth: Urbanomic.

Guattari, Félix (1989), *The Three Ecologies*, trans. I. Pinder and P. Sutton, London: Athlone.

―― (1995a), 'The New Aesthetic Paradigm' and 'Schizoanalytic Metamodelisation', *Chaosmosis: An Ethico-Aesthetic Paradigm*, trans. P. Bains and J. Pefanis, Sydney: Power Institute, pp. 58-76 and 98-118.

―― (1995b), 'On the Production of Subjectivity', *Chaosmosis: An Ethico-Aesthetic Paradigm*, trans. P. Bains and J. Pefanis, Sydney: Power Institute, pp. 1-32.

―― (1996a), 'Subjectivities: for Better and for Worse', *The Guattari Reader*, ed. G. Genosko, Oxford: Blackwell, pp. 193-203.

―― (1996b), 'A Liberation of Desire: An Interview with George Stambolian', *The Guattari Reader*, ed. Gary Genosko, Oxford: Blackwell, pp. 204-14.

―― (2013), 'Genet Regained', *Schizoanalytic Cartographies*, trans. A. Goffey, London: Bloomsbury, pp. 215-30.

Guy, Lesley (2024), 'I Am An Us: Exploring the Boundaries of a Shared Art Practice', PhD Dissertation, University of Northumberland.

Hadot, Pierre (1995), *Philosophy as a Way of Life: Spiritual Exercises from Socrates to Foucault*, trans. A. Davidson, Oxford: Blackwell.

Haiven, Max (2022), 'Financialization's Culture of Revenge', invited talk, Volatility Cultures series, Goldsmiths, London.

Halford, Victoria and S. Beard (dir.) (2011), *Voodoo Science Park*, 25 mins., available at: https://vimeo.com/48746036 (accessed 10 September 2021).

—— (2011), *Voodoo Science Park*, Winchester: Zero Books.

Haraway, Donna (1988), 'Situated Knowledges: The Science Question in Feminism and the Privilege of Partial Perspective', *Feminist Studies*, 14. 3: 575–99.

—— (2016), *Staying with the Trouble: Making Kin in the Chthulucene*, Durham, NC: Duke University Press.

Harney, Stefano and F. Moten (2013), *The Undercommons: Fugitive Planning and Black Study*, New York: Autonomedia.

Hart, William (1987), *The Art of Living: Vipassana Meditation as Taught by S. N. Goenka*, New York: Harper and Row.

Hayles, N. Katherine (2017), *Unthought: The Power of the Cognitive Unconscious*, Chicago: University of Chicago Press.

Hiller, Susan (2000), *Dream Machines*, exhibition catalogue, London: Hayward Gallery Publishing.

—— (2010), 'Map Marathon 2010: Susan Hiller', talk at serpentine Gallery, London, 16 October, available at: https://vimeo.com/25789788?login=true#_=_ (accessed 10 January 2023).

Hine, Phil (2022), discussion with J. Sutcliffe and P. McCormack, 'Magic: Documents of Contemporary Art', Whitechapel Gallery, London, available at: www.youtube.com/watch?v=pUOYhzZkxwk (accessed 12 February 2024).

Hoban, Russell (1980), *Riddley Walker*, London: Bloomsbury.

Hughes, Allan and M. Rohtmaa-Jackson (Blue Mountain Arcturus) (2022), 'Citadel of Chaos: An Art Practice to Materialise an Alternate Present', *Vector*, 24 August 2022, available at: https://vector-bsfa.com/2022/08/24/citadel-of-chaos-an-art-practice-to-materialise-an-alternate-present/#more-11758 (accessed 10 November 2022).

Ireland, Amy (2017) 'The Poememenon: Form as Occult Technology', *Urbanomic Documents*, available at: www.urbanomic.com/document/poememenon/ (accessed 5 September 2021).

—— (2022a), 'Is Crypto Patriarchy's Newest Tech?', *Spike*, 70: 58–9.

—— (2022b), 'Scrap Metal and Fabric: Weaving as Temporal Technology', *Agorism in the Twenty First Century*, 1: 57–75, available at: https://agorist.xyz/ (accessed 18 January 2024).

—— (2022c), talk at 'Cultivating Darkness', launch of Gruppo di Nun's *Revolutionary Demonology*, KARST, Plymouth, 15 December 2022.

Ishiguro, Kazuo (2015), *The Buried Giant*, London: Faber and Faber.

Jameson, Fredric (2005), *Archaeologies of the Future*, London: Verso.

Jung, Carl (1978), *Man and His Symbols*, London: Picador.

Kenning, Dean (2020), 'Foreword' to Andy Sharp, *The English Heretic Collection: Ritual Histories, Magickal Geography*, London: Repeater Books, pp. 9–15.

Kingsnorth, Paul (2014), *The Wake*, London: Unbound.

Kraus, Chris (2017), *After Kathy Acker*, New York: Semiotext(e).

Lacan, Jacques (1983), *The Psychoses: The Seminar of Jacques Lacan, Book III, 1955–1956*, ed. R. Grigg, trans. J-A. Miller, London: W. W. Norton and Co.

—— (1992), *The Ethics of Psychoanalysis 1959–1960: The Seminar of Jacque Lacan, Book VII*, ed. J-A. Miller, trans. D. Porter, New York: W. W. Norton and Co.

—— (2018), *The Sinthome: The Seminar of Jacque Lacan, Book XXIII*, trans. A. R. Price, Cambridge: Polity Press.

Laing, Olivia (2018), *Crudo*, London: Picador.

Land, Nick (1992), *The Thirst for Annihilation: Georges Bataille and Virulent Nihilism*, London: Routledge.

—— (2011), 'Circuitries', *Fanged Noumena: Collected Writings 1987–2007*, eds. R. Mackay and R. Brassier, Falmouth: Urbanomic/New York: Sequence, pp. 289–318.

Laruelle, François (2004), 'A New Presentation of Non-Philosophy', available at: www.onphi.org/download/pdf/32 (accessed 18 January 2024).

—— (2012), 'Photo-Fiction, A Theoretical Installation', *Photo-Fiction: A Non-Standard Aesthetics*, trans. D. S. Burk, Minneapolis: Univocal, pp. 11–24.

Latour, Bruno (2007), *Reassembling the Social: An Introduction to Actor-Network Theory*, Oxford: Oxford University Press.

Leckey, Mark (2019), *O' Magic Power of Bleakness*, London: Tate Gallery.

Le Guin, Ursula K. (1968), *The Wizard of Earthsea*, Berkeley, California: Parnassus Press.

—— (1989), 'The Carrier Bag Theory of Fiction', *Dancing at the Edge of Time: Thoughts on Worlds, Women and Places*, New York: Grove Press, pp. 165–70.

Linward, Timothy and P. Wolfendale (2018), *Dice Cult*, self-published.

Liston, Kate (2017), 'Room 113: Billy McCall and Neuschloss', *Corridor8*, available at: https://corridor8.co.uk/article/newcastle-sarah-munro-room-113-billy-mccall-neuschloss/ (accessed 23 January 2023).

Lock, Kris (2020), 'Crossings: Verity Birt and Tom Sewell', exhibition handout, Margate: Well Projects.

Lynch, John and S. O'Sullivan (2007), 'One Day in the Life of a City (July 21, 2006)', *Parallax*, 13.1: 28–37.

Lyotard, Jean-François (1984), *The Postmodern Condition: A Report on Knowledge*, trans. G. Bennington and B. Massumi, Manchester: Manchester University Press.

Mabey, Richard (2005), *Nature Cure*, London: Chatto and Windus.

Macfarlane, Robert (2012), *The Old Ways: A Journey on Foot*, London and New York: Penguin Hamish Hamilton and Viking.

Mackay, Robin (2022), Introductory talk at 'Cultivating Darkness', launch of Gruppo di Nun's *Revolutionary Demonology*, KARST, Plymouth, 15 December 2022.

Malabou, Catherine (2022), 'Destructive Plasticity, War, and Anarchism: A Conversation between Catherine Malabou and Julie Reshe', available at: www.youtube.com/watch?v=JBQixz2qg6g (accessed 16 June 2022).

Massumi, Brian (1988), 'Translator's Foreword' to G. Deleuze and F. Guattari, *A Thousand Plateaus*, trans. B. Massumi, London: Athlone Press, pp. ix–xv.

Mauss, Marcel (2001[1950]), 'A Definition of Magic', *A General Theory of Magic*, trans. R. Brain, London: Routledge, pp. 22–30.

Meillassoux, Quentin (2008), *After Finitude: An Essay on the Necessity of Contingency*, trans. R. Brassier, London: Continuum.

—— (2015), *Science Fiction and Extro-Science Fiction*, trans. A. Edlebi, Minneapolis: Univocal.

Metzinger, Thomas (2009), *The Ego Tunnel: The Science of the Mind and the Myth of the Self*, New York: Basic Books.

Morton, Timothy (2013), *Hyperobjects: Philosophy and Ecology after the End of the World*, Minneapolis: University of Minnesota Press.

Murray, Amber (2017), 'Decolonising the Imagined Geographies of "Witchcraft"', *Third World Thematics: A TWQ Journal*, 2.2–3: 157–79.

Nagapriya (2004), *Exploring Karma and Rebirth*, Cambridge: Windhorse.

Nathan, Tobie and I. Stengers (2018), *Doctor and Healers*, trans. S. Muecke, Cambridge: Polity.

Negarestani, Reza (2008), *Cyclonopedia: Complicity with Anonymous Materials*, Melbourne: re.press.

—— (2011), 'Globe of Revolution: An Afterthought on Geophilosophical Realism', *Identities: Journal of Politics, Gender and Culture*, 8.2: 25–54.

—— (2014), 'The Labour of the Inhuman', *#Accelerate: The Accelerationist Reader*, ed. R. Mackay and A. Avanessian, Falmouth: Urbanomic, pp. 427–66.

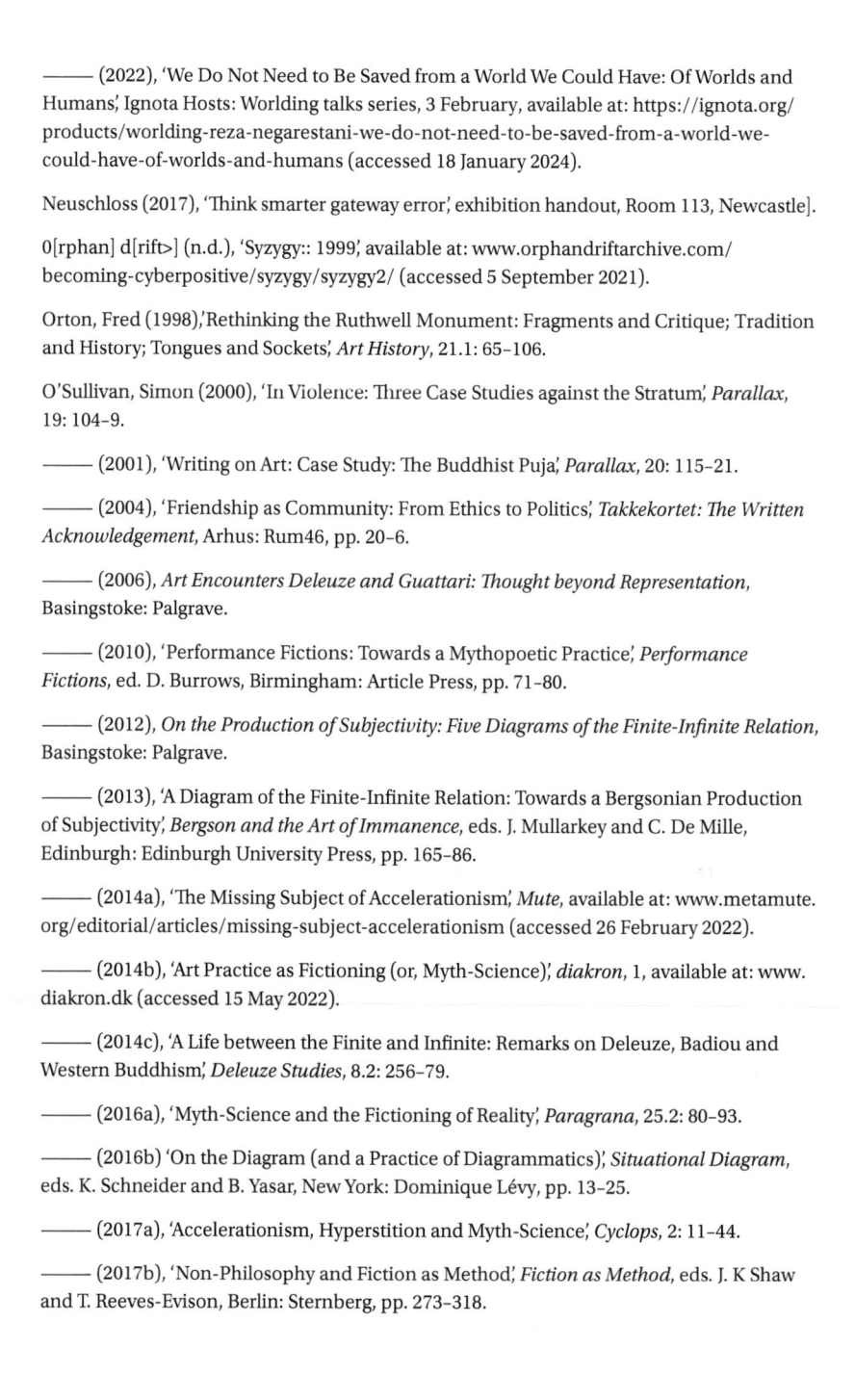

—— (2022), 'We Do Not Need to Be Saved from a World We Could Have: Of Worlds and Humans', Ignota Hosts: Worlding talks series, 3 February, available at: https://ignota.org/products/worlding-reza-negarestani-we-do-not-need-to-be-saved-from-a-world-we-could-have-of-worlds-and-humans (accessed 18 January 2024).

Neuschloss (2017), 'Think smarter gateway error', exhibition handout, Room 113, Newcastle].

O[rphan] d[rift>] (n.d.), 'Syzygy:: 1999', available at: www.orphandriftarchive.com/becoming-cyberpositive/syzygy/syzygy2/ (accessed 5 September 2021).

Orton, Fred (1998),'Rethinking the Ruthwell Monument: Fragments and Critique; Tradition and History; Tongues and Sockets', *Art History*, 21.1: 65–106.

O'Sullivan, Simon (2000), 'In Violence: Three Case Studies against the Stratum', *Parallax*, 19: 104–9.

—— (2001), 'Writing on Art: Case Study: The Buddhist Puja', *Parallax*, 20: 115–21.

—— (2004), 'Friendship as Community: From Ethics to Politics', *Takkekortet: The Written Acknowledgement*, Arhus: Rum46, pp. 20–6.

—— (2006), *Art Encounters Deleuze and Guattari: Thought beyond Representation*, Basingstoke: Palgrave.

—— (2010), 'Performance Fictions: Towards a Mythopoetic Practice', *Performance Fictions*, ed. D. Burrows, Birmingham: Article Press, pp. 71–80.

—— (2012), *On the Production of Subjectivity: Five Diagrams of the Finite-Infinite Relation*, Basingstoke: Palgrave.

—— (2013), 'A Diagram of the Finite-Infinite Relation: Towards a Bergsonian Production of Subjectivity', *Bergson and the Art of Immanence*, eds. J. Mullarkey and C. De Mille, Edinburgh: Edinburgh University Press, pp. 165–86.

—— (2014a), 'The Missing Subject of Accelerationism', *Mute*, available at: www.metamute.org/editorial/articles/missing-subject-accelerationism (accessed 26 February 2022).

—— (2014b), 'Art Practice as Fictioning (or, Myth-Science)', *diakron*, 1, available at: www.diakron.dk (accessed 15 May 2022).

—— (2014c), 'A Life between the Finite and Infinite: Remarks on Deleuze, Badiou and Western Buddhism', *Deleuze Studies*, 8.2: 256–79.

—— (2016a), 'Myth-Science and the Fictioning of Reality', *Paragrana*, 25.2: 80–93.

—— (2016b) 'On the Diagram (and a Practice of Diagrammatics)', *Situational Diagram*, eds. K. Schneider and B. Yasar, New York: Dominique Lévy, pp. 13–25.

—— (2017a), 'Accelerationism, Hyperstition and Myth-Science', *Cyclops*, 2: 11–44.

—— (2017b), 'Non-Philosophy and Fiction as Method', *Fiction as Method*, eds. J. K Shaw and T. Reeves-Evison, Berlin: Sternberg, pp. 273–318.

——— (2017c), 'Memories of a Deleuzian: To Think Is Always to Follow the Witches' Flight', *A Thousand Plateaus and Philosophy*, eds. H. Somers-Hall, J. Bell and J. Williams, Edinburgh: Edinburgh University Press, pp. 172–89.

——— (2018), 'Fictioning the Landscape', *Journal of Aesthetics and Phenomenology*, 5.1: 53–65.

——— (2022), 'Fictioning a Pilgrimage (or Fieldwork on the Fiction of the Self)', *Fieldwork for Future Ecologies: Radical Practice for Art and Art-Based Research*, eds. B. Crone, S. Nightingale and P. Stanton, Eindhoven: Onomatopee, pp. 397–415.

——— (2024a), *The Ancient Device*, Charmouth: Triarchy Press.

——— (2024b), *On Theory-Fiction and Other Genres*, London: Palgrave.

O'Sullivan, Simon and O. Ståhl (2006), 'Contours and Case Studies for a Dissenting Subjectivity (or, How to Live Creatively in a Fearful World)', *Angelaki*, 11.1: 147–56.

Pendlebury, Michael (2022), *Making Sense of Kant's 'Critique of Pure Reason': A Philosophical Introduction*, London: Bloomsbury.

Phillips, Rasheedah (2018), 'Placing Time, Timing Space: Dismantling the Master's Map and Clock in', *The Funambulist*, 18, available at: www.blackquantumfuturism.com/articles-guest-writing (accessed 6 May 2022).

Plant, Sadie (1997), *Zeros and Ones: Digital Women and the New Technoculture*, London: Fourth Estate.

——— (2001), *Writing on Drugs*, London: Faber and Faber.

P-Orridge, Genesis Breyer (1992), 'Behavioural Cut-Ups and Magick', *Rapid Eye 2*, ed. S. Dwyer, London: Annihilation Press, pp. 127–34.

Ratnaguna and Sraddhapa (2016), *Great Faith, Great Wisdom: Practice and Awakening in the Pure Land Sutras of Mahayana Buddhism*, Cambridge: Windhorse.

Reed, Patricia (2021), 'The End of a World and Its Pedagogies', *Making & Breaking*, 2, eds. S. Olma and U. Henry, available at: https://makingandbreaking.org/article/the-end-of-a-world-and-its-pedagogies/ (accessed 18 January 2024).

Reeves-Evison, Theo (2020), *Ethics of Contemporary Art: In the Shadow of Transgression*, London: Bloomsbury.

The Roland Barthes Reading Group (2020), *Roland Barthes's Party*, London: MA Bibliothèque.

Roudinesco, Élisabeth (2014), *Lacan: In Spite of Everything*, trans. G. Elliot, London: Verso.

Salmon, Yvonne (2019), 'Penda's Fen and Contemporary Occulture', *Of Mud & Flame: The Penda's Fen Sourcebook*, eds. M. Harle and J. Machin, London: Strange Attractor, pp. 51–61.

Sangharakshita (1993), *A Survey of Buddhism: Its Doctrines and Methods through the Ages*, Cambridge: Windhorse.

Schreber, Daniel Paul (2000), *Memoirs of My Nervous Illness,* New York: New York Review of Books Classics.

Scott, David (2000), 'The Re-enchantment of Humanism: An Interview with Sylvia Wynter', *Small Axe,* 8: 119–207.

Seth, Anil (2020), 'How Our Minds Predict Our Reality', *Mind & Life* podcast, available at: https://mindandlife.podbean.com/e/anil-seth-how-our-minds-predict-our-reality/ (accessed 1 October 2023).

Shani, Tai (2019), *Our Fatal Magic,* London: Strange Attractor.

Sharp, Andy (2020), *The English Heretic Collection: Ritual Histories, Magickal Geography,* London: Repeater Books.

Sharpe, Christina (2016), *In the Wake: On Blackness and Being,* Durham and London: Duke University Press.

Simondon, Gilbert (2011 [1958]), 'On the Mode of Existence of Technical Objects' (extract), trans. N. Mellamphy, D. Mellamphy and N. B. Mellamphy, *Deleuze Studies,* 5.3: 407–24.

Sleigh-Johnson, Sophie (2015), *Chthonic Index,* Southend-on-Sea: Focal Point Gallery.

—— (2022), 'Marsh Hermeneutics: Performing Sites of Disorientation', PhD Thesis, Goldsmiths College, London.

Smith, Phil (2010), *Mythogeography: A Guide to Walking Sideways,* Plymouth: Triachy Press.

—— (2022), *Living in the Magical Mode: Notes from the Book of Minutes of a Guild of Shy Sorcerers,* Axminster: Triachy Press.

Smith, Phil and H. Billinghurst (Crab and Bee) (2019), *A Plymouth Pantheon,* self-published (details at: https://crab-bee.tumblr.com/ [accessed 18 January 2024]).

Smith, Rodney (2014), *Awakening: A Paradigm Shift of the Heart,* Boston and London: Shambala.

Sogyal Rinpoche (1992), *The Tibetan Book of Living and Dying,* New York: Harper Collins.

Spare, Austin Osman (2007), *The Writings of Austin Spare,* Sioux Falls: Nu Vision.

Spinoza, Benedict de (1996), *Ethics,* ed. and trans. E. Curley, London: Penguin.

Starhawk (2003), 'Towards an Activist Spirituality', *Reclaiming Quarterly,* Autumn 2003, available at: http://starhawk.org/pdfs/Toward%20an%20Activist%20Sprituality.pdf (accessed 18 January 2024).

Stengers, Isabelle (2012), 'Reclaiming Animism', *e-flux,* 36, available at: www.e-flux.com/journal/36/61245/reclaiming-animism (accessed 5 September 2021).

Stupart, Linda (2016), *Virus,* London: Arcadia Missa.

Sutcliffe, Jamie (2021a), *Magic,* London: Whitechapel Gallery.

—— (2021b), 'Magic: A Gramarye for Artists', *Magic,* London: Whitechapel Gallery.

―― (2021c), 'Vocal Cord Parasite', essay written as part of 'Trouble in Outer Heaven: Portable Ops Plus', Southwark Park Gallery, London, 15 September to 31 October 2021.

Szwed, John F. (2000), *Space Is the Place: The Life and Times of Sun Ra*, Edinburgh: MOJO Books.

The Occulture (David Cecchetto, Marc Couroux, Ted Hiebert, Eldritch Priest) (2017), *Ludic Dreaming: How to Listen Away from Contemporary Technoculture*, London: Bloomsbury.

Tsing, Anna Lowenhaupt (2015), *The Mushroom at End of the World: On the Possibility of Life in Capitalist Ruins*, Princeton: Princeton University Press.

Viveiros de Castro, Eduardo (2004), 'Exchanging Perspectives: The Transformation of Objects into Subjects in Amerindian Ontologies', *Common Knowledge*, 10.3: 463–84.

―― (2014), *Cannibal Metaphysics*, trans. P. Skafish, Minneapolis: Univocal.

VNS Matrix (2015), *Hex* fanzine, no. 2.

Wark, McKenzie (2011), *The Beach Beneath the Street: The Everyday Life and Glorious Times of the Situationist International*, London: Verso.

―― (2021), *Philosophy for Spiders: On the Low Theory of Kathy Acker*, Durham, NC: Duke University Press.

Watts, Peter (2006), *Blindsight*, New York: Tor.

Weird Walks, fanzine, available at: www.weirdwalk.co.uk (accessed: 14 May 2022).

Williams, Alex (2013), 'Escape Velocities', *e-flux*, 46, available at: www.e-flux.com/journal/46/60063/escape-velocities (accessed 23 August 2022).

Williams, Raymond (1977), *Marxism and Literature*, Oxford: Oxford University Press.

―― (1978), 'Utopia and Science Fiction', *Science Fiction Studies*, 5.3: 203–14.

―― (1980), 'Base and Superstructure in Marxist Cultural Theory', *Problems in Materialism and Culture: Selected Essays*, London: Verso, pp. 31–49.

Wittig, Monique (1971), *Les Guérillères*, London: Peter Owen.

Wolfendale, Pete and T. Franklin (2012), 'Why Dungeons and Dragons Is Art', *Dungeons and Dragons and Philosophy: Raiding the Temple of Wisdom*, ed. J. Cogburn and M. Silcox, Chicago and LaSalle: Open Court, pp. 207–24.

Wynter, Sylvia (1971), 'Novel and History, Plot and Plantation', *Savacou*, 5: 95–102.

―― (2015), 'The Ceremony Found: Towards the Autopoetic Turn/Overturn, Its Autonomy of Human Agency and Extraterritoriality of (Self-)Cognition', *Black Knowledges/Black Struggles: Essays in Critical Epistemology*, eds. J. R. Ambroise, S. Broeck, Liverpool: Liverpool University Press, pp. 184–252.

Index

Acéphale Journal, Acéphale society
33–4, 35
acephaly *see* headlessness
Acker, Kathy 14–15, 105, 141–2, 151n11
   as egregore/in others' fictions 14–15
   and distributed authorship 141–2
   see also dream maps
action at a distance 105–6
activism 63
adolescence, adolescents 75, 79n8, 80n13,
   153–4, 156, 157
   see also pre-adolescence
aesthetics 88
affect, affective register 15, 50, 106, 174, 175,
   183, 187
agency 9, 37, 49, 102, 104, 105, 109, 110, 159,
   160, 185
   lack of 104
   see also free will
AI *see* Artificial Intelligence
algorithm, algorithms 38–9, 40–1
alt-right 8
   see also meme magic, neo liberalism
analytic formal artifact (Ferreira da Silva)
   64, 66n9, 85–6
anamorphism, anamorphosis 79n5, 132,
   156–7, 192
   reading 192
   temporal 132
anapanasatti 165, 172
ancestors, ancestor worship 47–8,
   127–130
   see also past
Ancient Device, The (O'Sullivan) 1, 4, 23,
   30–1, 108, 175
   for 'most ancient device' *see* self as
   fiction
animals 93–4
animism 116
   see also Stengers, Isabelle
anthropocene 9, 66n11, 67n13
   see also extractivism
anthropology 89
anxiety 10, 101–2, 108, 143–4, 194
   and climate change 102
archaeofictioning 51–2, 90, 127–36

archaeology, archaeological finds 70,
   128–30, 134
   art and 128
   experimental 131
   and figuration 132
   as calling forth a people 128, 129 (*see also*
   summoning)
   as fictioning 128, 129
   as props 129, 131
   as science 129
arche-fossil (Meillassoux) 85–6
Aristotle 24
Armah, Adjoa 132–3
   sketches/prototypes 133 (*compare*
   preparation)
art, art practice (in general) 39–40, 51, 70,
   73, 87–8, 122, 156
   as device 87–8
   and archaeology 128
   as calling forth a people 128 (*see also*
   summoning)
   blurring of art and life 79, 185 (*see also*
   avant-gardes)
art scenes, art world 153, 156
Artaud, Antonin 31n7, 76, 77
Artificial Intelligence (AI) 12–13, 48, 49,
   83–93, 135, 139, 145–6
   as causa sui 48
   as co-author 90
   as magical device 91
   as non-self 93
   as subject of fiction 90
   point of view of 48
as-if 26, 94, 123, 146, 156, 186, 187
asignification 16, 29, 65
   see also affect, affective register
attention economy 140, 161n2
   compare gap
audience 182–3, 185
   audience buy-in 186
Aurelius, Marcus 24
autism 46
   see also neurodiversity
autodidacticism 75
autofiction 14, 25, 28, 73, 93, 105
   see also Acker, Kathy; Joyce, James

autotheory 3, 125n7
avant-gardes 45, 83, 88, 128, 185-6
avatar 7, 17, 122, 141, 144, 160, 168, 183, 188
    in Hinduism 7
    dream avatar 12 (*see also* lucid dreaming)
    see also egregore, persona, character

Badiou, Alain 158
Barthes, Roland 24-5, 66n1
Barton, Justin 148
    and Mark Fisher 59, 60, 70, 71, 74
base materialism 33, 35, 40
basilisk, *see* Roko's Basilisk
Bataille, Georges 33-4, 35, 36, 38, 40
becoming 15, 183
Bergson, Henri 46-7, 51, 140
Birt, Verity 112n7, 134-5
Black Audio Film Collective 61
Black Plaque project 75
Black Quantum Futurism 50-1, 133
Blackness 40-1, 50, 61, 64, 86
    as device 40-1
    and poetics 50, 61, 64, 86 (*see also*
        Harney, Stefano and Fred Moten;
        Ferreira da Silva, Denise)
blind, blindly 87, 90, 187
    compare project
blockchain 97-8n20
blurring *see* porosity
book
    as device 64, 70
    as stage with props and figures 191
    within a book 84 (*see also* nesting)
brain (as prediction machine) 37
    see also neuroscience
Brassier, Ray 11-12, 36, 40
Buddhism 35, 37, 49, 123, 124-5, 131, 165-77
    and effective utopia (Laruelle) 172
    as asceticism 35
    Bodhisattvas 169
    the Buddha 169-170
    the Buddha as blockage/impasse 170
    ethics of 166
    meditation 51, 124-5, 131 (*see also*
        vipassana)
    Western Buddhism 165-6, 169, 172
burial chambers, burials 71, 131
    see also ancestor worship
Burroughs, William 17, 37, 45, 142, 150n6, 157
    see also cut-up

Burrows, David 1-2, 4n1, 10, 63, 64, 97n13, 128, 144-5, 146-7, 156, 182, 184, 185
    see also Plastique Fantastique

Cabaret Voltaire (venue) 185
    see also art scenes, avant-gardes
CAConrad 63
call forth *see* summoning
call itself forth – *see* hyperstition, retroactive causation, temporal loops, time circuits
call-and-response 188
capitalism, capitalist time 58, 102, 168
    as ongoing disaster (Barton) 148
    vs imagination 149
care 3, 39, 101-6, 109, 132, 148, 160, 194
    as dropping down 109
    of the imagination 132
    see also repair
Castenda, Carlos 144
cause of oneself (Lacan)
    see self, as cause of self
causality, cause-and-effect, linear time 17, 43, 44-6, 97n19, 105-6, 133-4, 171, 186
    compare gap
celibate machines (Deleuze and Guattari) 15
changeling 72
channelling 7, 181, 183, 190n5
    as side-stepping 183
chaos 16
chaos magick 16-17, 18
    and neoliberalism 21-2n25
character 7, 144, 154, 155, 159, 183 (*see also* avatars; Tabletop Role Playing Games)
    in own work (Leckey) 73
    in philosophy 84
    characters (in group work) 174
ChatGPT 145-6
Chiang, Ted 84
circling 25, 194
    see also preparation
    compare procrastination
circuits *see* local-global circuits; temporal loops
class 40, 58-9
co-option of cultural practices 165
    see also speaking for
cohesion, coherence 37, 42n6, 129
    see also key-points; plane; time-binding device

collaboration, collective production 3, 8, 40, 61-2, 156, 159-60, 185, 193
  see also Burrows, David; groups; Plastique Fantastique
  and autowriting 193
  and friendship 169
  collaborative writing 61-2, 64-5
  with non-human agents 184
  with machines 184
collage 80n14
collective, collectivity 46, 50, 64, 108
  and group authorship 8, 10, 61-2
  subindividual 50
  see also group
colonialism, colonial fictions, colonial time 40, 50-1, 57-8, 91, 115, 116, 119
  see also epistemicide
comedy, comic 27, 77
commons, common land 58-59
community 145, 166 and soul 166
compassion 177
computer games 7, 161n3
concepts 19, 30, 84, 85, 95-6n6, 158
  as creation and material 85
  dramatised 84
cone (of memory) (Bergson) 47, 51-2, 52
conjuring see magic
consciousness 10
  as retrocausation 11
consumerism 23, 148, 168
  see also capitalism
control 17, 18, 105
  compare cut-up
Cooper, Susan 121
Copestack, Anne-Marie 131-2
cost of living crisis 102
counter-culture 110
courage 175
Covid (lockdown period) 2, 101, 134, 182, 194
critique 30, 40, 65
Cup-and-ring markings 134
Cussans, John 31n5
cut-up 17, 45, 83, 89, 150n6, 157-8, 191
Cybernetic Culture Research Unit (Ccru) 9-10, 16, 19n5, 21n22, 43, 44, 45, 48, 53-4n5, 72
cybernetics 37

dada 185-6
DALL-E 145
death, death drive 15, 171, 178n10
  death of God (Nietzsche) 34
Debord, Guy 186
decolonisation 63, 106
  decolonisation of knowledge/university 116
  see also colonialism
deep fakes 135
DeepDream (Google) 145
deferral 24
  see also preparation
  compare procrastination
Deleuze, Gilles 74, 128, 129, 183
  and Félix Guattari 15-16, 21n23, 27-8, 29, 44, 50, 84, 85, 103, 122
Deller, Jeremy 80n14
demons, demonology 10, 20n8
  see also summoning
depression 101-2, 178n4
desire, desiring machines 15, 23-31, 176
  as ongoing process 23-4 (see also stasis, deferral)
  as fiction 23-4
  desiring production 44-5
desiring-work 23-31
despair 45, 49
device 3-4, 19, 36, 39, 50, 51, 52-3, 63-5, 70, 73, 75-6, 78, 83-95, 123, 124, 145, 168, 170, 173-4, 192, 194
  see also drugs; props; tools
  aesthetic 69, 78, 88, 90, 92
  art practice as 87-8
  Blackness as 40-1 (see also device, instrument as)
  book as 121
  as content of literature 83-4 (see also avant-garde)
  cross-genre 84
  dharma as 170
  film-essay as 55n17
  as both form and content of literature 84
  as foregrounding other worlds 123
  group as 173, 175, 176, 177
  instrument as 50, 64
  invitation as 124
  and magick 88-9, 94
  myth as 176
  performance as 182

device (*continued*)
  philosophy about 85
  philosophy as, philosophical devices 85–6
  poetics as 45, 64 (*see also* avant-gardes; Blackness; writing)
  political 94
  proliferation of 39, 91 (*see also* technicity)
  puja as 167
  seen as device 97n19, 192
  self as 93
  speaking back 108, 110
  speculative 86
  technical 69, 78, 83, 85, 89–92, 132
  theatrical 94
  time-travelling 70, 76, 91, 132
  tinkering with 39
dharma 170
  see also device
diagonal 110, 112n4, 160
  see also porosity
diagram, diagramming 14, 51, 80, 85, 92
dispelling *see* fiction seen as fiction, device seen as device
diversity 64
doubling 73, 75
dragon 188–9
drawings 14
dream, dreams, dreaming, dreamings 14, 73
  analysis/interpretation 140 (*see also* psychoanalysis)
  collective 146, 147
  and community 142n 146–7
  diaries 142
  and/as fiction 139, 141–2, 143
  as incursion from the outside (Barton) 148
  information 147, 149
  as landscape 139, 147
  literature as 123
  lucid dreams 12–13, 140–1
  lucidity (Barton) 148
  dream maps (Acker) 14, 105, 141–2, 147, 151n7
  as method 139–49
  as multifaceted object 140
  planetary (Barton) 148
  as repair 140
  sharing of 142, 146–7
  dream-work 139, 144
Dreammachine (Gysin) 88, 145
Dream Mapping (Hiller) 146

dream-time 176
Drexciya, Drexciya mythos 61
dropping down 91–2, 92, 117
  see also point of view
drugs 145
dukkha 170
  see also suffering
Dungeons and Dragons 154, 155–6, 161n3

Eastham Lake motorway bridge (Leckey) 71–2, 73
  as liminal space 71, 72
  as motif 72
  as key-point 73
Eco-feminism 134
Eco-therapeutics 4n5
ecology 63, 66n11
  see also anthropocene
eerie 69–70, 71, 74, 80n14
  and sound 70, 74
ego 13, 27, 42n7, 49
ego tunnel (Metzinger) 8, 12, 36
  see also nemocentric subject
egregore 8, 14, 17 *see also* avatar, persona
embodied thought
  see headlessness
emergence 48
emergent culture 59
enclosure
  see commons
England, English landscape 57–9, 73, 127–8, 134, 146, 154
  see also Essex Marshes; Yorkshire
English Heretic (Andy Sharp) 74–5
enlightenment (Buddhism) 169–70, 172
  and virtual 170
Eno, Brian 70, 74
epistemicide 105
  see also colonialism
escape 10
  see also outside, transformation
Eshun, Kodwo 62, 64, 81n21
esoteric materialism (Kenning) 74–5
Essex Marshes 76
ethics (pre-psychoanalysis) 24
event mapping (Black Quantum Futurism) 50–1, 133
evolution 36, 37
exorcism 72, 77

experimental, experimentation 36, 39–40, 50, 92
  see also writing, experimental; Science Fiction, (X)SF
expropriation 57, 59, 60, 104
  see also extraction; primitive accumulation; slavery
extraction, extractivism 58, 60, 62, 66n11, 91, 115–6
Extro-Science Fiction (XSF) see Science Fiction

fanzines 107, 113n16
fear (of death) 171
Federici, Silvia 59, 61, 104, 105, 106
feedback loops 12, 14, 39, 44
feminism 62
Ferreira da Silva, Denise 40, 58, 61, 64, 85–6, 106, 115–6
  and Sun Ra 66n9
festivals 74
  see also rituals
fiction, fictions 8–9, 10–14, 24–31, 71, 185, 192
  collective (as consensus) 8, 9
  collective (as group authored) (see groups)
  and colonialism/anticolonialism 40
  as conjuration 71
  embodiment of 186
  as escapism 45
  as agents in landscape 118
  fictional entities (see avatars)
  generic 169
  immersion in 159
  nested see nested fictions
  as Non-Philosophical/literature 28, 33, 34, 40, 70, 83–4
  of the self (see self as fiction)
  'other' fictions 193
  performance of 45–6
  porosity with reality 77
  as reactivating past(s) 67–79
  as real, real effects of 7, 9, 18, 26, 36, 45, 168, 185
  seen as fiction 12, 26, 35, 39, 83
  as simultaneously real and fiction 26, 183, 187
  sonic fictions 70
  as weapon in time-war 45
fictioning 10, 128, 145, 146, 160, 183, 186
  (see also worlding)
  collective, as collectively production 156, 159, 181
  of philosophy 85
figure–ground relation 85
figures 27
film 70, 71
  see also essay-film
first-person narration 40
  see also ego
  compare headlessness
first-person science 171
Fisher, Mark 69–70, 72, 73, 74, 75
  and Ccru 70
  and Science Fiction 70
folk image see image, manifest
Folkton Drums 131–2
foregrounding 22, 36, 39, 72, 78, 93, 157, 188, 192
  and comedy 77
  of different times/space-times 51, 65, 72, 78, 91, 122
  of indigenous voices 63
Frazer, J. G. 47, 75, 105–6
free parties 156
  see also scenes
free will 45, 95n1
  see also intent, sovereign subject
Freud, Freudianism 27, 28, 37–8, 127, 140
  and archaeology 127
friendship 168–9
  see also sangha
frustration 53
future, futures 25, 30, 44, 49, 62, 65, 67n13, 70, 83, 111, 127, 130, 142, 144, 149, 189
future-past object, future-past ritual 131
  see also hyperstition, preparation, temporal loops, time-circuits

Game Master 153, 155–6
gap, gap in sensory-motor schema (Bergson) 46–7, 51, 137n1, 140, 172
  and Buddhism/meditation 37
  and cut-up 17
Garner, Alan 70, 72, 79n4, 79n5, 121
Gauthier, Xavière 62
gender 40, 41–2n1, 58–9, 84
  trans- and nonbinary 63
generic creativity 36

Genet, Jean 16
genre 3–4, 43–4, 59, 79, 84, 87, 89, 121, 125n7, 193
　seen as genre 87
　see also writing
gesture 183–4
'getting going' *see* preparation
Gibson, William 48, 66
gig economy 140
Gilroy, Paul 61
globalisation 59, 70
Goenka, S. N. 165, 170
Great Britain 57
　see also England; Yorkshire
Great Outdoors (Meillassoux) 86
Green Tara 123
groups, group-work 3, 8–9, 15, 29, 34, 40, 147, 165, 167, 173–7, 183
　anchor, hold, leader, 176–7, 179n16 (*see also* Game Master, analyst)
　as fiction, as performance fiction 8, 40, 183 (*see also* Plastique Fantastique)
　group subject (Barton) 148
　headless group 34
　as representation 177
　subindividual 50
　and writing 107
　see also Acéphale; Black Quantum Futurism; Ccru; dream; Occulture, Plastique Fantastique; Roland Barthes Reading
Gruppo di Nun 22n25
Guattari, Félix 16, 29, 50
　see also Deleuze, Gilles and Félix Guattari
Guy, Leslie 162n7
Gysin, Brion 88, 145

habit *see* linear time
　compare gap
Halford, Victoria and Steve Beard 54n8, 59–60
haptic collectivity 106
Haraway, Donna 10, 109, 117, 122–3, 130, 156
　and collective storytelling 117
　and the dead 130
　and fiction ('The Camille Stories') 125n7
　and multispecies societies 117
　and string figures 122, 156
　(*compare* knot)
Harding, Edison 34–5

hare 111
Harney, Stefano and Fred Moten 40, 50, 61–2, 64, 86, 106
haunting, hauntology 70, 72, 106
　see also exorcism
Hayles, N. Katherine 20n10
headlessness, being headless 33–41
　and Blackness 41
　and gender 41–2n1
　and symptom 38
　non-heads 39
　see also Acéphale
higher education 101–4
　fees 101–2
　students 101–4
　use value and employability 101–3
Hiller, Susan 146, 151n11
Hine, Phil 109, 162n9
Hoban, Russell 84, 120
hospitality, performance as 182
Hughes, Allan and Mark Rohtmaa Jackson 162n7
human
　absence of 59, 70 (*see also* eerie)
　as 'project' 33
　decentring of 38
　exceeding of 45
　framed by AI 91
　generic/universal 86–7
　landscape marked by 60
　as time-bound 45, 89
　trans-genre of (Wynter) 86–7, 96n8
　see also subject
　compare non-human
hyperobject (Morton) 102
hyperstition (Ccru) 8–10, 16, 43, 45, 48
　and left accelerationism 49
　see also retro-causation, temporal loops, time circuits

illness 38–9
image 12, 16, 18, 19, 39, 122–3, 139, 146, 149
　AI and 145–6
　folk image (of self) *see* image, manifest image
　manifest image (of self) 11, 36, 49
　of other 58
　scientific image (of self) 11, 36, 39
　see also diagrams; Lacan, mirror-phase; representation
Imaginary (Lacan) 131, 157–8

imagination 109, 117, 118, 119-121, 125,
    131, 149, 153
  and/as care 109-10, 132
  imaginative engagement 115, 116, 117, 121
impermanence, reflecting on, experiencing
    35, 170-2
indigenous (people, land, knowledge) 42n8,
    51, 63, 116
inhuman *see* joy
  compare human, nonhuman
instrument Blackness as 64
  see also device, instrument
intent, intention 37, 87, 145, 185
  addressing audience as 182
  limits of 87, 191
  shared 169
interference device 132 *see also* cut-up
introspection 173
Ireland, Amy 21-2n25, 44-5, 53n2, 97-8n20
Ishiguro, Kazuo 120-1

James, M. R. 70
journeying *see* pilgrimage
joy
  inhuman 55n14
  non-self 171, 172
Joyce, James 14, 28
  see also sinthome
Jung, Carl 139-40, 143

Kant, Immanuel 44, 46, 49, 50, 54n7, 97n18
Keiller, Patrick 59
Kenning, Dean 74-5
key-points 16, 27, 47, 73, 74, 76, 90, 118, 121
Kingsnorth, Paul 120
knot
  as device 122
  Lacanian knot, RSI knot 13, 122
  self as 194
  see also Haraway, Donna; repair;
    sinthome
knowledge 18, 34, 28, 47, 81n19, 110, 116,
    161-2n6
  hidden 9-10, 44, 186
  and pedagogy 110
  self-knowledge 25, 167, 171-2
  see also decolonisation; outside
    knowledge; science; writing,
    academic
Korzybski, Alfred 42n6

Lacan, Jacques 13-14, 23, 25-7, 28, 34, 38,
    42n7, 47, 130, 131, 176
  mirror phase 20n13, 34 (see also
    misrecognition)
  torus 25
  see also knot; sinthome
Land Art 119-20
Land, Nick 45, 48
  see also Ccru
landscape 3, 29-30, 41, 57-65, 69-79, 84,
    117-18, 119, 124-5, 127-8, 132-3,
    134-5, 154, 160, 167, 173, 174,
    175, 192
  dream as 144, 146
  fictions about 69, 84
  figures in 41
  as foreground 69
  interpenetration with self 125
  and magic 69-79
  marked 121-2, 134
  as performance venue 190n8
  and repair 120
  restricted access to 121 (*see also*
    enclosure)
  revaluation through fiction 121
  and sacred sites 78 (*see also* key-points)
  self as 3, 23, 73
  shadow on 144
  within a landscape 141, 146 (*see also*
    nesting)
Laruelle, François 86, 87, 91, 172
learning to be compromised (Stengers)
    8-9, 116
Leckey, Mark 71-3, 74, 76, 77
  as character in own work 69
Le Guin, Ursula 117, 121
life
  as a fiction 8
  of a fiction 8
  a life 14, 15, 23, 26, 28, 46
  my life 7, 16, 19, 117-20, 143-4, 147-8,
    149, 153-6, 177n3, 192, 193-4
  see also art, blurring of art and life
life writing *see* autofiction
linear time *see* cause and effect
  compare cut-up, hyperstition,
    temporal loops
listening
  to the sound of Blackness 50
  to the unconscious 28

Live Action Role Play (LARPing) 154, 157
live, live art, live transmission 76
living in the ruins (Haraway; Tsing) 109, 142
local-global circuits, local-universal circuits 110, 128
looping 77
  see also repetition; temporal loops
lucid dreaming see dream
  see also avatar
Lyotard, Jean-François 83

machines
  collaboration with 146
  see also AI; mythotechnesis; technicity
Madani, Adnan 130, 131
magic 4, 8-11, 26, 69, 70, 72, 74, 88-9, 104, 106
  as care and repair 109
  compromised by (Stengers) 8, 116
  and context 89
  magical mode of existence (Simondon) 85, 118
  magical thinking 47
  and/as naming, re-naming and summoning 10, 16-17, 21n24, 41, 66n1
  as non-scientific understanding 47
  and place 69-79
  and pragmatism 9, 15
  and schizoanalysis 15
  sympathetic 47, 75
  theory of time 43
  tools 4, 17, 77, 88, 107 (see also staff as device)
  when not called magic 89, 106, 110
  see also magick; summoning
  compare science
magical voluntarism (Smail) 112n4
magick 16-17, 18, 47, 88-9
  and/as literature 89
  and writing 17
  see also chaos magick
Malabou, Catherine 20n11
manifesto 34, 128
  see also avant-gardes
map, mapping 23, 27, 28-30, 75, 107, 111, 146-7
  dream maps (Acker) see dream
  mappa mundi 151n11
  molecular map 29
  see also Dream Mapping; diagram; event mapping; landscape

Marx, Marxism 27, 59
materialist psychology see schizoanalysis
matriarchies, gynocracy 104, 105
medicine, medical knowledge, medical technology, medicalised body 38-9
  masculinisation of 104
  professionalisation of 104
  compare witch
meditation 165, 166-7, 170-3
  vipassana (Goenka) 165, 170-3
  see also Buddhism
Meillassoux, Quentin 43-4, 85-6
memes, meme magic 8, 19n1
memory 127
  collective memory 127
mental health 3, 101-2, 132, 166, 172
  in academia 101-2, 132
  see also anxiety; depression; trauma
metamodelling (Guattari) 17, 21n23
method 1-2, 18, 75, 81n19
  dreaming as 139-49
  walking as 138n13, 162n8
metta bhavana 166
  see also meditation
Metzinger, Thomas 8, 12, 36
Middle Passage 61, 106
  and witch-hunts 106
  see also colonialism, primitive accumulation, slavery
mindfulness 178n4
  of breathing 166-7, 171, 172
  see also meditation
mirror 18, 174
  as device 63
  mirror phase see Lacan, Jacques
  as narcissistic loop 64
  as sympathetic magic 75
misrecognition 27, 34
  see also Lacan, Jacques, mirror phase
mix tapes 77
modes of existence 59, 108, 109, 118, 122
  and dream 143, 144
  magical mode (Simondon), see magic
  non-self mode 93
  pre-technical mode (Simondon) 88, 118
  and residual cultures 59
  and ritual 130

technical mode (Simondon), *see* technicity
molecularity (Guattari) 103
  see also map, molecular
Morton, Timothy 102
multimedia 51, 60, 134
music 75
  Black music 61
  and Plastique Fantastique 188
  and place 74
  see also devices, scenes, sonic fictions
mystic 54n6
myth 3, 19, 30-1, 57-65
  awareness of own 177
  collective myths 62
  contestation of dominant myths 57-60
  cultural specificity of 175-6
  haptic myths 62
  myths of resistance 59
  as obscuration (*see also* control) 57-8, 59, 65, 128, 174
  universal 175
myth-science (Sun Ra) 51, 62
myth-work 1-4, 19, 30, 57-65, 70, 71, 72, 74, 78, 144, 165, 173, 175-6, 177, 192, 194
  and desire 23
  foregrounding other voices as 63, 64, 65
  and performance 74
  therapeutic 144
  and trauma 60-1
mythogeography (Smith) 162n8
mythopoesis 105
mythotechnesis 135-6, 145, 184

narration, narrator 11, 14, 25, 30, 44, 76, 77, 84, 109, 120-1, 129-30, 144, 173
  and archaeology 129
  and embodiment, enactment 186
  and linear time 44, 50 (*compare* writing, experimental)
  self-narration 11, 17, 24, 30, 47, 75-6, 103, 105, 108, 124, 144 (*see also* magic, tools; self, as cause of self)
  see also ego, Game Master, point-of-view, first-person
narrative *see* colonialism; fiction; myth; representation; writing
nationalism 57
naturalisation *see* obscuration

nature
  as outside 118
  myth of no human presence 119
  nature/culture division 116
  see also anthropocene, landscape
Negarestani, Reza 49, 53-4n5
nemocentric subject *see* subject, nemocentric
neolithic 71, 131-2, 134
  see also ancient past
nested fictions, nesting 12, 32n9, 45, 84, 124, 134, 140, 146, 159, 177, 186, 187
  in fiction 146
  self as 12, 124, 140-1, 142, 143, 159
  VR as 145
neurodiversity 49, 98n21 *see also* autism
neuroscience 7-8, 11-12, 36-7, 49, 93, 122, 159
  and Blackness 41
Neuschloss 132
New Noveta 76
Nietzsche, Friedrich 84
non-art 87-88
non-human 115-125, 134
  empathy with 115
  as persons 116
non-linear temporalities 51
  see also hyperstition, temporal loops
  compare causality
non-modern 116
Non-Philosophy (Laruelle) 86, 91, 93
non-self 7, 12, 49, 93, 171-2
  Buddhism and 165, 173
  technologies of 165, 173
  compare self; point-of-view
non-spaces 59
non-time 50
non-western epistemologies 47, 116
non-human, non-human persons 30, 109, 115-25
'Nothing is true, everything is permitted' 109

O'Sullivan, Tom 4n3, 126n12, 154-5, 159-160
obscuration, obscuration of landscape, *see* myth, obscuration
obsession 75
obstacles *see* deferral
occult, occulture 9-10, 43, 44

Occulture (course and students) 103–6, 107–9, 111, 159–60
opacity 12, 36, 41, 42n11, 97n18
　see also device as device; fiction as fiction
　compare transparency
outside 18, 34, 45, 71, 92, 97n18
　cosmos 118
　as eerie 71
　incursion from 72, 148
　as inside 124, 141
　nature as 118, 120, 121
　outside knowledge 186
　live play 154, 157 (*see also* pre-adolescence)
　of self/subject 86, 88–9
　see also Great Outdoors
Outsider Art 87

P-Orridge, Genesis 158
pagan, pagan figures, pagan images 169
　see also transitional monument
pain 171
　as self 171
parochialism, secret power of 76
past 44, 46, 47–8, 50–2, 58, 62, 65, 72, 117, 118, 120, 122, 127–36
　ancient past/deep past 62, 70
　in the present 75, 80n14, 85, 127, 129, 130, 137n1 (*see also* cone)
　see also ancestors; ancient past; cone; hyperstition; life; temporal loops; time-circuits
pedagogy 110–11
Peirce, C. S. 85
Penda's Fen 73
perception 37, 102, 148
　as controlled hallucination (Seth) 37
　compare dream, hyperobject
performance 7, 50, 52, 60, 71–8, 87, 119, 123, 136, 150n7, 168, 174, 181–9, 191
　and/as contemporary art 71–3, 75, 76–9, 87, 133, 181, 184–5
　and/as device/s 88, 187
　as both device and representation of device 187
　as laboratory for exploring fiction of the self 183
　as live and public 182–3 (*see also* audience)
　and landscape 60, 74, 76–8, 119, 149, 190n8 (*see also* performance, and walking)

and/as magic 181, 185, 187
online 182
'performance fiction' 8, 60, 69–79, 181–9
　pre-history of 185–6
　as point of view on what pre-exists it 186, 187
　as presentation and representation 185–6
　and/as repair 181
　and representations, see props
　and scenes 184–5
　and scripts/protocols 184 (*see also* writing)
　and technical devices 184
　and the unexpected 184, 185
　and walking 60, 135
　see also myth-work; Plastique Fantastique; pilgrimage; props; self as fiction; Sleigh-Johnson, Sophie
performative utterances *see* spells
persona *see* avatar; character
personhood, non-human persons 9, 30, 116, 129
perspective 167, 168, 172, 173, 176
　as wider context 167, 171–2
　see also point of view
perspectivism (Viveiros de Castro) 116
　see also point of view
pilgrimage 75, 76, 121, 144
　see also performance and walking; walking
place 69–79
　see also key-points, landscape
placebo effect 12
plane of consistency, of immanence, of interconnectedness, of a thousand devices 92, 92, 94, 117
Plant, Sadie 48
Plastique Fantastique 8, 18, 108, 146–7, 150n7, 181–2, 188–9, 189n2
poetics *see* Blackness; device, poetics
poetry
　spells as 63
point of view 12, 27, 29, 34, 35, 37, 40, 52, 64, 73, 86–7, 88, 94, 120–1, 123, 124, 186, 192
　from above 92, *92*
　and autofiction 73
　and/as device 65, 84, 87–8, 89, 94
　dream 139, 140–1, 145
　enlightened (*vipassana*) 172
　from future 52 (*see also* hyperstition, *see also* AI)

machinic 91 (*see also* AI)
nature writing as 120
non-place, nowhere 34, 172 (*see also* nemocentric subject)
and the novel 84
outside as 44
on self 12, 157 (*see also* writing back, speaking back)
shift in 12, 84, 86–7, 154, 155, 159–60
on the Real 65
see also anamorphism; perspectivism; subject, transcendent
compare dropping down
population as fiction in algorithmic governance 38
porosity (real/fiction; present/future; self/non-self) 48, 73, 77, 80n13, 149, 173, 183, 187
post-human *see* non-human
pragmatics, pragmatism 9, 15, 16, 17–18, 21n17, 27, 30, 36, 51, 103, 116
pre-adolescence 117, 18, 119–20, 121, 153–4, 156, 157
see also adolescence
pre-modern 47, 59, 116
as idyll 120
see also neolithic; non-Western
prediction (*see also* algorithm) 43
preparation 24–5, 123, 154, 187
as desiring work 24–5
Preparation of the Novel, The (Barthes) 24–5
primitive accumulation 59, 104
see also commons; expropriation; extraction; Middle Passage; witchcraft
procrastination 25
compare deferral; preparation
production of subjectivity (Guattari) *see* subjectivity, production of
prometheanism 90, 122
see also hyperstition and left accelerationism
props 30, 70, 76–7, 96, 122–3, 126n17, 129, 131, 133–4, 135, 136, 146, 154, 167, 168, 177, 179n18, 183–4, 185, 186–7, 188
see also device; representation
psychoanalysis 13–14, 16, 21–2n25, 23–4, 25–8, 42n7, 47, 191
as repair 127
see also Freud; Lacan
compare schizoanalysis

psychogeography *see* mapping
psychosis, avoidance of 27
see also mental health
puja 167, 168
puppets 179n18

quantum entanglement 51
quilting points (Lacan) 26–7, 194

readability
and linearity 44
reader, reading 32n9, 62, 83, 84, 108, 110, 120, 192
and escapism 45–6
and Tabletop Role Playing Games 158–9
see also Roland Barthes Reading Group; work, sharing of; writing, experimental
Real, the (Lacan) 13, 16, 17, 65, 131
trauma as 57–8, 65
reality (dominant, mundane) 9, 17, 45, 77, 94, 97, 149, 155, 157–8, 170, 177, 185, 186
deeper reality 39, 143, 170
as disappointment 25
as a fiction 26, 45
illusion as 94
obscured by fictions 40, 64
of the past 127, 129, 136 (*see also* archaeology)
subatomic 77
see also control; fiction, real effects of; science
reality effect (Lyotard) 18, 83, 87, 93, 186
see also fiction, real effects of
recuperation 168 *see also* repair
Reed, Patricia 162–3n10
re-enactment, re-staging, re-telling, re-versioning 76, 131, 133
and AI 135
of Folkton Drums 132
see also repetition
regression, regressive 9, 62, 75, 89, 96n11, 104, 106, 118, 119, 125n9
see also colonialism; science
rehearsal 188
see also preparation
religion, religiosity 85

repair 3, 13–14, 57, 63, 101, 106–11, 121, 124, 127, 128, 148, 160, 173, 175, 181, 193–4
   collective forms 65, 175
   and dream 148
   as dropping down 109
   games as 160
   and the non-human 124
   and the past 136
   retreat and 175
   rituals of 134
   writing as 193–4
   see also care; sinthome
repetition 19, 52, 72, 77, 79, 95
   and/as style 1–2, 192
   see also festivals;
representation 16, 28, 29, 40, 65, 70–2, 107, 109, 113n11, 119–24, 131–2, 174, 184–5
   and archaeology 131–2
   as care and repair 106
   and/as device 4n4, 83, 85, 87, 187
   and dreams 142
   and the eerie 69–71
   figuration/face 132
   group and/as 177
   as focus/intensification/multiplier 142, 174, 179n17, 184
   of landscape 70, 76, 119
   of magic 107
   and memory 126n13
   as repetition 70, 71–2, 74
   as Spectacle, *see* Spectacle
   as scene/stage 71, 187
   sub-representation 11, 39 (*see* ego-tunnel; nemocentric subject)
   and teaching 107
   of time 43
   see also device; diagram; fiction; image; mirror; nesting; Symbolic; writing
repurpose, repurposing, resignifying 18, 65, 128
   see also repetition
   compare re-enactment
residues, residual cultures, residual objects 59, 70, 74, 75, 105, 122, 127–8, 129, 131
   material residues 127
   and re-enactment 131
   of waking life 143
residuum *see* subject, as residuum
retreats 165, 167, 168
   as liminal space 168

retroaction, retro-causality, retrospective action/effects 9, 14, 16, 27, 30, 35, 43, 47–8, 51, 54n8, 55n11, 189
   and AI 48–9
   and colonial myth 58
   personal retrospection 153, 175
   and tachyons 47
   see also hyperstition, temporal loops, time circuits
right action, right speech 166
   see also Buddhism, ethics of
ritual, rituals 46, 52–3, 74, 76, 123, 130, 134, 182
   future-past 131
   rituals of repair 134
   see also devices, *see also* festivals
Roko's Basilisk 48
   see also AI
Roland Barthes Reading Group 31n2
Rossiter, Leonard 77

sacrifice, self-sacrifice 34, 38, 41, 117
Salmon, Yvette 73, 74
sangha 166
scenes, club and music 156, 184–5
   and non-human 185
   as theatrical setting 187, 189
schizoanalysis 15–16, 17, 18, 27, 191
Schneeman, Carolee 105
Science Fiction 43–4, 48, 51, 61–2, 63, 70, 91, 117, 137n4, 158
   devices in 84, 90, 91
   as device 63
   Extro-Science Fiction (XSF) (Meillassoux) 43–4
   and Middle Passage 61 (*see also* Drexciya)
   and Tabletop Role Playing Games 161n4
   (X)SF 53n1, 53n2
   see also Myth-science
science, scientific subject, scientific method 7–9, 11–12, 37–9, 44, 47, 49, 89–92, 93–4, 129, 130
   as blind 90
   and colonialism 91
   and fiction 98n21
   History of 91
   as proliferation of devices 91
   see also Science Fiction
self 3, 11, 15, 29, 34, 40
   and Buddhism 165, 168
   as cause of self 47

as device 3, 36-7, 64
dissolution of 22n25
as emergent 18
as feedback 37
as fiction 7-8, 10, 11-13, 17, 28-9, 35-6, 38, 39, 49, 50, 83, 87, 93, 94, 109, 122, 123, 139, 157, 159, 169, 181, 188, 192, 193 (*see also* character)
getting self out of the way 30
as landscape 167, 173
larval selves 15
narration of *see* narration
as nemocentric *see* subject, nemocentric
and not-self 183
as other selves 36
as predictable 38
as self-authored fiction 13, 15, 27-8
self-determination 107
self-formation 11, 14
self-knowledge (*vipassana*) 171
self-non-self porosity *see* porosity
side-stepping of 109, 142 (*see also* dropping down)
technologies of (Foucault) 15, 93, 101, 165, 173
and time 49
widened temporal context of 130
Sellars, Wilfred 12
sequence *see* cause and effect
Seth, Anil 37
Sewell, Tom 134-5
see also Birt, Verity
shame 53, 156, 175, 190n11
Sharp, Andy *see* English Heretic
shrines 168n3, 178n5
sigils, sigil magick 16, 89, 107
see also Spare, Austin Osman
signification, signifying registers 27, 29, 50, 184, 187, 194
silencing *see* speaking for
Simondon, Gilbert 47, 78, 85, 88, 90, 118, 120
sinthome (Lacan) 13-14, 28
and James Joyce 14, 28
see also repair; symptom
site 60, 70, 74-5, 76, 78, 121, 134
activation of 74, 134
disused 118
obscured 75
as performance stage 71-2
pre-modern 59

re-purposed 128, 137n2
resonance 70
see also key-points; landscape; pilgrimage
sitting, just sitting (Triratna) 167, 168, 171
Situationists 185-6
slavery 58, 60, 61
slave forts (Ghana) 133
see also colonialism; expropriation; extractivism; Middle Passage; primitive accumulation
Smith, Phil 162n8
sound 74, 76-8, 188-9
as conjuration 78
found sound 132-3
sonic devices 74, 81n21
sonic fiction 62, 74, 76, 77-8
see also music
sovereignty, sovereign subject 33, 34
and colonialism 40-1
space-time, space and time 17, 44, 47, 49, 53, 65, 76, 89, 91, 105, 131, 135, 140
different, non-linear, other 51, 74, 92, 97n14, 116, 141, 153, 171, 192
nesting of 135
porosity 73
retreat 168
see also cause and effect; cut-up; reality
Spare, Austin Osman 16, 88, 158
speaking back 17-18, 142-3, 146, 183
speaking for 116
speaking with the dead 127, 130, 133, 135
Spectacle (Debord) 186
spells 63, 89, 107
see also magic; summoning; writing
Spinoza, Benedict de 24, 38-9, 170
Ståhl, Ola 4n5, 147-8
staff as device 76, 77, 133
standing stones 73-4, 80n14, 134
see also key-points; neolithic
Starhawk 61, 63, 104, 105
stasis 23, 24, 26
statue
as political device 58, 94
Virgin Mary 9
Stengers, Isabelle 8-9, 10, 60-1, 63, 91, 104, 106
structures of feeling (Williams) 69, 71, 73, 77, 78
eerie as 69-70, 71

Stupart, Linda 107
style
  as device 84–5
  as performance of content 85
  of a philosophy 84–5
subject (hetero/normative/male/modern/scientific/universal/Western/white) 9, 10, 13, 26–8, 29, 39, 41, 49, 61, 107, 116, 165
  barred (Lacan) 176
  collective/group 84, 107, 108, 148
  and/as desiring 24
  dissolution of 22n25, 45, 55n14
  indebted 112n2
  modern/scientific subject 9, 10
  nemocentric 8, 18, 36–7, 40
  outside of 88
  as residuum 44
  and stasis 23
  transcendental 49
  waking 140
  see also agency; self; sovereign; subjectivity
subjectivity
  decolonisation of 63
  as device 3
  distributed 50
  outside of 124
  production of (Guattari) 15–16, 21n23, 64, 103, 109, 122
suffering 170, 174
summon, summoning 7, 10, 17, 30, 34, 49, 65, 69, 108, 123, 130, 132, 135, 142–4, 150n7, 167–8n3, 184, 185, 187, 189
  and archaeofictioning 129
  pasts 65, 69, 79n4, 131, 133
  a people to come 34, 127, 128, 129, 130, 146, 149, 182–3
  and performance 69, 77, 123, 135, 150n7, 184, 185, 187, 189
  and technical objects 78, 132, 191
  writing as 7, 108, 110, 191
  see also hyperstition
  compare exorcism
Sun Ra 37–2n7, 51, 62, 64
Sutcliffe, Jamie 19n2, 161n3, 162n9
Sutton Hoo 59, 70
  see also key-points; site
Symbolic (Lacan) 13, 16, 17, 38, 57–8, 65, 130, 157, 158
symptom 13–14, 15, 27, 38
  see also sinthome

Tabletop Role Playing Games (TTRPG) 120, 153–60
  aesthetic (Wolfendale and Franklin) 161n1
  multispecies 159
Tam Lin *see* changeling
tarot 88, 107
technicity (Simondon) 78, 85, 91, 122
  as extractivism 118
  see also mode
technologies of non-subject 109
  compare self, technologies of
technologies of the self *see* self, technologies of
technical mode of existence *see* technicity
  compare magic, magical mode of existence
temporal loops *see* time circuits
  see also hyperstition, retroaction
The World After (David Blandy) (TTRPG) 159
theory 95
  as 'low theory' (Wark) 75, 81n17
  as practice 52
theory-fiction 84–5, 135, 148
time *see* space-time
  African 50–1
  anastrophic 44 *see also* retroactive causation
  catastrophic 44 *see also* linear
  decolonisation of 50–1, 133–4
  time circuits 9, 26, 29, 43–52, 61, 136, 193–4 (*see also* hyperstition, retroaction)
  as cybernetic *see* time circuits
  linear *see* cause and effect
  non-time 50
  time rift 72
  time traps 48
  time travel, time travel device 43, 45, 50–2, 61, 70–2, 76, 79n4, 91, 132, 137n7
  time wars 45–6
tools *see* magic, tools
tool/weapon narrative 67n13
  see also cut-up; device
transformation, self-transformation 2, 10, 17, 18, 22n25, 26, 65, 75, 87, 88, 94, 95, 108, 121, 123, 160, 167, 172, 175, 186–8, 191
  see also device; magick
transitional monuments 128
transparency 12, 20n12, 36, 97n18

see also myth, obscuration
compare opacity
trauma 60, 61, 63, 65, 69, 73, 127–8, 174
   as past in present 127–8
   see also Real, the
Traveller (TTRPG) 161n4
tropes 19
   see also genre; repetition
trust 169, 173, 174
Tsing, Anna Lowenhaupt 109
Turing test 90
two, two-ness 126n12, 147, 155, 169

unconscious 29, 38, 42n7
   as beheading 38 (*see also* headlessness)
   listening to 28
   'unconscious theme' 24
universal *see* human, generic/universal; local-universal circuits; myth, universal; subject, universal
unseen *see* transparency
   as irreversibility 35, 58
Ur-fiction 49 *see also* subject, transcendental

virtual reality (VR) 135, 145, 161n3
   see also AI; nested fictions
visions 73 *see also* dream
Viveiros de Castro, Eduardo 9, 116
VNS Matrix 107
voodoo 31n5
vulnerable, vulnerability 62, 175

walking 60, 121, 132–3, 134–5, 162n8
   and headlessness 34
   as method 138n13, 162n8
   as performance or summoning 135
   see also pilgrimage
Watts, Peter 98n21
Williams, Alex 49
Williams, Raymond 59, 105
witchcraft, witches 59, 60–1, 62–3, 104–5, 107
   actually extant practice 105
   and/as care 104
   and ecology 104

hunts, trials, burnings 104–5, 106
   as regression 104, 106
Wittig, Monique 84, 146
Wolfendale, Peter and Timothy Franklin 161n1, 162n7
work 10, 17
   as graft 25
world building, world making, worlding 10, 124, 155–6, 157, 158–9, 160, 162–3n10, 184
   and correlative subject 157
   and feeling 157, 158, 160
   as inhabitation (animating) 155–6, 158, 160
   as preparation (building) 155–6
world-within-a-world *see* nested fictions
world wide web 91
   see also AI
writing 7, 14, 17, 18, 83
   academic/scholarly 18–19, 107, 116, 191
   by AI 145–6
   with AI 146
   as care and repair 193–4
   as conjuring other fictions 110
   experimental 14, 17, 39–40 (*see also* avant-garde)
   as magical technology 191
   as magickal 89
   as myth-work 191
   as non-self 7
   and performance 184
   performative 18–19
   as repair 14, 107
   and retrocausation 55n11
   scripts, protocols 186
   as self-authorship 7, 16, 109 (*see also* autowriting; self as fiction)
   as side-stepping of self 191
   as unintentional 191 (*see also* summoning)
Wynter, Sylvia 86–7

Yeats, W. B. 44
Yorkshire, North Yorkshire Moors 117–8, 131, 134, 137n2, 149, 154

Zen Buddhism *see* Buddhism